LATE NINETEENTH-CENTURY AMERICAN LIBERALISM

Representative Selections, 1880-1900

The American Heritage Series

The American Heritage Series

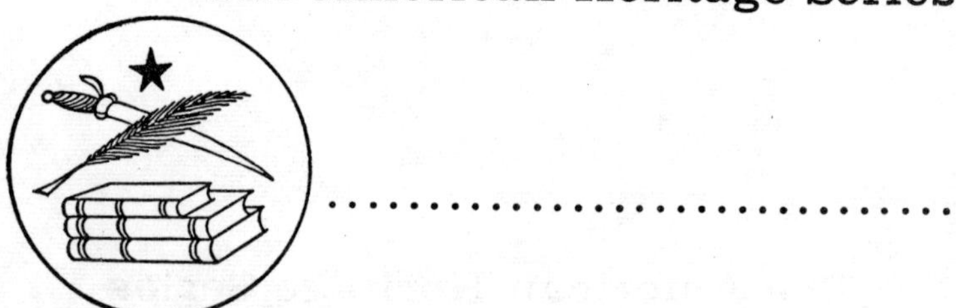

LATE NINETEENTH-CENTURY AMERICAN LIBERALISM

Representative Selections, 1880-1900

Edited, with an introduction, by

LOUIS FILLER

Professor of American Civilization, Antioch College

The American Heritage Series

published by

THE BOBBS-MERRILL COMPANY, INC.
A SUBSIDIARY OF HOWARD W. SAMS & CO., INC.
Publishers • INDIANAPOLIS • NEW YORK

Printed in the United States of America
Library of Congress Catalog Card Number: 61-18060

PREFACE

Liberalism is not only one of the most complex of concepts; it has carried different weight and connotation at various points in its history. This has been particularly true in the United States. Here, there has been no notable Liberal party to act as a point in space for social and political forces. The major parties have all been able to claim some stake in liberalism. Nevertheless, there is a discernible liberal tradition in American affairs. It can be traced through the changing history of the country; it can be measured in terms of its varying dimensions and effectiveness.

The present volume focuses upon a period roughly encompassing the years 1880-1900. Events of consequence to later liberals precede 1880. Thus, the Bland-Allison Act of 1878 can be classified as a liberal effort to deal with the "silver" issue. The present editor has, however, made efforts to deal with liberal tendencies and personalities at their high and unusual moments. The silver question is, therefore, displayed in William Jennings Bryan's celebrated peroration of 1896. Another notable milestone in late nineteenth-century American liberalism might have been the election in 1884 of Grover Cleveland: the first Democratic President since the Civil War. Cleveland was not an outstanding liberal, but he was a change from the uninspiring litany of Presidents Grant, Hayes, Garfield, and Arthur. To have begun the collection in 1884, on the other hand, would have lost us worthy references of value to the liberalism of the period. Therefore, 1880 to 1900. The latter date closes the century. It offers no striking evidence that a great (and enigmatic) reform movement is shortly to thrill the country. But by that token it suggests the need for more closely examining the liberalism of the years preceding, in order to discover the roots of muckraking and Progressivism.

The 1890's and before are often seen as a "transitional

period"—transitional, that is, to the Era of Reform. The present writer has no great regard for the concept of "transition." It assumes more determinism in human affairs than evidence generally warrants, certainly, in the present case. Still, once one has dismissed the idea that Americans in the 1890's lived only that the 1900's might flourish, it is possible to agree that much which the reformers of the earlier time projected, their twentieth-century followers were able to test. This fact alone should justify a closer attention to the aims and views of liberals of the late nineteenth century than they have often received.

L. F.

CONTENTS

PART ONE—POLITICS AND SOCIETY

PART TWO—THE SPIRITUAL UNREST

PART THREE—THE SOCIAL QUESTION

INTRODUCTION

EAST AND MIDDLE WEST

EAST AND MIDDLE WEST

CONCEPTS OF LIBERALISM IN AMERICA DURING THE LATE NINETEENTH CENTURY

We seem, today, to be re-evaluating our national heritage in terms of world needs and perspectives, and, usually, in the name of liberalism. Our history texts, to be sure, now tend to display more tolerance of American radicalism than one can discover, let us say, in Ellis P. Oberholtzer's *History of the United States;* but the emphasis is surely less upon the positive qualities of the Molly Maguires, for instance (assuming, for the moment, that they were radicals), than upon the social and economic conditions which drove some of them to mayhem. In other words, there appears to be an effort in the making—and not only by historians—to define a liberal position with strength and substance, that will be neither a pretty appendage of a social conservatism, nor a petty foil to radicalism; and that can point the way to a more promising world than that which created the Mollys.

The problem is to define our heritage. Harold Stassen once urged us to export our concept of freedom. But what is it? There appears to be a general belief that it is equivalent to liberalism. But what is *liberal?* The *New York Herald Tribune* made a commendable attempt to determine its meaning, and threw open its columns to interested readers. The replies, though numerous, and including correspondence from well-known persons, were remarkably thin. The two most interesting responses were neither by historians nor political scientists: one was a poem, and the other a brief definition, "A liberal is a radical with a wife and two children." [1] The newspaper

[1] *New York Herald Tribune,* "What Is a Liberal?" Feb. 16, 1949; see also editorial of Feb. 8, 1949, and letters, Feb. 10, 13, 15; editorial, Feb. 17,

even assigned a reporter to interview a variety of people, including Republicans, Democrats, Liberals (capitalized), Progressives, Communists, and "non-partisans," and ask them to define a liberal. The chairman of the board of the United States Steel Corporation asked to be excused, and the president of the National Maritime Union thought it "too big a question to answer these days." A cleric agreed to try a definition, but, unfortunately, had to catch a train only four hours after being asked. Some of the completed definitions, including contributions by professional historians, showed signs of toil and earnestness but, as the *Herald Tribune* observed in a wise summing up, all were marked by a peculiar vagueness, were weak on specific policy or program, and, unlike communism, which appealed for authority to such theoreticians as Marx and Engels, seemed unaware of the commanding figures of Jeremy Bentham, Adam Smith, John Stuart Mill, and later liberal philosophers.

> One suspects [continued the *Herald Tribune* editorial] that as a partisan political principle, "liberalism" has largely lost its meaning, partly because its doctrinal foundations have been undermined by history, partly because its great humanistic and liberating implications have been too universally accepted by all thoughtful men.

1949, and letter of March 2. Harold Zlotnik's sonnet on "The Liberal," appearing in a letter of Feb. 13, merits reproduction here:

Attuned attentively to every sound
  Within the polyphonic human range,
The liberal, unbiased and unbound,
  Discovers harmony on scales of change.
And he applies a probing stethoscope
  Of righteousness to all society,
Hearing a rhythm as the people grope
  Toward justice, toward a social piety.
So circumspect of freedom, he will stalk
  The predatory claw upon the land,
Cry evil to the world and bravely walk
  In tatters with the flagellated band.
No clock of compromise, no time of fear
  Will mark divisions in his honest year.

Yet liberalism continues to be a word which challenges thought. Many people, certainly, have an idea of an America which was greater-hearted and better than the Haymarket Riot, the cyclical depressions, and the Pullman Strike would indicate. "America was promises." But was the promise radical or liberal? This is no mere question of semantics. Communism has been declared, in Earl Browder's famous phrase, to be twentieth-century Americanism. A fairly popular volume of recent vintage claims to be true to the spirit of American liberalism, and appears to approve the careers of John Brown, Emma Goldman, and John Reed. It can make a difference, what one means by calling oneself a liberal.

Professor Rubin Gotesky has observed that it is more accurate to talk of *liberalisms,* than of liberalism, since it takes in so many others connoting liberalism, from free enterprise to antimilitarism.[2] The word is peculiarly open to the error of synecdoche—of substituting the part for the whole. Liberals are not, today, in most locales of presumed intelligence, put under fire for being liberals, except in gross cases of abuse; they are denounced for being something else, perhaps "leftists" or "rightists"—the reader must think through some specific situations for himself. Yet liberalism itself has no democratic origin: *artes liberales,* for example, referred to a course of studies fit for gentlemen, at one time. In Dr. Johnson's day, it still defined a person who opposed aristocracy or despotism, but favored a democracy strictly controlled in the interests of a small ruling class. Gentlemen still quoted Milton gladly: "License they mean when they cry liberty." But already their aristocratic emphases were being undermined by the growing power of the middle classes, with their insistence upon liberal constitutionalism.[3]

[2] Rubin Gotesky, "Liberalism in Crisis," *European Idealogies,* ed. Feliks Gross (New York, 1948), pp. 231 ff.

[3] Frederick Watkins, *The Political Tradition of the West. A Study in the Development of Modern Liberalism* (Cambridge, Mass., 1948), pp. 119 ff., 149 ff. Cf. Franklin C. Palm, *The Middle Classes Then and Now* (New York, 1936), pp. 46 ff., and *passim.*

With the early decades of the nineteenth century and the rise of industrialism—with its proletarian concomitant—the Manchester Liberals made a principle of free enterprise. But even before them, liberals, like the elder Pitt, who rejoiced that three million Americans were unwilling to be slaves, had made their reputation by fighting monopolies in the name of liberty.

Richard Cobden, who scourged the English grain growers, continued the tradition. By his time, however, "liberalism" threw a wider net than ever before, and in subsequent Victorian decades, its advocates undertook to regularize its meaning, and give it universal application.

Once more to refer to Professor Gotesky's admirable essay, briefly, its analysis of liberal tenets formulated in 1911 by L. T. Hobhouse divides them into nine categories, as follows: *Civil liberty*—government by law, not men; *fiscal liberty*—"no taxation without representation"; *personal liberty*—giving us freedom of thought, speech, religion; *social liberty*—equality. Here Professor Gotesky observes that equality is not necessarily liberty—everyone can be equally in chains. *Economic liberty* is, of course, the classical liberty of *laissez faire*. Then comes *liberty for women and children*—once more, not really liberties, our analyst points out, but actually restraints, on the right, for instance, of a child to go to work instead of to school, if he so chooses. The list may here be quickly, but momentously, completed by referring to *equality of nations*—again, not necessarily ensuring them freedom; *antimilitarism;* and the great freedom of *popular sovereignty*.

Here is a formidable list of liberties and restraints, guaranteed to disseminate freedom wherever people might be found. No wonder that capitalism, which had arisen more or less with liberalism, more and more dissociated itself from it, and, in Europe, took a course which created a proletariat, revolutionary movements, and theoreticians who denounced liberals as bankrupt or reactionary.

The American Scene

How did Americans fare? The industrial revolution came later to them than to western Europeans, and so did its social effects. It is not until the post-Civil War period that one can, properly, speak of a "new industry"; and even then its impact upon the working and middle classes was not comparable to what happened in Europe.[4] Karl Marx sent his First International over here to be buried; such was his opinion of American radicalism. This is by no means to say that there were no radicals here. The radicals of this period can be identified as those who took a doctrinaire position looking to a change in the American social structure, the position being inherited or adapted from European experience. As Laurence Gronlund wrote: "Socialism—*modern* Socialism, *German* Socialism, which is fast becoming *the* Socialism the world over—holds that the impending reconstruction of Society will be brought about by the Logic of Events; teaches that *the Coming Revolution is strictly an Evolution.*"[5] As the quotation suggests, it was possible for a radical *in thought* to be no more than moderately radical *in fact:* a "parlor pink." He could, however, affect the thinking of persons who were more than that, and it was when radical thought was fused with working-class action that it attained significance. A workingman was not necessarily a radical, even when he engaged in violence, as during the railroad riots of 1877. It was the mental outlook, the tactics, the logic of events which determined the radical or liberal nature of the worker, or, indeed, his reactionary aspects.

To the extent that labor drew together co-operative, experi-

[4] Factory operatives did, to be sure, experience real difficulties in the pre-Civil War period, particularly in the ranks of the "old" immigration, and especially in the large eastern cities. The farm, however, acted as a buffer; Norman Ware, *The Industrial Worker, 1840-1860* (Boston, 1924), *passim.*

[5] Laurence Gronlund, *The Co-operative Commonwealth* (Boston, 1884), p. 8.

mental, craft union tendencies of the earlier period preceding the Civil War, it was liberal. To the extent that it struggled, under the new industrial dispensation, to preserve the individual, whether by secret organizations, rituals, or strikes, it was liberal. To the extent that it sought to adjust the laborer to new conditions of life and labor, it was, again, liberal. But to the extent that it merely accepted the machine, and showed itself willing to accept a "class" relationship to the corporation, it was no more, if no less, liberal than the corporation. The sharp opposition of capitalism and unionism can be said to have ground out a species of liberalism in the long run; to that extent one can accept the Selig Perlman theory of labor which saw it as a reformer of capitalism, a down-to-earth solvent of industrial unrest.[6] But labor, which repudiated "producer consciousness" and was indifferent to the anti-monopoly campaign, and which concerned itself only with its very own job, was no creator of social programs and could be merely neutral, and, on occasion, even illiberal. What it might do in its latter role depended on circumstances. It might, mistaking effect for cause, riot against the Chinese and humiliate southern European immigrants. It might accept the ward heeler's two-dollar bill in exchange for its vote. It might hail Samuel Gompers as a labor statesman and join him in an organized elite of labor. In 1896, notably, it might vote McKinley into the Presidency.[7] And, on the other hand, it might, when composed of unorganized workers, or workers in poorly organized industries, see itself as a victim of fundamental injustice, and accept in theory or fact the slogans and perspectives of the *Communist Manifesto.*

Militancy or non-militancy, to repeat, defines neither class nor action. Liberalism does not condemn its adherents to sweet reasonableness while its opponents sweep the field.

[6] Selig Perlman, *A Theory of the Labor Movement* (New York, 1928), p. 314 and *passim.*

[7] Cf. Edgar E. Robinson, *The Presidential Vote, 1896-1932* (Stanford, 1934), pp. 4-5.

Liberal forces can engage in war for a liberal principle; to what extent they did so during the Civil War, it would be interesting to consider. The farmers of the San Joaquin Valley who, in the post-Civil War period, took up arms against the Southern Pacific Railroad were contending for liberal principles. However, this action was less characteristic of them than was the Populist Revolt. Generally, the liberal farmer was less effective when resisting monoply with arms, than when resisting it at the polls. It was otherwise with the workers.

In the light of the above, to whom may the terms *liberal* and *radical* be applied? For example, can we speak of Edward Bellamy's program as an example of "native American radicalism"? Or would it stretch the word out of all proper sense and meaning to do so? Bellamy was, indeed, opposed to the unhampered rule of trusts; but to say that this defines the radical is to accept the definition of liberalism made by the trustmakers themselves. Bellamy's program actually appealed to broad classes of conservatives, as well as certain radicals.[8] The most "radical" aspects of Bellamy's program, in a practical sense, the nationalization of railroads and telegraph lines, was a strictly limited program which had already been accomplished, completely or in part, by some conservative governments of Europe. Bellamy was a liberal, one who was concerned for the liberties of aspects of the middle class.

What in America of the latter decades of the nineteenth century, if anything, connected the various protagonists of liberalism? At first glance, they made up a motley assembly. E. L. Godkin was for free trade, civil service reform, and peace, among other things. William Dudley Foulke was for women's rights and civil service reform; he was mildly free trade, and he approved of McKinley and the territorial gains of the Spanish-American War. Theodore Roosevelt, before he became President, professed contempt for the *New York Post*

[8] Cf. Louis Filler, "Edward Bellamy and the Spiritual Unrest," *American Journal of Economics and Sociology*, VIII (1949), 246.

and the so-called goo goos,[9] though he was a goo goo himself in the liberal phases of his thought. James B. Weaver was for free trade and other causes noted above, as well as additional ones in the Populist Platform—a fact which separated him from the liberals who have already been mentioned. Henry George was a free trader, but opposed to the Populists, as they were to him. Bellamy's "nationalizing" program permitted him to co-operate with the Populists, but not with the genteel reformers, and he lacked interest in George's program. George, on his side, considered Bellamy a utopian.

A closer comparison of American conditions and liberal tenets is in order. The English liberals had fought mercantilism, that is, monopoly, in the interests of free trade, that is, capitalism. By the closing decades of the nineteenth century, the situation had been completely reversed. The capitalists had become monopolists themselves, and were demanding the "liberty" to remain monopolists. Nowhere was the "divine right of capital," as Professor Clarence E. Ayres has called it, established more firmly than in America: in government under a melancholy succession of presidents; in law under the aegis of the Supreme Court; in education under the so-called classical economists, the Social Darwinians, and the general defenders of the *status quo*.

In theory, and to the extent that the latter believed in law, representative government, *laissez faire,* anti-militarism—they were liberals. It was to some extent the Social Darwinian element in their thinking which distorted their perspective. They feared restraints on child and woman labor. Memory of the low-grade Jukes family prejudiced them against equality. Anglo-Saxon pride troubled those who foresaw yellow, black, and other perils and tides. In practice, a person like William Graham Sumner could scarcely be called a liberal at all; that is, there was hardly any liberty, from civil right for radicals to

[9] See William Dudley Foulke, *A Hoosier Autobiography* (New York, 1922), pp. 112-13, for a characteristic statement by Roosevelt on his position. "Goo goos" was a contemptuous name applied to partisans of the Good Government Clubs of the era.

popular sovereignty, which was actually safer in his hands than in those of individuals who dreamed of a dictatorship of the proletariat. The interesting fact is that this state of affairs, in which government and business became substantially one, had not created a strong radicalism in the United States. It had, rather, created a variety of interest groups, each of which was concerned with its own stake in freedom, and which met with others at some points, but rarely all.

Reform now obtrudes upon the liberal picture. Doctrinaire liberalism had originally been a fight for a hands-off policy; and in the American version of the free trade, free enterprise, Manchester Liberalism, it continued to be. E. L. Godkin was not a congenital reformer: he was interested in seeing that nature's laws, as he conceived them, be given free play. His cure for an ignorant electorate, for example, was not schools, but restrictions at the polls. But even Manchester Liberals found it necessary to go out and work for free trade, good government standards, and other measures that pleased them. Their efforts in behalf of liberalism were more and more supplemented by those of interest groups which were less reverent toward classical liberalism, more concerned with social measures of specific interest to themselves, and no less liberal—in that they helped to preserve liberty—for that reason.

Charles Edward Russell

Liberalisms, not liberalism. One wonders how many fitter instruments one can discover for revealing inner social structures and relationships in the post-Civil War period than Charles Edward Russell. This figure has been slighted without warrant in American liberal historiography. It would be interesting to know why. Had he died with his own times, say, in 1912, when he ran for Governor of New York on the Socialist ticket, his historical consequence might have been more apparent. His long trail of causes, crowned with his brilliant services during the muckraking period, might have set him in a certain perspective. But he went on. He disillusioned some of his radical followers by supporting American participation in World War I. He added a long and bewildering array of books to an already long list—new books which dealt with the Philippine question, the orchestra conductor Theodore Thomas, poetry, Blaine, Julia Marlowe, among others. He lent his name to societies favoring the abolition of capital punishment and of vivisection, advocating Zionism, interracial co-operation in the District of Columbia, recognition of the Irish Republic. He actively adhered to the Johnstown Flood Correspondents Association, the Silurians, and many fraternal organizations. Furthermore, he continued to preach the socialism he had accepted in the Progressive era, and to his stubborn end threw his lampoons and sarcasm about from the pages of the *New Leader*. It was, no doubt, difficult to think of Russell as an historical character.

Yet his autobiography, *Bare Hands and Stone Walls* (1933), might have given students of his period greater pause than it apparently did. The light from Lincoln Steffens' autobiography apparently interfered with the attention properly due Russell's book. Still, it was an extraordinarily well-written story, with perceptions which Steffens did not always attain, and should have made clearer than it did Russell's peculiar usefulness in understanding American liberalism. He had begun with free trade in Iowa, in the 1870's. He had perceived the truth in Henry George's analysis of fundamental social wrong, and he had sympathized with the Greenbackers. As a big city reporter, he had learned the horrors of tenement life, and the dubious activities of real estate and public utilities corporations. As a muckraker, he had come into his kingdom of reform and had written with great effect on an amazing number of themes: Beef Trust depredations, railroad manipulations, the prison system, Trinity Church tenements, among many others. As a socialist, he became a critic of his own earlier nostrums. He studied colonialism in India, and arbitration in New Zealand, aided in the founding of the National Association for the Advancement of Colored People, and blasted at trusts until the muckraking movement was submerged by natural and unnatural forces. It was only right, as will appear, that his last muckraking book should have been *The Story of the Non-Partisan League* (1920); after the deluge, reform re-established its bastion in the Northwest.

Anyone having even a cursory literary acquaintance with Russell and his works must, perhaps involuntarily, wonder whether he was indeed a liberal. Russell would hardly satisfy those who like to think of liberals as wishy-washy and uncertain characters. Nor could he be termed broad-minded in any sense. A not untypical statement by him reads: "All Englishmen hate America, whatever they may pretend when American help is needed." In old age, he maintained an elaborate contempt for book reviewers, asking whether there was "any spectacle more absurd than that of the American public reading the *New York Times Book Review* and the *Saturday* Something—I forget what they call that particular tissue of nonsense—and being in any way moved except to sardonic mirth?"[10] He was extremely suspicious of his enemies, and ready to believe the worst of them. And not only of notorious politicians and businessmen. It tells us something, perhaps, to know that he considered Theodore Roosevelt "the greatest enemy" of the muckrakers.[11]

However, we are not here concerned with liberalism in its more flaccid and colloquial senses, but in its relationship to liberty. Russell's causes make up a roster of the liberal causes of the Eighteen Eighties and Nineties—one which he simply intensified when, in the pre-World War I period, he became the leader of the muckrakers. Which of his causes did one whose domestic trail ran from Davenport, Iowa, to New York consider most significant?

[10] Charles Edward Russell to the editor, Dec. 24, 1937.

[11] The above does not, of course, reflect upon Russell's extreme generosity of character, and fineness of intention. Russell had sterling qualities of appreciation and loyalty to which many persons were indebted. Indeed it may be said that much of his journalistic ruthlessness was compounded of indignation and a need for hiding his sensitivity. His first publication, a book of verse, was entitled *Such Stuff as Dreams* (1902).

> I suppose only those that lived in the West through the seventies and eighties can understand how and why [muck-raking] really started. . . . It grew out of the rank despotism and oppression, now unknown and unbelievable, long exercised by the railroad companies first, and then by other great corporations. . . . The East had no full knowledge of the process until years afterward and then never in its full tide of audacity. It had nothing to do with the corruption in municipal politics, except so far as the corporations used corruption there.[12]

Again:

> It was one thing to attack low-browed and ignorant political thugs and vice-mongers. To do so was safe and along easy ways. To all the "better elements," the intelligentsia, the educated and the well-to-do it was immensely gratifying. It appealed strongly to their sense of caste superiority, it confirmed their pet belief that the evils of the country were due to the fact that they and their class were not running it, and to all nativists it was sweet balm because it showed that these iniquities were committed by persons with foreign names. Therefore, it was welcomed and applauded and viewed as a great public service. It was a far different thing to attack the men that had most been honored as shining beacons of success under the American system, the men that were universally lauded for integrity, character and success, and to show that they were in fact just thieves and swindlers.[13]

Here we encounter an element which seems to separate liberals—not merely on the basis of causes, but of geographical sections. One need only turn to the *Chapters of Erie* written by Charles Francis Adams, Jr., to observe the difference. The sordid story of railroad graft, bribery, double-dealing at its worst told by Adams is well known. Henry Cabot Lodge, in a memorial address on Adams, credited him with drawing up and heading the first effective railroad commission—whatever it was that "effective" meant to the gentleman from Massachusetts.[14] But

[12] Russell to the editor, Sept. 28, 1938.

[13] *Idem*, Dec. 26, 1938.

[14] *Charles Francis Adams, 1835-1915, An Autobiography* (Boston, 1916), p. xxxiv. Lodge's own view of the railroad situation is instructive.

it was the crude character of the Gould-Drew administration which dismayed its New England critic. The shippers received exactly three pallid lines of attention in his essays. Adams himself in due time resigned from the Massachusetts Commission to become President of the Union Pacific Railroad (from which post he was appropriately evicted by Jay Gould), and still later made clear just what regulation of railroads meant to him. He had once appeared to write open-mindedly on the future of governmental relationships to railroads and had reported foreign experiments dispassionately. Now, he deplored "the desire of the man in the street to get things done and, as he imagines, once-and-for-all disposed of." And he opposed "the growing tendency to excessive legislation . . . in which the supposed popular will is crystallized and penalized." He never had believed in it, he affirmed, and for that reason had lacked sympathy for what he sarcastically termed "the sturdy champions of the 'Dear Peepul.' " [15]

We have thus travelled some distance from Charles Edward Russell. We travel further if we turn to a friend of the Adamses, the appropriately surnamed E. L. Godkin, on the railroads. Godkin requires more thought than his lucid and informed journalism might appear to ask, at first glance; and it is to be hoped that useful studies of this important figure will begin to appear at last. He can often appear to say all that a reasonable man might demand, and as often mean less. Thus, he writes appealingly of the workingman, on occasion, for one who holds the lower classes in considerable contempt. Strikes, he tells us in 1867, are "remarkable indications of the general eagerness of men of all classes to get rid of the arbitrary rule of individuals, and get under the government of *law*." [16] Here, one thinks, is the beginning of human compromise, of mutual understanding. But then, in the *Nation* for January 28, 1875, Godkin turns to the Granger Laws—and the picture changes:

[15] *Idem*, pp. 175-76.

[16] Rollo Ogden, ed., *Life and Letters of Edwin Lawrence Godkin* (New York, 1907), II, 44-45.

> We maintain . . . that the principle of the Potter Law [of Wisconsin] . . . is either confiscation, or, if another phrase be more agreeable, the change of railroads from pieces of private property, owned and managed for the benefit of those who have invested their money in them, into eleemosynary or charitable corporations, managed not for the profit of the owners, but for the benefit of a particular class of applicants for outdoor relief—the farmers; and more than this [Godkin adds somewhat gratuitously] such farmers only as happen to live along the line. . . .
>
> We feel it our duty to warn all investors that they will be very foolish to trust any of their money to legislatures which pass such laws as the Potter Act, to judges who decide such laws constitutional. . . .

Godkin was very clear that the farmer who could not support himself on terms dictated by the railroad had no right to be in farming; he does not appear to have been concerned with what the farmer might do instead, nor does he seem to have been aware that when he talked of the farmer—even the farmer who lived "along the line"—he was talking about a substantial portion of the western and midwestern population. Charles Edward Russell seems never to have forgotten it; and we thus come upon a fundamental difference between western and eastern liberalism. The western farmer was, of course, no radical; on the contrary, he was the ultimate individualist. He was not interested in socialism; it was independence of the railroad for which he yearned. His apparent radicalism lay in his solution: regulation suggested socialism. But it was the Jeffersonian farmer he aimed to preserve: his liberalism lay in his class intent, and the moderation intrinsic to his actual tactics and strategy.

Regulation in the East meant far less than in the West because in the former case railroads lacked central significance. The East, as Lincoln Steffens saw, was older. Corruption—or urbanization—went deeper.[17] There, administrative irresponsibility on the railroads was spectacular, but still not so important as railroad rates; and these depended not so much on the relation of railroads to farmers, as upon that of railroads

[17] *The Autobiography of Lincoln Steffens* (New York, 1931), pp. 464 ff.

to corporations. Railroads could undermine middle-class business; but this did not distinguish them from other monopolies which they thereby served. Nor did it force a union between farmers, and workers, and what Karl Marx would have called petty bourgeois business elements, which suffered from the policies of the railroads and their business allies. The eastern farmer, far from co-operating with the laborer, politically or for economic ends, did not even sympathize with the western farmer, whose Granger Laws he saw as providing competition with himself. Labor, of course, had no great apparent stake in the issue of carrying charges. As for William Graham Sumner's famous "forgotten man," he could as easily despise the farmer as he could the worker—the "hick" as well as the "Mick"—and saw no clear gain in affiliating with either. Yet a liberal solution for their respective troubles had to be compounded out of their respective needs, if the threatened Europeanization of America—the creation of an America of caste and class—was to be avoided.

Free Trade and Freedom

Free trade was not a movement indigenous to the West; but seen as Charles Edward Russell saw it, it all but was:

> Almost any other industry could claim some fostering care or substantial help of government. Farming, the industry upon which all the rest depended, could go hang. Manufacturers of articles in iron, steel, wood, textiles, ceramics, were enriched by a tariff that shielded them from competition. The farmer not only had no such shield but in a way vital to his interests he must face in a foreign market the fierce rivalries of the world. The cost of everything he must buy was artificially enhanced for him by the tariff that swelled the profits of the manufacturers; the price of his staple products was fixed for him by an uncontrolled competition.[18]

[18] Russell, *Bare Hands and Stone Walls* (New York, 1933), p. 28. This volume is particularly useful in the present discussion because it concerns itself with Russell's role as a "side-line reformer." Other aspects of his life are treated in his *These Shifting Scenes* (1914), and elsewhere.

A Godkin might sardonically remark that the farmer's plaint was not that protection was unfair, but that it did not include him. Godkin seemed to himself to stand on higher moral ground when he denounced protection in principle. But this was the trouble with Manchester Liberalism in America in general: it was largely uninterested in people, particularly common people.[19] Godkin, David A. Wells, his pupil Henry Adams, Edward Atkinson, Horace White, and Grover Cleveland approached the tariff problem not with the passion of a John Bright, but with the enthusiasm of a gadgeteer, the earnestness of a baseball fan. It was otherwise with them when they turned to the defense of the gold standard: then they fought as men do who defend their homes. They could find nothing good to say of the greenback and silver repudiationists: in the terms of the times, they were, to the gold champions, anarchists, or abettors of anarchy, knaves or fools, and dangerous in any case.

They had the logic of classical economy on their side, but it condemned the farmer to foreclosure or ruin. A frame of mind which approved free trade, but condemned currency manipulation, was created in the laboratory—or, rather, in the drawing rooms of genteel students of economics who disliked the *nouveaux riches* and their agents, but detested the mob. Let the elegant Henry Adams voice their feelings for them. Writing to his friend John Hay in November of 1893, he criticizes the "gold bugs," but only because of what he deems to be their incompetence:

> I would pardon them their rascality on the stock-exchange and their imbecility in politics [he adds], but I can't forgive them their massacre of my friends who are being cleaned out and broken down by dozens.

He mocks Hay for "uniting Schurz and David Wells and Perry Belmont and Grover Cleveland and all the wise and

[19] The *Nation* prided itself on its "objectivity"; see, for example, the review of John Stuart Mill's career, in the May 18, 1882, issue which found a contradiction between his "intellectual perceptions" and his "emotional" ideas, as on Nature.

good, and me, in paeans of praise for the Major [McKinley], who is undoubtedly the greatest and best of all Americans since the immortal Washington," in 1896; but there is only the shadow of a joke in his assurance that he will "shout for the Major, and no one shall charge me with indifference to the best interests of Wall Street." And there is no joke at all when he writes to his brother Brooks of the situation, as he sees it, in 1898:

> As for the capitalists and their powers, *je m'en fiche pas mal.* The capitalists have been licked out of their hides in every test of strength of late. It is the socialist—not the capitalist—who is going to swallow us next, and of the two I prefer the Jew. I am always thinking of the next Presidential election, and of what we are to say two years hence. Hanna will drive us to Bryan—and then! Much as I loathe the regime of Manchester and Lombard Street in the nineteenth century I am glad to think I shall be dead before I am ruled by the Trades Unions of the Twentieth. Luckily society will go to pieces then.[20]

Adams and his kind deserve their due. They maintained standards of right and wrong at a time when such standards went begging. They were intelligent during a period of brutal expansion. They made keen contributions to letters, as in the case of Adams, and social science, as in the case of Wells, and to such worthy causes as civil service reform, good government, the free trade issue, and others which will be noted. But they were egregious egotists, they were blind to large social realities. Of the two types, it was the Populists who saw, and felt, most deeply.

For if it was true that the farmers were interested in survival, rather than in abstract justice, it was the survival of the individual for which they fought. Here were no peasants; unlike the farmers of the Vendée, it was for themselves alone that the Americans took up arms. It was a government of the people they demanded. Free trade, greenbacks, and silver did not, in the West, derive from a theory, but from a condition.

[20] Harold Dean Cater, ed., *Henry Adams and His Friends* (Boston, 1947), p. 438; see also pp. 294-95, 387.

The farmers were, no doubt, less than consistent in their attitude toward the tariff. They played, to some extent, the game of the Silver Kings in defending the panacea to end all panaceas. But there was no questioning their need, and the unwillingness of the gold and protectionist patriots to respect it. To that extent, the farmers heralded the New Deal: its assumption that no one must starve, that experiments within the competitive system were desirable, and that the burden of proof during economic crises was on the self-appointed leaders of American industry, rather than upon those who suffered most acutely by its operations.[21]

Seen separately, the free trade, greenback, and silver agitations were panaceas. Seen together, they were part of a persistent and many-sided effort to maintain free enterprise—or, better still, the freedom of enterprise. The West, not the East, became the focus for liberal thought in America not because liberal forces were less active in the East, but because the liberal equation there was more complex, and tended to break down into goo gooism or worse.

Henry George

It is as an expression of concern for the future of the most basic of all commodities—land—that Henry George's crusade first commands attention. The fact that free land was disap-

[21] This somewhat negative definition of the New Deal is offered in terms of what the New Deal actually accomplished or attempted, rather than in what it professed. Mr. Roosevelt, from time to time, enumerated a number of "rights" which he claimed for the common citizen which go far beyond those implied in the above points. One philosophic analysis of these "rights"—including the "right" to a "useful and remunerative job," to a "decent home," medical care, "adequate protection from economic fear of old age, sickness, accident, and unemployment," among other "rights"—is included in William Aylott Orton, *The Liberal Tradition: a Study of the Social and Spiritual Conditions of Freedom* (New Haven, 1945), p. 42 and *passim*. The New Deal is viewed with more approval, in the light of a discussion of liberalism, in Harold Laski, *The Rise of Liberalism* (New York, 1936), pp. 284 ff.

pearing was notorious long before Frederick Jackson Turner announced his frontier thesis. That the public domain was being despoiled was one of the outstanding complaints of the Greenback Labor party in 1880. Recognition of the high percentage of fraud in land negotiations in the West appears and reappears during the Eighteen Eighties. Cleveland took reformist measures looking to the return of government property illegally acquired, but, characteristically, with no more vigor and penetration than he expended in the later phases of his free trade crusade.[22]

The Henry George analysis derived from the same condition that excited the anti-railroad fight: monopoly. And because land was so basic to life, this analysis provided a stimulus to social thought. As Russell explained:

> While we had been urging the main battle charge against Protection as a governmental policy, Henry George had been stating a far higher view of the same subject. *Progress and Poverty,* that epochal work, had gone of its own momentum from one thinking mind to another. . . . We had proposed to end Protection; he hoped to end also poverty, the slums, the huge degradation of the masses, the acute inequalities of condition that curse and threaten all modern social structures.[23]

The genesis of George's plan in far western conditions has been traced, though it bears further study, and George's exposure to the power of monopoly in New York, his shocked view of tenement conditions, must also be taken into account. Yet George's period of sensational influence was not among the western farmers, who persisted in regarding themselves as landed, if harrassed, proprietors, and therefore uninterested in taxes on land. *Progress and Poverty* stirred action among the landless workers in the cities who suffered in their relations with realtors and tenement owners. Suffice it here to call attention to its remarkable effect upon urban liberal thought,

[22] Alfred N. Chandler, *Land Title Origins* (New York, 1945), pp. 510-11.
[23] Russell, *Bare Hands and Stone Walls,* p. 46.

and especially upon an outstanding triumvirate of middle western urban reformers.[24] Tom Johnson of Cleveland was, of course, directly inspired by George, and had personal reason for understanding the role of the public utilities in municipal affairs. But Samuel Jones of Toledo, and Hazen Pingree of Detroit before him appear to have stumbled upon that knowledge simply by persisting in giving democratic government to their constituents. The significant fact is that they should have acquired the kind of following they did, and become symbols of reform. They differed *in kind* from "reform" mayors of New York, for example. The latter emphasized election frauds, preferably by the opposition, moral delinquency, police laxity—goo goo causes. George's ideas seemed highly theoretical to Charles Edward Russell, but had George won his mayoralty election fight of 1886, it would have made a difference: he, and the trade unions that supported him, had concrete ideas about what they planned for New York. It made a difference when George's follower Tom Johnson won in Cleveland, and when Jones and Pingree won in their respective cities. For these men emphasized valid franchises, proper rates for public utilities, democratic processes. *They emphasized, in fact, an urban modification of what concerned the farmers.*

None of them brought the millennium. Jones preached a Golden Rule which, in terms of large-scale, eastern, industrial and economic conditions might be called oversimplified, though it seems to have been moderately effective. Johnson, with his candid reminiscences of former franchise grabs, supplied his constituents with valuable information. Unfortunately, the conditions which had permitted him to become a millionaire, permitted him only to set a brave example of what a municipal reformer should be. Pingree, the maverick of them all, requires, for understanding, the most careful study of all. A bold and bluff "friend of the people," despite

[24] For eastern appreciation of their work, and evidence of their relationship to other reformers, see "Mul" (William H. Muldoon), *Mark Hanna's "Moral Cranks" and—Others. A Study of Today* (Brooklyn, 1900).

his self-made fortune (all three reformers had strikingly similar backgrounds), Pingree fought the municipal monopolists in their name, devised the Georgian scheme for the unemployed which charmed admirers throughout the land—planting potatoes in vacant lots—and otherwise put vigor into Detroit's civic affairs. Yet he was thrown into the breach by Republicans in 1896 to save Michigan from Bryan, and he did. He received more votes for Governor than McKinley did for President, and principally by keeping mum on the subject of gold.[25]

Thus, these were practical men in many ways; it was the middle western temper which permitted them to function in a manner not quite conceivable in the East. They were not only elected, they were re-elected, and without the aid of a powerfully organized socialist and labor vote which had made Henry George such a threat in the far East. Eastern cities had the same problems of high utility rates, unfair franchises, and corrupt councils; but though their larger industrial populations, their "new" immigration, their longer traditions of party politics created genteel reformers and radicals of stature, they created no Tom Johnson.

Socialism

A variety of other reformers—both East and West—could here be properly considered with reference to the liberalisms of the hesitant Nineties. Edward Bellamy and his program of "nationalism" are pertinent. The eastern and western elements in John P. Altgeld's crusade would be to the point, as would a comparison with that of Tom Johnson and the others of his region. Both eastern and western elements were present in Altgeld. They were not rigidly dependent on geography, and Chicago was perhaps more "eastern" in its ways and the character of its problems than were some areas of, let us say, Ohio. Richard Welling, too, would repay analysis, if only to

[25] Muriel Florence Bernitt, "The Defeat of Michigan Democracy in 1896" (M.A. thesis, University of Chicago, June, 1931).

demonstrate that all goo goos were not necessarily anemic characters who rushed to the police whenever a football was kicked through their windows. William Allen White would also make an interesting case study, his Penrod-like folksyness and laggard reformism entitling him to a kind of second-class liberal status. But there will be enough to criticize in a more profound liberalism than White could ever fathom, without dealing with him.

If we turn to Henry Demarest Lloyd, it is to note the socialist element in his liberalism, and consider its significance. Lloyd was a liberal who moved from Manchester causes which he had picked up from the aged and unprofound Francis Lieber to a profound concern for the democratic process. He seized upon monopoly as the enemy, and wrote vigorously against combines of many types. But relatively early, he grasped the idea that labor suffered by monopoly as well as agriculture, and that it was not sufficient to discourage the organization of monopolies: it was also desirable to encourage the organization of trades-unions and support labor's demands. Accordingly, he was critical of the Omaha Platform of 1892 because it said too little of organized labor, and approved the public ownership–State intervention ideas of both Populism and labor. In short, he accepted the gradualist socialism advocated by the Fabians, and made every effort to further its acceptance in America.

Fabianism was also accepted by Edward Bellamy, who introduced the original *Fabian Essays* to America. But Bellamy was theory-ridden, and conceived himself as more of a socialist than the socialists; as he said:

> Nationalists are socialists who, holding all that socialists agree on, go further, and hold also that the distribution of the co-operative product among the members of the community must be not merely equitable, whatever that term may mean, but must be always and absolutely equal.[26]

[26] G. Bernard Shaw, ed., *Socialism: the Fabian Essays . . . with . . . an Introduction to this American Edition by Edward Bellamy* (Boston, 1894), p. xvi.

Bellamy's distinction, aside from having organized a large public opinion in favor of public ownership, lay in the fact that he popularized the idea of socialism in America, for all that he was wary of it, and, in the utopian terms he chose, made it many things to many people. The more specific Christian Socialists shared with him this responsibility.[27] Lloyd had idealogical and religious relations to both, though he was slower to commit himself to socialism. He held on to the basic realities of the laborer and the farmer, and struggled to bring them together. He struck at big business as the foe of both, in his famous *Wealth against Commonwealth.* He tried, in other words, to develop a liberalism which would be adequate for a time of machinery and trusts. The difficulties he encountered remind us that it was sometimes easier to espouse frankly radical solutions to social problems than to struggle with a liberal equation.

Charles Edward Russell hailed Lloyd as a precursor of the muckrakers, and he did have a farsighted awareness of the social direction in which America was moving. But for the Eighteen Nineties, his campaign was premature, and condemned to relative failure. Socialism was too strong a draught for Americans even of the depressed Nineties, even in its Fabian version. With Richard T. Ely, they feared socialism as a menace to liberty: as a process of levelling down, not up, as an encouragement to "unchecked and unfettered power." [28]

[27] Notably George D. Herron, whose views excited western conservatives adversely during his tenure at what became Grinnell College. As "Mul" noted: "Previous to Professor Herron's appearance upon the stage of public affairs the chief exponents of Socialism in this country were in the main German-Americans, and others of foreign birth. In the minds of the public Socialism was associated with long-haired men and beer saloons, discontent and un-Christian thought" ("Mul," *op. cit.,* p. 3 and *passim).* Cf. James Dombrowski, *The Early Days of Christian Socialism in America* (New York, 1936). This latter volume must be used cautiously; in failing to define its terms carefully it provides difficulties. For instance, in placing Henry George with the Christian Socialists, it does not note the anti-socialist element in his thought *(idem,* pp. 35 ff.).

[28] Richard T. Ely, *Socialism . . . with Suggestions for Social Reform* (New York, 1895), pp. 206 ff. and *passim.*

Middle-class America preferred to endure Cripple Creek, Homestead, and the Pullman Strike, rather than to face the question of what they signified and how they were to be made unnecessary. Agrarian liberalism was sufficiently drastic, to the most needy among them: a liberalism which called in the South for Negro-white co-operation against monopoly; in the commanding West for a variety of reforms; and, nationally, for the mirage of free silver.

Nationalism

A queer lot they made, the western "radicals," so called, though it has long since been established that they were the genuine statesmen of the time, whose program of direct election of senators, the sub-treasury plan, a graduated income tax, and the rest, would be appreciated by posterity.[29] More difficult to judge is the intense nationalism which can be discerned in the attitudes of the most liberal westerners, and which sharply distinguishes them from their Manchester opponents. The genteel liberals were not only not nationalistic; they were, at times, positively anti-American. As E. L. Godkin wrote, in 1889, during a visit to England:

> The people here are so polite, and there are so many well-dressed, educated men, and life is so well ordered, I am thinking I am not worth a cent as a "good American." *This is confidential.*[30]

It was otherwise with Charles Edward Russell, who was proud of his heritage as an American, and passionately resented criticism of his country, particularly from an Englishman. Considering that he himself was not gentle when he came to deal with his country's faults, his bitterness in the following passage from his letters is striking:

> I like to think of the two visits Charles Dickens paid . . . because they are the first conspicuous manifestations of a

29 John D. Hicks, *The Populist Revolt* (Minneapolis, 1931).
30 Ogden, ed., *Life and Letters of . . . Godkin*, II, 143.

> trait that among the educated and the well-to-do has since become familiar. We may be sure that in no other country in the world would a critic so venomous, persistent and implacable have been received with such warmth and welcome. . . . No doubt it is a beautiful trait in a Christian people to like to be kicked in the face. But I cannot help reflecting upon the difference if the case were reversed. Suppose some American writer had said of England things one tenth as bitter as Dickens said of America, if the offender should visit the land he traduced he would be pilloried or ostracized or both. The sweet, gentle and submissive American spirit I have often observed at week end parties in England where the favorite topic for conversation—if an American is present—is the appalling depravity of my native land, in which the vis[i]tor is expected to acquiesce and usually does. . . . This turning of the other cheek may make for peace. I do not know. But I can testify that in an American that isn't ashamed of his country it makes for mental nausea.[31]

Russell was aware of Dickens' critical attitudes toward English institutions; and since Russell himself handled roughly not only American institutions, but also those of the English (who do not seem to have ostracized him for it), it is evident that an unthinking resentment against *foreign* criticisms as such expressed itself in these lines written in old age. Yet Russell was probably as much an internationalist as could be found in all the West, which, in the Eighteen Nineties became implicated in the momentous adventure of imperialism. It is an adventure which has been inadequately analyzed, and which can only be treated here as the fatal flaw in the liberalism of the Eighties and Nineties.

Liberal nationalism had, of course, for much of the nineteenth century—as in Italy and Hungary—been identified with progress and reform, but it may be doubted if anywhere the alliance attained the fierce assurance which it displayed in America. Liberals identified their causes with those of Jeffer-

[31] Russell, ms. (n.d.; 1939?). For a typical and undistinguished example of western—in this case southwestern—nationalism and anti-English bias, see *The Writings of W. C. Brann* (Waco, 1905). See, for example, "Those Blawsted Hawmerican Men," II, 225 ff.

son, Jackson, and Lincoln. They retained the spirit of patriotism which had been whipped up during the Civil War. The pre-eminence of the Republic in matters of freedom was a major premise with them. Brand Whitlock was to recall "a remarkable sight" which was pointed out to him during his days as a reporter: James G. Blaine while Secretary of State informally receiving farmers, reporters, "all sorts and conditions of men" in a train coach. "There is the premier of a great government," it was pointed out to Whitlock, "and yet the commonest man may approach him without ceremony, and talk to him as though he were nobody." [32] This was a very different reaction from that of Henry Adams, who in his novel, *Democracy,* expressed disgust at the mediocrity of Blaine and the vulgar familiarity which characterized politics in America.

There was promise in the multiplicity of liberalisms: Manchester, labor, agrarian, southern, as well as those of George, Bellamy, "Coin" Harvey, and others. Unfortunately, they did not, separately or collectively, make up an internationalism which could meet and master the imperialism of such worthies as Captain Mahan, Homer Lea, and Theodore Roosevelt, among others. The best that they had to offer was the free trade internationalism of the Manchester Liberals. But it was a bloodless, doctrinaire thing: it did not respect colonial peoples, except, perhaps, in the abstract; [33] and it gyrated between paternalism and a feeling that there was enough for all great nations without bloody and uncivilized conflict. Such must be the verdict on a generation which gave the Nobel Peace Prize to the author of the Roosevelt Corollary, the man who boasted expensively that he had taken the Panama Canal,

[32] Brand Whitlock, *Forty Years of It* (New York, 1920), p. 50.

[33] Though how well, in the abstract. See, for example, the *Nation* for March 16, 1882, on "The Republican Party and the Chinese Bill," which marshalled arguments with point and precision. It denounced the bill as discriminatory, upbraided the Republican party for doing what the South had itself done fifteen years before, and what the Chinese with their doctrine of "racial purity" were doing. For good measure, it denounced the anti-Jewish laws which "disgraced" the Russian statute books.

the man who sent the American Fleet around the world. Manchester Liberals wrote eloquently against imperialism. E. L. Godkin, Moorfield Storey, Oswald Garrison Villard, and their familiars made contributions to the theory of pacifism and arbitration and international accord, as well as to its practice in the Venezuelan crises and the Philippine situation. But their lack of interest in the masses—any masses—disqualified them for leadership in building a serious peace movement from the grass roots up.

As for those who were immediately in touch with the grass roots, their sympathies seem to have barely stretched to the American frontiers. It was too easy for Americans to conceive of themselves as a superior people, and to congratulate lesser races on having achieved a relationship to themselves. Finley Dunne, the best of his generation in this respect, wrote sardonically, even bitterly, about American imperialism, but the cynicism which was his strength was no substitute for a program. Much more typical of western liberals was Albert J. Beveridge, who was in the forefront of the warmongers. It must here suffice that they were not alone. Pulitzer and Hearst and their working-class readers do not deserve all the credit for creating a war spirit which was not there already. Hanna, who opposed war, and who may be said to have bought the presidency for McKinley, was unable to buy peace because there was no substantial interest in peace—in the nationalistic West, as elsewhere. Bryan's peculiar course in the Spanish-American War has been ascribed, in part, to his lack of brainpower; but it is in no way different from that of William Allen White, who also kept his western ear to the ground.

To be sure, the election of 1900 may have been no clear verdict in favor of imperialism.[34] But it will take much more work to disentangle anti-imperialism from isolationism—and even from imperialism. Westerners, like sentimentalists in the East, did momentarily forget Sherman's march to the sea in

[34] Thomas A. Bailey, "Was the Presidential Election of 1900 a Mandate on Imperialism?" *Mississippi Valley Historical Review* (Cedar Rapids, Ia.), ch. 14, pp. 43 ff.

their enthusiasm for *Cuba Libre;* but their interest in the Philippines was not wholly altruistic. By 1898, it was only relatively funny to have a letter arriving in Manila from the West requesting information about "farming land" in the islands.[35]

There were die-hard voices of Populism which saw no good in our victory or its consequences.[36] But Ray Stannard Baker, fresh from Michigan and Chicago, and soon to be a leading reform journalist, could write as follows in 1900 to a magazine audience which was about to revel in muckraking sensations:

> The march towards "prosperity" was already under way when the *Maine* was blown up in Havana harbor and war with Spain was declared. . . . [The Government spent money; it relieved unemployment.] And then the war had the interesting and yet powerful effect of diverting the mind of the American from his own woes—his currency troubles, his tariffs, his hard times. . . . He began to think of glory and patriotism and expansion; he went into throes of hero worship over Dewey, Sampson, Roosevelt, Wood; and when the war was over he returned to business in a cheerful, confident frame of mind, believing himself to be quite the bravest and most successful man on earth. . . . In a lesser degree also it had the effect of stimulating certain American industries of the productive order. The war in Cuba by the destruction of the plantations, had cut down the world's supply of sugar and tobacco. As a result, tobacco-planting and to a certain extent the sugar industry in the United States were given a new impetus.[37]

Such was the viewpoint of one soon to be among the most famous of the muckrakers. It differed only in degree from the point of view expressed in the *St. Louis Post-Dispatch:* "The Filipino is treacherous and deceitful. Besides, we want his country." [38] It reflected a short-sighted democracy which was to feel every ache and pain in our domestic society, but lacked

[35] Thomas Beer, *Hanna* (New York, 1929), p. 207.

[36] See, for example, Wharton Barker, *The Great Issues, Reprints of Some Editorials from the American, 1897-1900* (Philadelphia, 1902).

[37] Ray S. Baker, *Our New Prosperity* (New York, 1900), pp. 23-24.

[38] Quoted in Bailey, *The Man in the Street* (New York, 1948), p. 195.

the imagination to feel those in other people. It capped a process which was to leave our State Department in such utter control of its own affairs—so free of any correction by public opinion—that even liberals in diplomacy were to feel no rein upon their actions, responsible or irresponsible. The gross example is, again, Bryan, who could understand that it was a catastrophe for two great nations to wage war under modern conditions; but was unable to understand that the diplomatic dogs he unleashed to cow Nicaragua would not suffer themselves to be restrained or directed when the nation in question became Germany or England. Charles Edward Russell was infinitely more intelligent, dedicated and informed than Bryan. But the best he could suggest, when the time came for him to support our entrance into World War I, was that we would be fighting Junkerism abroad as we must fight Junkerism in the Colorado mines.[39] This was, perhaps, more true than false; but he failed to define who "we" were. Nor would it have helped if he had. Few American liberals, East or West, had a more substantial point of view to offer. Most of them had nothing but a helpless patriotism to contribute.

Perspective: The Era of Reform

Liberalism of the latter decades of the nineteenth century, then, was a mixture of liberalisms which achieved a delusive consummation in the Nineteen Hundreds and the first Wilson Administration. The genteel reformers had their day of "throwing the rascals out" from Philadelphia to San Francisco, and instituting reigns of "good government": the short ballot, the initiative and referendum, and all the other paraphernalia of efficiency that would, ultimately, serve machine politicians as well as reformers. A beginning was made in housing legislation, insurance legislation, conservation legislation, and similar matters. A very significant oversight--one which provides a sharp contrast with what was done under the

[39] His defense of his course during World War I may be examined in *Bare Hands and Stone Walls*, pp. 279 ff.

New Deal—was the government apparatus, in the midst of reform, remaining in conservative hands: there seems to have been little awareness that a liberal revolution ought to have sympathetic administrators to carry out the mandates of Congress. Gifford Pinchot was forced out of a Government bureau, La Follette never got into one, and a host of experts on political, social, and economic questions were never asked. The grossest failures were, of course, in the handling of the trust problem, and in the total lack of an international perspective, which would have put a healthy damper on liberal optimism and faith in progress and its reputed handmaiden, science.

The trouble with liberalism in the Nineteen Hundreds was its trouble in the preceding decades: it was completely a victory of the western wing of liberalism, at its most individualistic. It looked askance at those who, like David Graham Phillips, sought to probe, not only the manifestations of economic disease, but the American patient himself, and his scale of values. It preferred the values of a Booth Tarkington. It failed to use the limited, but provocative, point of view of a Henry Adams. It did not assimilate the labor problem.

It never knew what hit it when, early in the Nineteen Tens, organized business interests set out to end the peculiarly high standards of free speech which it had created. It is a mistake to say, as does one thesis, that muckraking was a "fad." [40] But it is as unhelpful to gloss over its failures and interpret it glibly as a "prelude" to the New Deal. The pendulum theory of reform—that progressive times must alternate with reactionary times—is treacherous, and is unlikely to console anyone who survives an atom-bomb attack. It would seem preferable to take an age for what it actually offers, rather than as an integer in a nebulously satisfying theory of progress.

The Eighties and Nineties were rich in liberal experiments which added up to a comprehensive defense of liberty. The relationship of *laissez faire* to civil, social, and personal liberties was clearly posed by a variety of laws and actions. The

[40] C. C. Regier, *The Era of the Muckrakers* (Chapel Hill, 1932), p. 214.

question of the status of women and children was presented in humanitarian and political terms. Popular sovereignty struggled to express the will of the people in the face of theories that this would mean the end of civilization, the creation of a mob mind. It would have been well if, in addition, these liberal actions had been better synchronized: they might have corrected popular American attitudes toward Chileans, Italians, Hawaiians, Englishmen, and others, which made the history of our foreign diplomacy a less than brilliant page in our annals.

Thus, in seeking to preserve the individual, our liberals failed to organize a liberalism able to cope with the powerful challenge which World War I offered. To that extent liberalism failed. Even New Deal liberalism failed, according to a volume with a title as curious as was the cordial reception it received from the American historical profession. Liberalism had failed, this work asserted, and would continue to fail to maintain "freedom of contract," freedom of competition, and freedom from monopoly.[41] Its error was that it conceived of liberalism solely in economic terms and failed to see even these in context. It is true that liberalism had emphasized Granger laws, free trade, anti-monopoly, the right to strike, and economic panaceas. But liberalism had never meant bread alone, nor was it committed to any one way of earning it. Henry George and Edward Bellamy linked their several social solutions to religious objectives. Ignatius Donnelly saw a moral issue in the silver question. Eugene V. Debs went to prison because he deemed the notorious "blanket injunction" issued against the striking Pullman workers unconstitutional. The liberty of speech was recognized as fundamental by all the reformers, and was the most distinctive accomplishment of the reform era. Mr. Chamberlain, secure in the wheels of *Fortune Magazine,* did not, apparently, feel deprived of any liberties; but in bidding farewell to reform for himself, he did not necessarily speak for all other liberal forces in the land.

[41] John Chamberlain, *Farewell to Reform: the Rise, Life and Decay of the Progressive Mind in America* (second ed.; New York, 1933), p. vii.

Liberalism, in the time that has been considered, massed large forces in defense of its historical aims, but did not seize them firmly. A proper combination of the liberalisms of the reform era might well have produced the "mixed economy" which today is offered by some theorists as an answer to international and domestic paradoxes which disturb mankind. In any case, the true "promise of American life" lay not in a theory, concocted by an intellectual efficiency expert, which might mystically appease the laborer, the farmer, the entrepreneur, and the modern bureaucrat. It lay in an expansion of the several liberties which hard times and intellectual confusion had clarified for Americans in the latter decades of the nineteenth century: liberties which all classes of the population required, restraints which kept those liberties in sight; and a renewed appreciation of the need for exporting, not only these concepts, but the liberties themselves, overseas.

LOUIS FILLER

CHRONOLOGY

1879

May 24. Death of William Lloyd Garrison.

Dec. 13. The Territory of Wyoming gave women the vote.

Henry George's *Progress and Poverty* first published.

1880

April. Organization of the National Farmers' Alliance.

June 9. The Greenback Labor party nominated James B. Weaver, of Iowa, for the Presidency. He received 308,578 votes.

Nov. 17. Signing of the Chinese Exclusion Treaty.

Publication of Henry Adams' novel, *Democracy,* a criticism of the results of mob influence in government.

The United States Census showed a population of 50,155,783.

1881

July 2. President James A. Garfield shot by a disappointed office-seeker; died September 19. This event spurred demand for a civil service act.

July 4. Tuskegee Institute established at Tuskegee, Alabama.

Nov. 15. Labor convention organized the Federation of Trades and Labor Unions, precursor of the American Federation of Labor.

Publication in *Atlantic Monthly* of Henry D. Lloyd's "Story of a Great Monopoly."

Publication of Helen Hunt Jackson's *A Century of Dishonor.*

1882

Jan. 2. The Standard Oil Trust first organized. The "trust" was created by Samuel C. T. Dodd, a corporation lawyer.

John F. Slater gave a million dollars for education of Negroes in the South.

Publication of Helen Campbell's *The Problem of the Poor.*

1883

Jan. 16. Passage of the Pendleton Act, establishing the Civil Service Commission.

Depression of 1883. It continued without significant upturn till 1885; its effects continued to be felt for several years after.

Publication of John Hay's *The Breadwinners.* This first American novel about labor opposed organized labor.

1884

Nov. 4. The 150,369 votes of the Prohibition party helped give the State of New York to the Democrats, and elected Grover Cleveland to the Presidency.

The Knights of Labor, an industrial union, open to skilled and unskilled workers, mounted in influence as leaders in a great strike movement to resist results of economic depression.

Publication of John P. Altgeld's *Our Penal Machinery and Its Victims.*

Publication of Laurence Gronlund's *Modern Socialism.*

1885

Publication of Josiah Strong's *Our Country,* a major patriotic and religious appeal for imperialism.

Publication of George W. Cable's *The Silent South.*

1886

May 4. Explosion of a bomb among police at a labor rally at the Haymarket, in Chicago. Trial in June resulted in seven death sentences, even though the bomb-thrower was not identified.

Oct. 28. Bartholdi's statue of "Liberty Enlightening the World" unveiled in New York Harbor.

Nov. 2. Workingmen in New York nominated Henry George for mayor. He received 68,110 votes against Abram Hewitt's 90,552 and Theodore Roosevelt's 60,435.

Dec. 8. Organization of the American Federation of Labor.

Publication of Richard T. Ely's *The Labor Movement in America.*

1887

Jan. 21. Passage of the Interstate Commerce Bill.

Feb. 8. Passage of the Dawes Act, offering a more positive program than before to the Indian population.

Feb. 15. Women vote in Kansas municipal elections.

Mar. 4. The anti-Catholic American Protective Association founded in Iowa.

July 8. Excommunication of Dr. Edward McGlynn in New York for advocating Henry George's program.

Sept. American Tariff Reform League incorporated.

1888

Mar. 26. First meeting of the International Convention of Women, in Washington, D. C.

May 15. Equal Rights Convention at Des Moines, Iowa, nominated Belva A. Lockwood for President.

June 13. Establishment of a Department of Labor, without Cabinet status.

Publication of James Bryce's *American Commonwealth.*

Publication of Edward Bellamy's *Looking Backward, 2000-1887.*

1889

Mar. 23. Oklahoma officially opened to settlers.

Sept. 14. Hull House established in Chicago.

The General Federation of Women's Clubs instituted.

Publication of Terence V. Powderly's *Thirty Years of Labor.*

1890

Jan. 23. Organization of the Woman's Christian Temperance Union.

July 2. Passage of the Sherman Anti-Trust Act.

July 10. Wyoming is the first state to grant women the suffrage.

July 14. Passage of the Sherman Silver Purchase Act.

Oct. 1. The McKinley Tariff Bill, highest in the history of the country, signed by the President.

Population of the United States 62,947,714.

Publication of Jacob A. Riis' *How the Other Half Lives.*

1891

Mar. 3. Amendment to Immigration Acts established a Superintendent of Immigration, and excluded several classes of criminals and other undesirable aliens.

April 4. American Academy of Political and Social Science organized.

May 19. The People's Party created, Cincinnati, Ohio.

Publication of Hamlin Garland's *Main-Travelled Roads.*

Publication of Ignatius Donnelly's *Caesar's Column: a Story of the Twentieth Century.*

1892

Jan. 1. Ellis Island opened as a receiving station for immigrants.

Mar. 22. Death of Walt Whitman, in Camden, New Jersey.

July 5. The People's party, at Omaha, Nebraska, nominated James B. Weaver for the Presidency. He received 1,027,329 popular votes, and twenty-two electoral votes.

July 6. At Homestead, Pennsylvania, a gun-battle took place between union men on strike and strikebreakers sent by the Pinkerton Detective Agency. The strike continued until November 20.

Oct. 23. Dedication of the World's Columbian Exposition, in Chicago.

Publication of George D. Herron's *A Plea for the Gospel.*

1893

Jan. 17. Revolution in Hawaii, instigated by United States Minister John L. Stevens, and a protectorate proclaimed. Though welcomed by the outgoing Harrison Administration, it was denounced by the newly-elected President Cleveland.

June 26. Newly elected governor of Illinois, John P. Altgeld, in a notable message, freed anarchists imprisoned for complicity in the Haymarket bombing of 1886.

June 27. Stock market crash. The ensuing economic crisis the worst in American history till then: 491 banks, over 15,000 businesses failed that year. The depression continued until 1897.

July 12. Frederick Jackson Turner delivered his paper on "The Significance of the Frontier in American History" at a meeting of the American Historical Association.

Publication of Stephen Crane's *Maggie: a Girl of the Streets,* a contribution to American literary realism.

1894

April 30. "Coxey's Army," headed by Jacob S. Coxey, marched from Ohio to Washington, D. C., seeking aid for the unemployed. Other units converged from different areas of the country. Dispersed for trespassing on Capitol grounds.

May 11. Beginning of the Pullman Strike, headed by Eugene V. Debs, of the American Railway Union. He and others were later arrested for defying a court order, under the Sherman Anti-Trust Act. Imprisoned, Debs became a socialist. The strike was lost, the union dissolved.

Aug. 27. First graduated income tax passed; declared unconstitutional the next year.

Dec. 31. The Lexow Committee completed its investigation of municipal corruption in New York: a forerunner of later muckraking exposés.

Publication of Henry D. Lloyd's *Wealth against Commonwealth.*

Publication of William H. Harvey's *Coin's Financial School,* a sensational "free silver" pamphlet.

1895

Jan. 21. Supreme Court decided that E. C. Knight Company, the "Sugar Trust," was neither a conspiracy nor in restraint of trade, and therefore not subject to prosecution under the Sherman Anti-Trust Act.

Feb. 24. Cuban revolt broke out against Spain.

Sept. 18. Booker T. Washington's Atlanta Exposition Address.

Dec. 21. Congress authorized President Cleveland to appoint a Venezuelan Boundary Commission. The President had endorsed the notorious message of his Secretary of State, Richard Olney, to Great Britain, claiming to be "practically sovereign" in the Americas.

Publication of Albert Shaw's *Municipal Government in Great Britain.*

1896

Jan. John Dewey's experimental University Elementary School opened in Chicago.

July 11. The Populist wing captured the Democratic Party; nominated William Jennings Bryan for the Presidency. His whirlwind campaign netted him 6,502,925 popular votes, 176 electoral votes, against McKinley's 7,104,179 popular votes, 271 electoral votes.

Aug. 12. Discovery of gold in Alaska; the gold rush took place the following year.

1897

Oct. 29. Death of Henry George.

Publication of Charles M. Sheldon's *In His Steps;* feeble as fiction, sensational at home and abroad in its appeal for militant Christianity.

1898

Feb. 15. Blowing up of the *Maine* in the harbor of Havana.

April 21. A state of war declared with Spain.

May 22. Death of Edward Bellamy.

June 15. Joint Resolution for Annexation of Hawaii passed.

Aug. 9. The Spanish government accepted American peace terms, freeing Cuba, giving the United States Puerto Rico, Guam, and the Philippine Islands.

Publication of Finley P. Dunne's *Mr. Dooley in Peace and in War.*

Publication of E. L. Godkin's *Unforeseen Tendencies of Democracy.*

1899

Jan. 15. Edwin Markham's "The Man with the Hoe" first published.

Feb. 4. Filipino insurrectionists attacked United States troops at Manila. The rebellion continued until March 23, 1901.

Feb. 17. Founding of the Anti-Imperialist League.

May 18. Meeting of the first Hague Peace Conference. A Permanent Court of International Arbitration was established.

July 21. Death of Robert G. Ingersoll.

Sept. 6. Secretary of State John Hay circulated a memorandum declaring for an "Open Door Policy" in respect to foreign spheres of influence in China.

Publication of John Dewey's *School and Society.*

Publication of Thorstein Veblen's *The Theory of the Leisure Class.*

1900

Mar. 6. Convention of the Social Democratic Party nominated Eugene V. Debs for the Presidency.

Mar. 14. Bill establishing the gold standard became law.

May. Boer delegates visited the United States seeking sympathy and aid in their battle against Great Britain.

Nov. 4. President McKinley re-elected. He was shot, September 6, 1901, died eight days later; succeeded by Theodore Roosevelt.

Population of the United States 76,303,387.

Publication of William V. Moody's "An Ode in Time of Hesitation."

SELECTED BIBLIOGRAPHY

Abell, Aaron I. *The Urban Impact on American Protestantism, 1865-1900*. Cambridge, 1943.

Barnard, Harry. *Eagle Forgotten: The Life of John Peter Altgeld*. Charter Books. Indianapolis and New York, 1962.

Bliss, W. D. P. (ed.). *The Encyclopedia of Social Reform*. New York, 1897.

———. *The New Encyclopedia of Social Reform*. New York, 1910.

Bryce, James. *The American Commonwealth*. London, 1891.

Cherrington, Ernest H. (ed.). *Standard Encyclopedia of the Alcohol Problem*. Westerville, Ohio, 1925-1930.

Commons, John R. (*et al.*, eds.). *History of Labour in the United States*. New York, 1918-1935.

Dabney, Virginius. *Liberalism in the South*. Chapel Hill, 1932.

Dombrowski, James. *The Early Days of Christian Socialism in America*. New York, 1936.

Ekirch, Arthur A., Jr. *The Decline of American Liberalism*. New York, 1955.

Faulkner, Harold U. *Politics, Reform and Expansion, 1890-1900*. New York, 1959.

Filler, Louis. *Crusaders for American Liberalism*. Yellow Springs, Ohio, 1961.

Flower, B. O. *Progressive Men, Women and Movements in the Past Twenty-five Years*. Boston, 1914.

Ginger, Ray. *Altgeld's America*. New York, 1958.

Gompers, Samuel. *Seventy Years of Life and Labor*. New York, 1925.

Haynes, Frederick E. *Social Politics in the United States*. Boston, 1924.

Hicks, John D. *The Populist Revolt*. Minneapolis, 1931.

Higham, John. *Strangers in the Land*. New Brunswick, 1955.

Hofstadter, Richard. *Social Darwinism in American Thought*. Philadelphia, 1944.

Josephson, Matthew. *The Politicos, 1865-1896.* New York, 1938.

Knight, Grant C. *Critical Period in American Literature.* Chapel Hill, 1951.

Mann, Arthur. *Yankee Reformers in the Urban Age.* Cambridge, Mass., 1954.

May, Henry F. *Protestant Churches and Industrial America.* New York, 1949.

Millis, Walter. *The Martial Spirit.* Boston, 1931.

Moon, Parker T. *Imperialism and World Politics.* New York, 1926.

Nye, Russel B. *Midwestern Progressive Politics.* East Lansing, 1951.

Peck, Harry T. *Twenty Years of the Republic.* New York, 1907.

Quint, Howard H. *The Forging of American Socialism.* Columbia, S. C., 1953.

Rhodes, James F. *History of the United States,* Vol. VIII. New York, 1919.

Russell, Charles E. *Bare Hands and Stone Walls.* New York, 1933.

Schlesinger, Arthur M. *The Rise of the City, 1878-1898.* New York, 1933.

Stanton, Elizabeth C., *et al. The History of Woman Suffrage.* New York, 1881-1922.

Steffens, Lincoln. *Autobiography.* New York, 1931.

Sullivan, Mark. *Our Times; the United States, 1900-1925.* Vols. I, II. New York, 1926-1927.

Washington, Booker T., and W. E. B. Du Bois. *The Negro in the South.* Philadelphia, 1907.

Welling, Richard. *As the Twig Is Bent.* New York, 1942.

Whitlock, Brand. *Forty Years of It.* New York, 1914.

Woods, Robert A. *English Social Movements.* New York, 1891.

Wyckoff, Walter A. *The Workers: an Experiment in Reality . . . The East.* New York, 1897.

———. *The Workers: an Experiment in Reality . . . The West.* New York, 1898.

Yellen, Samuel. *American Labor Struggles.* New York, 1936.

NOTE ON THE TEXT

The following selections have been taken from primary or authoritative sources. In several cases, where speeches are reproduced, they are from works which the authors themselves supervised. Professor Filler's Introduction is based on an article of the same title which appeared in January, 1952, in *The American Journal of Economics and Sociology* (Vol. XI).

Aside from minor editorial alterations in modernizing spelling and punctuation, the materials have been reproduced as they were published. Professor Filler's footnotes are bracketed to distinguish them from those of the authors and earlier editors, and all ellipses indicate an omission by him. He has, for the reader's convenience, contributed Biographical Notes on the represented authors.

O. P.

LATE NINETEENTH-CENTURY AMERICAN LIBERALISM

Representative Selections, 1880-1900

PROLOGUE

I

THE MAN WITH THE HOE [1]

EDWIN MARKHAM

WRITTEN AFTER SEEING MILLET'S WORLD-FAMOUS PAINTING

God made man in His own image,
in the image of God made He him.—Genesis.

Bowed by the weight of centuries he leans
Upon his hoe and gazes on the ground,
The emptiness of ages in his face,
And on his back the burden of the world.
Who made him dead to rapture and despair,
A thing that grieves not and that never hopes,
Stolid and stunned, a brother to the ox?
Who loosened and let down this brutal jaw?
Whose was the hand that slanted back this brow?
Whose breath blew out the light within this brain?

Is this the Thing the Lord God made and gave
To have dominion over sea and land;
To trace the stars and search the heavens for power;
To feel the passion of Eternity?
Is this the Dream He dreamed who shaped the suns
And marked their ways upon the ancient deep?
Down all the stretch of Hell to its last gulf
There is no shape more terrible than this—
More tongued with censure of the world's blind greed—
More filled with signs and portents for the soul—
More fraught with danger to the universe.

1 [Edwin Markham, *The Man with the Hoe and Other Poems* (New York, 1921 ed.), pp. 15-18.]

What gulfs between him and the seraphim!
Slave of the wheel of labor, what to him
Are Plato and the swing of Pleiades?
What the long reaches of the peaks of song,
The rift of dawn, the reddening of the rose?
Through this dread shape the suffering ages look;
Time's tragedy is in that aching stoop;
Through this dread shape humanity betrayed,
Plundered, profaned and disinherited,
Cries protest to the Judges of the World,
A protest that is also prophecy.

O masters, lords and rulers in all lands,
Is this the handiwork you give to God,
This monstrous thing distorted and soul-quenched?
How will you ever straighten up this shape;
Touch it again with immortality;
Give back the upward looking and the light;
Rebuild in it the music and the dream;
Make right the immemorial infamies,
Perfidious wrongs, immedicable woes?

O masters, lords and rulers in all lands,
How will the Future reckon with this Man?
How answer his brute question in that hour
When whirlwinds of rebellion shake the world?
How will it be with kingdoms and with kings—
With those who shaped him to the thing he is—
When this dumb Terror shall reply to God
After the silence of the centuries?

II

AN ODE IN TIME OF HESITATION[1]

WILLIAM VAUGHN MOODY

(After seeing at Boston the statue of Robert Gould Shaw, killed while storming Fort Wagner, July 18, 1863, at the head of the first enlisted Negro regiment, the Fifty-fourth Massachusetts.)

I

Before the solemn bronze Saint Gaudens made
To thrill the heedless passer's heart with awe,
And set here in the city's talk and trade
To the good memory of Robert Shaw,
This bright March morn I stand,
And hear the distant spring come up the land;
Knowing that what I hear is not unheard
Of this boy soldier and his negro band,
For all their gaze is fixed so stern ahead,
For all the fatal rhythm of their tread.
The land they died to save from death and shame
Trembles and waits, hearing the spring's great name,
And by her pangs these resolute ghosts are stirred. . . .

IV

Alas! what sounds are these that come
Sullenly over the Pacific seas,—
Sounds of ignoble battle, striking dumb
The season's half-awakened ecstasies?

1 [William Vaughn Moody, from "An Ode in Time of Hesitation," *The Poems and Plays of William Vaughn Moody* (Boston, n.d.), I, 15-25.]

Must I be humble, then,
Now when my heart hath need of pride?
Wild love falls on me from these sculptured men;
By loving much the land for which they died
I would be justified.
My spirit was away on pinions wide
To soothe in praise of her its passionate mood
And ease it of its ache of gratitude.
Too sorely heavy is the debt they lay
On me and the companions of my day.
I would remember now
My country's goodliness, make sweet her name.
Alas! what shade art thou
Of sorrow or of blame
Liftest the lyric leafage from her brow,
And pointest a slow finger at her shame? . . .

VIII

Was it for this our fathers kept the law?
This crown shall crown their struggle and their ruth?
Are we the eagle nation Milton saw
Mewing its mighty youth,
Soon to possess the mountain winds of truth,
And be a swift familiar of the sun
Where aye before God's face his trumpets run?
Or have we but the talons and the maw,
And for the abject likeness of our heart
Shall some less lordly bird be set apart?—
Some gross-billed wader where the swamps are fat?
Some gorger in the sun? Some prowler with the bat?

IX

. . . Oh, by the sweet blood and young
Shed on the awful hill slope at San Juan,
By the unforgotten names of eager boys

Who might have tasted girls' love and been stung
With the old mystic joys
And starry griefs, now the spring nights come on,
But that the heart of youth is generous,—
We charge you, ye who lead us,
Breathe on their chivalry no hint of stain!
Turn not their new-world victories to gain!
One least leaf plucked for chaffer from the bays
Of their dear praise,
One jot of their pure conquest put to hire,
The implacable republic will require;
With clamor, in the glare and gaze of noon,
Or subtly, coming as a thief at night,
But surely, very surely, slow or soon
That insult deep we deeply will requite.
Tempt not our weakness, our cupidity!
For save we let the island men go free,
Those baffled and dislaureled ghosts
Will curse us from the lamentable coasts
Where walk the frustrate dead.
The cup of trembling shall be drainèd quite,
Eaten the sour bread of astonishment,
With ashes of the hearth shall be made white
Our hair, and wailing shall be in the tent;
Then on your guiltier head
Shall our intolerable self-disdain
Wreak suddenly its anger and its pain;
For manifest in that disastrous light
We shall discern the right
And do it, tardily.—O ye who lead,
Take heed!
Blindness we may forgive, but baseness we will smite.

III

THE NEW COLOSSUS [1]

EMMA LAZARUS

Not like the brazen giant of Greek fame,
With conquering limbs astride from land to land;
Here at our sea-washed, sunset gates shall stand
A mighty woman with a torch, whose flame
Is the imprisoned lightning, and her name
Mother of Exiles. From her beacon-hand
Glows world-wide welcome; her mild eyes command
The air-bridged harbor that twin cities frame.
"Keep, ancient lands, your storied pomp!" cries she
With silent lips. "Give me your tired, your poor,
Your huddled masses yearning to breathe free,
The wretched refuse of your teeming shore.
Send these, the homeless, tempest-tost to me,
I lift my lamp beside the golden door!"

1 [Emma Lazarus, *The Poems of Emma Lazarus* (Boston, 1889), I, 202-3. (Written in aid of Bartholdi Pedestal Fund, 1883.)]

IV

THE STREETS AT MIDNIGHT[1]

ERNEST LACY

Rank vapors from the steaming earth arise,
  And swiftly past the laboring moon are blown,
  Which like a bauble in the rapids thrown,
Gleams bright, then sinks into the whitened skies.
Beneath the brilliant lamplight one descries
  A cat with fiery eyeballs limping down,
  And then a slattern woman of the town,
Poor soul! not lust but hunger in her eyes.

O friend, if you have never roamed the street,
  Aware your burdens must with years accrue,
Yet suffering for each suffering thing you meet—
  If you have never starward raised your view,
Fate questioning, and read your life's defeat,
  Turn o'er the page: it was not writ for you.

1 [Ernest Lacy, *Plays and Sonnets* (Philadelphia, 1900), p. 223.]

PART ONE

POLITICS AND SOCIETY

V

THE POPULIST PLATFORM OF 1892[1]

. . . Assembled upon the one hundred and sixteenth anniversary of the Declaration of Independence, the People's Party of America in their first National Convention, invoking upon their action the blessing of Almighty God, put forth, in the name and on behalf of the people of this country, the following preamble and declaration of principles:

The conditions which surround us best justify our cooperation. We meet in the midst of a nation brought to the verge of moral, political, and material ruin. Corruption dominates the ballot box, the Legislatures, the Congress, and touches even the ermine of the Bench. The people are demoralized; most of the States have been compelled to isolate the voters at the polling places to prevent universal intimidation or bribery. The newspapers are largely subsidized or muzzled, public opinion silenced, business prostrated, our homes covered with mortgages, labor impoverished, and the land concentrating in the hands of the capitalists. The urban workmen are denied the right of organization for self-protection; imported pauperized labor beats down their wages; a hireling standing army, unrecognized by our laws, is established to shoot them down, and they are rapidly degenerating into European conditions. The fruits of the toil of millions are boldly stolen to build up colossal fortunes for a few, unprecedented in the history of mankind, and the possessors of these in turn despise the Republic and endanger liberty. From the same prolific womb of governmental injustice we breed the two great classes—tramps and millionaires.

The national power to create money is appropriated to en-

1 [Edward McPherson, ed., *A Handbook of Politics for 1892* . . . (Washington, 1892), pp. 269-71. Chapter title supplied by editor.]

rich bond-holders; a vast public debt, payable in legal tender currency, has been funded into gold-bearing bonds, thereby adding millions to the burdens of the people.

Silver, which has been accepted as coin since the dawn of history, has been demonetized to add to the purchasing power of gold by decreasing the value of all forms of property as well as human labor, and the supply of currency is purposely abridged to fatten usurers, bankrupt enterprise and enslave industry.

A vast conspiracy against mankind has been organized on two continents, and it is rapidly taking possession of the world. If not met and overthrown at once, it forebodes terrible social convulsions, the destruction of civilization, or the establishment of an absolute despotism.

We have witnessed, for more than a quarter of a century, the struggles of the two great political parties for power and plunder, while grievous wrongs have been inflicted upon the suffering people. We charge that the controlling influences dominating both these parties have permitted the existing dreadful conditions to develop without serious effort to prevent or restrain them.

Old Parties Treated as One

Neither do they now promise us any substantial reform. They have agreed together to ignore, in the coming campaign, every issue but one. They propose to drown the outcries of a plundered people with the uproar of a sham battle over the tariff, so that capitalists, corporations, national banks, rings, trusts, watered stock, the demonetization of silver and the oppressions of the usurers may all be lost sight of. They propose to sacrifice our homes, lives and children, on the altar of mammon; to destroy the multitude in order to secure corruption funds from the millionaires.

Assembled on the anniversary of the birthday of the nation, and filled with the spirit of the grand general and chieftain who established our independence, we seek to restore the

Government of the Republic to the hands of the "plain people" with whose class it originated. We assert our purposes to be identical with the purposes of the National Constitution, to form a more perfect Union and establish justice, insure domestic tranquillity, provide for the common defense, promote the general welfare and secure the blessings of liberty for ourselves and our posterity.

We declare that this Republic can only endure as a free government while built upon the love of the whole people for each other and for the nation; that it cannot be pinned together by bayonets; that the civil war is over and that every passion and resentment which grew out of it must die with it, and that we must be in fact, as we are in name, one united brotherhood of [free men].[2]

Farmers' Demands

Our country finds itself confronted by conditions for which there is no precedent in the history of the world; our annual agricultural productions amount to billions of dollars in value, which must within a few weeks or months be exchanged for billions of dollars' worth of commodities consumed in their production; the existing currency supply is wholly inadequate to make this exchange; the results are falling prices, the formation of combines and rings, the impoverishment of the producing class. We pledge ourselves that, if given power, we will labor to correct these evils by wise and reasonable legislation, in accordance with the terms of our platform.

We believe that the powers of government—in other words, of the people—should be expanded (as in the case of the postal service) as rapidly and as far as the good sense of an intelligent people and the teachings of experience shall justify, to the end that oppression, injustice, and poverty shall eventually cease in the land.

While our sympathies as a party of reform are naturally

2 [*Handbook of Politics* reads "freedom."]

upon the side of every proposition which will tend to make men intelligent, virtuous and temperate, we nevertheless regard these questions—important as they are—as secondary to the great issues now pressing for solution, and upon which not only our individual prosperity, but the very existence of free institutions depend; and we ask all men to first help us to determine whether we are to have a Republic to administer, before we differ as to the conditions upon which it is to be administered; believing that the forces of reform this day organized will never cease to move forward, until every wrong is righted, and equal rights and equal privileges securely established for all the men and women of this country. We declare, therefore,

Perpetual Labor Union

First—That the union of the labor forces of the United States this day consummated shall be permanent and perpetual; may its spirit enter into all hearts for the salvation of the Republic, and the uplifting of mankind.

Wealth for Workers

Second—Wealth belongs to him who creates it; and every dollar taken from industry without an equivalent is robbery. "If any will not work, neither shall he eat." The interests of rural and civic labor are the same; their enemies are identical.

Ownership of Railways

Third—We believe that the time has come when the railroad corporations will either own the people or the people must own the railroads; and should the Government enter upon the work of owning and managing all railroads, we should favor an amendment to the Constitution by which all persons engaged in the Government service shall be placed under a civil service regulation of the most rigid character, so as to prevent the increase of the power of the national administration by the use of such additional Government employes.

Finance

First—We demand a national currency, safe, sound, and flexible, issued by the General Government only, a full legal tender for all debts, public and private, and that without the use of banking corporations; a just, equitable and efficient means of distribution direct to the people at a tax not to exceed two per cent per annum, to be provided as set forth in the Sub-Treasury plan of the Farmers' Alliance, or a better system; also by payments in discharge of its obligations for public improvements.

(A) We demand free and unlimited coinage of silver and gold at the present legal ratio of sixteen to one.

(B) We demand that the amount of circulating medium be speedily increased to not less than fifty dollars per capita.

(C) We demand a graduated income tax.

(D) We believe that the money of the country should be kept as much as possible in the hands of the people, and hence we demand that all State and national revenues shall be limited to the necessary expenses of the Government, economically and honestly administered.

(E) We demand that Postal Savings Banks be established by the Government for the safe deposit of the earnings of the people and to facilitate exchange.

Transportation

Second—Transportation being a means of exchange and a public necessity, the government should own and operate the railroads in the interest of the people.

The telegraph and telephone, like the post office system,

being a necessity for the transmission of news, should be owned and operated by the Government in the interest of the people.

Land

Third—The land, including all the natural sources of wealth, is the heritage of the people and should not be monopolized for speculative purposes; and alien ownership of land should be prohibited. All land now held by railroads and other corporations in excess of their actual needs, and all lands now owned by aliens, should be reclaimed by the Government and held for actual settlers only.

The following supplementary resolutions, not to be incorporated in the platform, came from the Committee on Resolutions and were adopted, as follows:

The Supplementary Platform

Whereas, Other questions having been presented for our consideration, we hereby submit the following, not as a part of the platform of the People's party, but as resolutions expressive of the sentiment of this Convention:

1. *Resolved,* That we demand a free ballot and a fair count in all elections, and pledge ourselves to secure it to every legal voter without Federal intervention, through the adoption by the States of the unperverted Australian or secret ballot system.

2. That the revenue derived from a graduated income tax should be applied to the reduction of the burden of taxation now resting upon the domestic industries of this country.

3. That we pledge our support to fair and liberal pensions to ex-Union soldiers and sailors.

4. That we condemn the fallacy of protecting American labor under the present system, which opens our ports to the pauper and criminal classes of the world, and crowds out our wage earners; and we denounce the present ineffective laws

against contract labor, and demand the further restriction of undesirable immigration.

5. That we cordially sympathize with the efforts of organized workingmen to shorten the hours of labor, and demand a rigid enforcement of the existing eight-hour law on Government work, and ask that a penalty clause be added to the said law.

6. That we regard the maintenance of a large standing army of mercenaries, known as the Pinkerton system, as a menace to our liberties, and we demand its abolition; and we condemn the recent invasion of the Territory of Wyoming by the hired assassins of plutocracy, assisted by Federal officials.

7. That we commend to the favorable consideration of the people and to the reform press the legislative system known as the initiative and referendum.

8. That we favor a constitutional provision limiting the office of President and Vice-President to one term, and providing for the election of Senators of the United States by a direct vote of the people.

9. That we oppose any subsidy or national aid to any private corporation for any purpose.

10. That this convention sympathizes with the Knights of Labor, and their righteous contest with the tyrannical combine of clothing manufacturers of Rochester, and declare it to be the duty of all who hate tyranny and oppression, to refuse to purchase the goods made by the said manufacturers, or to patronize any merchants who sell such goods. . . .

VI

TRUSTS[1]

JAMES B. WEAVER

A trust is defined to be a combination of many competing concerns under one management. The object is to increase profits through reduction of cost, limitation of product and increase of the price to the consumer. The term is now applied, and very properly, to all kinds of combinations in trade which relate to prices, and without regard to whether all or only part of the objects named are had in view.

Combinations which we now call trusts have existed in this country for a considerable period, but they have only attracted general attention for about ten years. We have in our possession copies of the agreements of the Standard Oil and Sugar Trusts. The former is dated January 2, 1882, and the latter August 6, 1887.

Trusts vary somewhat in their forms of organization. This is caused by the character of the property involved and the variety of objects to be attained. The great trusts of the country consist of an association or consolidation of a number of associations engaged in the same line of business—each company in the trust being first separately incorporated. The stock of these companies is then turned over to a board of trustees who issue back trust certificates in payment for the stock transferred. The trust selects its own board of directors and henceforth has complete control of the entire business and can regulate prices, limit or stimulate production as they may deem best for the parties concerned in the venture. The trust itself is not necessarily incorporated. Many of the

[1] [James B. Weaver, *A Call to Action. An Interpretation of the Great Uprising, Its Source and Causes* (Des Moines, 1892), pp. 387-494.]

strongest, such as the Standard Oil Trust, the Sugar Trust, and The American Cotton Seed Oil Trust and others are not. They are the invisible agents of associated artificial intangible beings. They are difficult to find, still harder to restrain and so far as present experience has gone they are practically a law unto themselves.

The power of these institutions has grown to be almost incalculable. Trustees of the Standard Oil Trust have issued certificates to the amount of $90,000,000, and each certificate is worth today $165 in the market, which makes their real capital at least $148,500,000, to say nothing of the added strength of their recent European associations. They have paid quarterly dividends since their organization in 1882. The profits amount to $20,000,000 per year. The Trust is managed by a Board of Trustees all of whom reside in New York. The combine really began in 1869, but the present agreement dates no further back than January, 1882. The only record kept of the meetings of these trustees is a note stating that the minutes of the previous meeting were read and approved. The minutes themselves are then destroyed. These facts were brought to light by an investigation before the New York Senate February, 1888. Colonel George Bliss and General Roger A. Pryor acted as council for the people and a great many things were brought out concerning the Standard, and a multitude of other combines, which had not before been well understood. John D. Rockefeller, Charles Pratt, Henry M. Rogers, H. M. Flagler, Benjamin Brewster, J. N. Archibald, William Rockefeller and W. H. Tilford are the trustees and they personally own a majority of the stock. Seven hundred other persons own the remainder. This trust holds the stock of forty-two corporations, extending into thirteen States. The Cotton Seed Oil Trust holds the stock of eighty-five corporations extending into fifteen States.

Trust combinations now dominate the following products and divisions of trade: Kerosene Oil, Cotton Seed Oil, Sugar, Oat Meal, Starch, White Corn Meal, Straw Paper, Pearled Barley, Coal, Straw Board, Lumber, Castor Oil, Cement, Linseed Oil, Lard, School Slate, Oil Cloth, Salt, Cattle, Meat Products, Gas, Street Railways, Whisky, Paints, Rubber, Steel, Steel Rails, Steel and Iron Beams, Cars, Nails, Wrought Iron Pipes, Iron Nuts, Stoves, Lead, Copper, Envelopes, Wall Paper, Paper Bags, Paving Pitch, Cordage, Coke, Reaping, Binding and Mowing Machines, Threshing Machines, Plows, Glass, Water Works, Warehouses, Sand Stone, Granite, Upholsterers' Felt, Lead Pencils, Watches and Watch Cases, Clothes Wringers, Carpets, Undertakers' Goods and Coffins, Planes, Breweries, Milling, Flour, Silver Plate, Plated Ware, and a vast variety of other lines of trade.

The Standard Oil and its complement, the American Cotton Oil Trust, were the advance guard of the vast army of like associations which have overrun and now occupy every section of the country and nearly all departments of trade. The Standard has developed into an international combine and has brought the world under its yoke. In 1890 the largest German and Dutch petroleum houses fell under the control of the Standard Oil Company, and the oil importing companies of Bremen, Hamburg and Stettin were united by the Standard into a German-American Petroleum Company, with its seat at Bremen. In 1891 the Paris Rothschilds, who control the Russian oil fields, effected a combination with the Standard Oil Trust, which makes the combine world wide; and so far as this important article of consumption is concerned, it places all mankind at their mercy. Our information concerning this international oil trust is derived from the report concerning the Petroleum Monopoly of Europe by Consul-General Edwards, of Berlin, made to the Secretary of State, June 25, 1891, and published in Consular Reports No. 131.

Now that the Petroleum Combine has accomplished the conquest of the world, what is to hinder every other branch of business from accomplishing the same end? The Standard has led the way and demonstrated the feasibility of such gigantic enterprises and others will doubtless be quick to follow. Already, indeed, the anthracite coal barons have followed their example so far as this country is concerned, and the "Big

Four," who control the meat products of this country, have reached out and subsidized the ship room and other facilities for international trade in that line. We hear also well authenticated rumors that other combinations, looking to the complete control of every branch of mercantile business, are already in existence and making what they regard as very satisfactory progress.

The Sugar Trust, which now fixes the price of 3,000,000,000 pounds of sugar annually consumed in the United States, is managed upon substantially the same plan as the Standard Oil Trust, and so, in fact, are all of the great combines. They rule the whole realm of commerce with a rod of iron and levy tribute upon the country amounting to hundreds of millions of dollars annually—an imposition which the people would not think for a moment of submitting to if exacted by their Government.

Are Trusts Legal?

It is clear that trusts are contrary to public policy and hence in conflict with the common law. They are monopolies organized to destroy competition and restrain trade. Enlightened public policy favors competition in the present condition of organized society. It was held in 1880, Central Ohio Salt Company *vs.* Guthrie, 35 Ohio St., 666, that a trust was illegal and void. The Pennsylvania courts held the same way against the Coal Trust of that State. Morris Coal Company *vs.* Vorday, 68 Pa. St., 173.

In 1869 a coal company in New York had contracted to buy coal from several firms upon condition that they would not sell coal to other persons in that locality. The party buying the coal did not pay for it, whereupon suit was brought to collect. The court refused to enforce the bargain, holding that the contract was illegal. Arnot *vs.* Pittison Coal Company, 68 N. Y., 558. The same rule was upheld by the courts at Louisiana in 1859. In Illinois a Grain Dealer's Combine was held to be illegal. The question arose in a suit brought to compel a proper division of the profits. The court refused to enforce the agreement. See Croft *vs.* McConoughy, 79 Ill., 346. The same character of decisions will be found in perhaps a majority of the States. Indeed, since the days when Coke was Lord Chief Justice of England, more than a century and a half ago, the courts in both England and America have held such combinations to be illegal and void. See "Case of the Monopolies," 11 Coke, 84.

It is contended by those interested in Trusts that they tend to cheapen production and diminish the price of the article to the consumer. It is conceded that these results may follow temporarily and even permanently in some instances. But it is not the rule. When such effects ensue they are merely incidental to the controlling object of the association. Trusts are speculative in their purposes and formed to make money. Once they secure control of a given line of business they are masters of the situation and can dictate to the two great classes with which they deal—the producer of the raw material and the consumer of the finished product. They limit the price of the raw material so as to impoverish the producer, drive him to a single market, reduce the price of every class of labor connected with the trade, throw out of employment large numbers of persons who had before been engaged in a meritorious calling and finally, prompted by insatiable avarice, they increase the price to the consumer and thus complete the circle of their depredations. Diminished prices is the bribe which they throw into the market to propitiate the public. They will take it back when it suits them to do so.

The Trust is organized commerce with the Golden Rule excluded and the trustees exempted from the restraints of conscience.

They argue that competition means war and is therefore destructive. The Trust is eminently docile and hence seeks to destroy competition in order that we may have peace. But the peace which they give us is like that which exists after the leopard has devoured the kid. This professed desire for peace is a false pretense. They dread the war of competition because the people share in the spoils. When rid of that, they always turn their guns upon the masses and depredate without limit or mercy. The main weapons of the trust are threats, intimidation, bribery, fraud, wreck, and pillage. Take one well authenticated instance in the history of the Oat Meal Trust as an example. In 1887 this Trust decided that part of their mills should stand idle. They were accordingly closed. This resulted in the discharge of a large number of laborers who had to suffer in consequence. The mills which were continued in operation would produce seven million barrels of meal during the year. Shortly after shutting down, the Trust advanced the price of meal one dollar per barrel and the public was forced to stand the assessment. The mills were more profitable when idle than when in operation.

The Sugar Trust has it within its power to levy a tribute of $30,000,000 upon the people of the United States by simply advancing the price of sugar one cent per pound for one year.

If popular tumult breaks out and legislation in restraint of these depredations is threatened, they can advance prices, extort campaign expenses and corruption funds from the people and force the disgruntled multitude to furnish the sinews of war for their own destruction. They not only have the power to do these things, but it is their known mode of warfare and they actually practice it from year to year.

The most distressing feature of this war of the Trusts is the fact that they control the articles which the plain people consume in their daily life. It cuts off their accumulations and deprives them of the staff upon which they fain would lean in their old age.

The Remedy

For nearly three hundred years the Anglo-Saxon race has been trying to arrest the encroachments of monopoly and yet the evil has flourished and gained in strength from age to age. The courts have come to the aid of enlightened sentiment, pronounced all such combinations contrary to public policy, illegal, and their contracts void; and still they have continued to thrive. Thus far repressive and prohibitory legislation have proved unavailing. Experience has shown that when men, for the sake of gain, will openly violate the moral law and infringe upon the plain rights of their neighbors, they will not be restrained by ordinary prohibitory measures. It is the application of force to the situation and force must be met with force. The States should pass stringent penal statutes which will visit personal responsibility upon all agents and representatives of the Trust who aid or assist in the transaction of its business within the State. The General Government, through its power to lay and collect taxes, should place an excise or internal revenue tax of from twenty-five to forty per cent on all manufacturing plants, goods, wares, or merchandise of whatever kind and wherever found when owned by or controlled in the interest of such combines or associations, and this tax should be a first lien upon such property until the tax is paid. The details of such a bill would not be difficult to frame. Such a law would destroy the Trust root and branch. Whenever the American people really try to overthrow these institutions they will be able to do so and to further postpone action is a crime.

What of the Future?

One of the main charges against Charles the First was that he had fostered and created monopolies. His head went to the block. Nearly every great struggle of the English race has been caused by the unjust exactions of tribute—against the extortions of greed. Our own war for Independence was a war against taxes. Our late internal struggle was for the freedom of labor and the right of the laborer to possess and enjoy his own. That struggle is still on and it is now thundering at our gates with renewed energy. It will not down, though the Trust heap Ossa upon Pelion. The people will rise and overturn the despoilers though they shake the earth by the displacement.

These vast struggles are great teachers and the world is learning rapidly. We are coming to know that great combinations reduce the cost of production and soon the world will grasp the idea that the people can combine and protect themselves. In this combine, in this co-operation of all, there will be no discrimination and the bounties of Heaven will be open alike to the weak and the powerful. We welcome the conflict. There is no time to lose nor can the battle begin too soon.

VII

HOW THE WORLD CAME TO BE RUINED[1]

IGNATIUS DONNELLY

We were uneasy, restless, longing for the night to come. To while away the time we conversed upon subjects that were near our hearts.

I said to Maximilian while he paced the room:

"How did this dreadful state of affairs, in which the world now finds itself, arise? Were there no warnings uttered by any intelligent men? Did the world drift blindly and unconsciously into this condition?"

"No," said Maximilian, going to his library; "no, even a hundred years ago the air was full of prophecies. Here," he said, laying his hand upon a book, "is *The Century Magazine*, of February, 1889; and on page 622 we read:

> For my own part, I must confess my fears that, unless some important change is made in the constitution of our voting population, *the breaking strain upon our political system will come within half a century*. Is it not evident that our present tendencies are in the wrong direction? The rapidly increasing use of money in elections, for the undisguised purchase of votes, and the growing disposition to tamper with the ballot and the tally-sheet, are some of the symptoms. . . . Do you think that you will convince the average election officer that it is a great crime to cheat in the return of votes, when he knows that a good share of those votes have been purchased with money? No; the machinery of the election will not be kept free from fraud while the

1 [Ignatius Donnelly, *Caesar's Column* (Chicago, n.d.), pp. 93-103. The novel has described an America of the late twentieth century which has fallen into the hands of an oligarchy. It is being opposed by a secret society, the Brotherhood.]

atmosphere about the polls reeks with bribery. *The system will all go down together.* In a constituency which can be bribed all the forms of law tend swiftly to decay.

"And here," he said, picking up another volume, "is a reprint of the choicest gems of *The North American Review.* In the number for March, 1889, Gen. L. S. Bryce, a member of Congress, said:

> We live in a commercial age—not in a military age; and the shadow that is stealing over the American landscape partakes of a commercial character. In short, *the shadow is of an unbridled plutocracy,* caused, created and cemented in no slight degree by legislative, aldermanic and congressional action; *a plutocracy that is far more wealthy than any aristocracy that has ever crossed the horizon of the world's history, and one that has been produced in a shorter consecutive period;* the names of those members are emblazoned, not on the pages of their nation's glory, but of its peculation; who represent no struggle for their country's liberties, but for its boodle; no contests for Magna Charta, but railroad charters; and whose octopus-grip is extending over every branch of industry; a plutocracy which controls the price of the bread that we eat, the price of the sugar that sweetens our cup, the price of the oil that lights us on our way, the price of the very coffins in which we are finally buried; a plutocracy which encourages no kindly relation between landlord and tenant, which has so little sense of its political duties as even to abstain from voting, and which, in short, by its effrontery, is already causing the unthinking masses to seek relief in communism, in single-taxism, and in every other ism, which, if ever enforced, would infallibly make their second state worse than the first.

"And here are hundreds of warnings of the same kind. Even the President of the United States, in that same year, 1889, uttered this significant language:

> Those who use unlawful methods, if moved by no higher motive than the selfishness that prompted them, may well stop and inquire, *What is to be the end of this?*

"Bishop Potter, of New York, in the national ceremonies, held April 30, 1889, which marked the centennial anniversary of the first inauguration of George Washington, spoke of the plutocracy, which had already reached alarming proportions, and expressed his doubts whether the Republic would ever celebrate another centennial. Afterwards, in explaining his remarks, he said:

> When I speak of this as the era of the plutocrats, nobody can misunderstand me. Everybody has recognized the rise of the money power. Its growth not merely stifles the independence of the people, but the blind believers in this omnipotent power of money assert that its liberal use condones every offense. The pulpit does not speak out as it should. These plutocrats are the enemies of religion, as they are of the state. And, not to mince matters, I will say that, while I had the politicians in mind prominently, there "are others." I tell you I have heard the corrupt use of money in elections and the sale of the sacred right of the ballot openly defended by ministers of the gospel. I may find it necessary to put such men of the sacred office in the public pillory.

"And Bishop Spalding, of Peoria, Illinois, about the same time, said:

> Mark my words, the saloon in America has become a public nuisance. The liquor trade, by meddling with politics and corrupting politics, has become a menace and a danger. Those who think and those who love America and those who love liberty are going to bring this moral question into politics more and more; also this question of bribery, this question of lobbying, this question of getting measures through state and national legislatures by corrupt means. They are going to be taken hold of. Our press, which has done so much to enlighten our people, which represents so much that is good in our civilization, must also be reformed. It must cease to pander to such an extent to the low and sensual appetites of man. My God, man is animal enough! You don't want to pander to his pruriency! You don't want to pander to the beast that is in him. . . . Our rich men —and they are numerous, and their wealth is great—their number and their wealth will increase—but our rich men *must do their duty or perish*. I tell you, in America, we will not tolerate vast wealth in the hands of men who do nothing for the people.

"And here is a still more remarkable article, by Dr. William Barry, in *The Forum,* for April, 1889. He speaks of—

> The concrete system of capitalism, which in its present shape is not much more than a century old, and goes back to Arkwright's introduction of the spinning-jenny in 1776—that notable year—as to its hegira or divine epoch of creation.

"And again he says:

> This it is that justifies Von Hartmann's description of the nineteenth century as "the most irreligious that has ever been seen"; this and not the assault upon dogma or the decline of the churches. There is a depth below atheism; below anti-religion, and into that the age has fallen. It is the callous indifference to everything which does not make for wealth. . . . What is eloquently described as "the progress of civilization," as "material prosperity," and "unexampled wealth," or, more modestly, as "the rise of the industrial middle class," becomes, when we look into it with eyes purged from economic delusions, the creation of a "lower and lowest" class, without land of their own, without homes, tools or property beyond the strength of their hands; whose lot is more helplessly wretched than any poet of the Inferno has yet imagined. Sunk in the mire of ignorance, want and immorality, they seem to have for their only gospel the emphatic words attributed to Mr. Ruskin: "If there is a next world they *will* be damned; and if there is none, they are damned already." . . . Have all these things come to pass that the keeper of a whisky shop in California may grow rich on the spoils of drunken miners, and great financiers dictate peace and war to venerable European monarchies? The most degraded superstition that ever called itself religion has not preached such a dogma as this. It falls below fetishism. The worship of the almighty dollar, incarnate in the self-made capitalist, is a deification at which Vespasian himself, with his *"Ut puto, deus fio,"* would stare and gasp.

"And this remarkable article concludes with these words of prophecy:

> The agrarian difficulties of Russia, France, Italy, Ireland, and of wealthy England show us that ere long the urban

> and the rural populations will be standing in the same camp. They will be demanding the abolition of that great and scandalous paradox whereby, though production has increased three or four times as much as the mouths it should fill, those mouths are empty. The backs it should clothe are naked; the heads it should shelter, homeless; the brains it should feed, dull or criminal, and the souls it should help to save, brutish. Surely it is time that science, morality and religion should speak out. A great change is coming. It is even now at our doors. Ought not men of good will to consider how they shall receive it, so that its coming may be peaceable?

"And here," Max added, "is the great work of Prof. Schelligan, in which he quotes from *The Forum,* of December, 1889, page 464, a terrible story of the robberies practiced on the farmers by railroad companies and moneylenders. The railroads in 1882 took, he tells us, one-half of the entire crop of Kansas to carry the other half to market! In the thirty-eight years following 1850 the railroad interest of the United States increased fifteen hundred and eighty per cent; the banking interest nine hundred and eighteen per cent, and the farming interest only two hundred and fifty-two per cent. A man named Thomas G. Shearman showed, in 1889, that 100,000 persons in the United States would, in thirty years, at the rate at which wealth was being concentrated in the hands of the few, own three-fifths of all the property of the entire country. The *American Economist* asserted, in 1889, that in twenty-five years the number of people in the United States who owned their own homes had fallen from five-eighths to three-eighths. A paper called *The Progress,* of Boston, in 1889, gave the following significant and prophetic figures:

> The eloquent Patrick Henry said: "We can only judge the future by the past."
>
> "Look at the past:
>
> When Egypt went down 2 per cent of her population owned 79 per cent of her wealth. The people were starved to death.

When Babylon went down 2 per cent of her population owned all the wealth. The people were starved to death.

When Persia went down 1 per cent of her population owned the land.

When Rome went down 1,800 men owned all the known world.

There are about 40,000,000 people in England, Ireland and Wales, and 100,000 people own all the land in the United Kingdom.

For the past twenty years the United States has rapidly followed in the steps of these old nations. Here are the figures:

In 1850 capitalists owned 37½ per cent of the nation's wealth.

In 1870 they owned 63 per cent.

"In 1889, out of 1,500,000 people living in New York City, 1,100,000 dwelt in tenement houses.

"At the same time farmlands, East and West, had fallen, in twenty-five years, to one-third or one-half their cost. State Assessor Wood, of New York, declared, in 1889, that, in his opinion, 'in a few decades there will be none but tenant farmers in this State.' [2]

"In 1889 the farm mortgages in the Western States amounted to three billion four hundred and twenty-two million dollars."

"Did these wonderful utterances and most significant statistics," I asked, "produce no effect on that age?"

"None at all," he replied. " 'Wisdom cries in the streets, and no man regards her.' The small voice of Philosophy was unheard amid the blare of the trumpets that heralded successful knavery; the rabble ran headlong to the devil after gauds and tinsel."

"Have there been," I asked, "no later notes of warning of the coming catastrophe?"

"Oh, yes," he replied; "ten thousand. All through the past century the best and noblest of each generation, wherever and whenever they could find newspapers or magazines that

[2] See *Popular Science Monthly,* November, 1889, p. 28.

dared to publish their utterances, poured forth, in the same earnest tones, similar prophecies and appeals. But in vain. Each generation found the condition of things more desperate and hopeless; every year multiplied the calamities of the world. The fools could not see that a great cause must continue to operate until checked by some higher power. And here there was no higher power that desired to check it. As the domination and arrogance of the ruling class increased, the capacity of the lower classes to resist, within the limits of law and constitution, decreased. Every avenue, in fact, was blocked by corruption. Juries, courts, legislatures, congresses, they were as if they were not. The people were walled in by impassable barriers. Nothing was left them but the primal, brute instincts of the animal man, and upon these they fell back, and the Brotherhood of Destruction arose. But no words can tell the sufferings that have been endured by the good men, here and there, who, during the past century, tried to save mankind. Some were simply ostracized from social intercourse with their caste; others were deprived of their means of living and forced down into the ranks of the wretched; and still others"—and here, I observed, his face grew ashy pale, and the muscles about his mouth twitched nervously—"still others had their liberty sworn away by purchased perjury, and were consigned to prisons, where they still languish, dressed in the hideous garb of ignominy, and performing the vile tasks of felons." After a pause, for I saw he was strangely disturbed, I said to him:

"How comes it that the people have so long submitted to these great wrongs? Did they not resist?"

"They did," he replied; "but the fruit of the tree of evil was not yet ripe. At the close of the nineteenth century, in all the great cities of America, there was a terrible outbreak of the workingmen; they destroyed much property and many lives, and held possession of the cities for several days. But the national government called for volunteers, and hundreds of thousands of warlike young men, sons of farmers, sprang to arms; and, after several terrible battles, they suppressed the revolution, with the slaughter of tens of thousands of those who took part in it; while afterwards the revengeful Oligarchy sent thousands of others to the gallows. And since then, in Europe and America, there have been other outbreaks, but all of them terminated in the same way. The condition of the world has, however, steadily grown worse and worse; the laboring classes have become more and more desperate. The farmers' sons could, for generations, be counted upon to fight the workmen; but the fruit has been steadily ripening. Now the yeomanry have lost possession of their lands; their farms have been sold under their feet; cunning laws transferred the fruit of their industry into the pockets of great combinations, who loaned it back to them again, secured by mortgages; and, as the pressure of the same robbery still continued, they at last lost their homes by means of the very wealth they had themselves produced. Now a single nabob owns a whole county; and a state is divided between a few great loan associations; and the men who once tilled the fields, as their owners, are driven to the cities to swell the cohorts of the miserable, or remain on the land a wretched peasantry, to contend for the means of life with vile hordes of Mongolian coolies. And all this in sight of the ruins of the handsome homes their ancestors once occupied! Hence the materials for armies have disappeared. Human greed has eaten away the very foundations on which it stood. And of the farmers who still remain nearly all are now members of our Brotherhood. When the Great Day comes, and the nation sends forth its call for volunteers, as in the past, that cry will echo in desolate places; or it will ring through the triumphant hearts of savage and desperate men who are hastening to the banquet of blood and destruction. And the wretched, yellow, under-fed coolies, with women's garments over their effeminate limbs, will not have the courage or the desire or the capacity to make soldiers and defend their oppressors."

"But have not the Oligarchy standing armies?" I asked.

"Yes. In Europe, however, they have been constrained, by inability to wring more taxes from the impoverished people, to gradually diminish their numbers. There, you know, the real government is now a coterie of bankers, mostly Israelites; and the kings and queens, and so-called presidents, are mere toys and puppets in their hands. All idea of national glory, all chivalry, all pride, all battles for territory or supremacy have long since ceased. Europe is a banking association conducted exclusively for the benefit of the bankers. Bonds take the place of national aspirations. To squeeze the wretched is the great end of government; to toil and submit, the destiny of the peoples.

"The task which Hannibal attempted, so disastrously, to subject the Latin and mixed-Gothic races of Europe to the domination of the Semitic blood, as represented in the merchant-city of Carthage, has been successfully accomplished in these latter days by the cousins of the Phoenicians, the Israelites. The nomadic children of Abraham have fought and schemed their way, through infinite depths of persecution, from their tents on the plains of Palestine, to a power higher than the thrones of Europe. The world is today Semitized. The children of Japheth lie prostrate slaves at the feet of the children of Shem; and the sons of Ham bow humbly before their august dominion.

"The standing armies of Europe are now simply armed police; for, as all the nations are owned by one power—the money power—there is no longer any danger of their assaulting each other. But in the greed of the sordid commercial spirit which dominates the continent they have reduced, not only the numbers, but the pay of the soldiers, until it is little better than the compensation earned by the wretched peasantry and the mechanics; while years of peace and plunder have made the rulers careless and secure. Hence our powerful association has spread among these people like wild-fire: the very armies are honeycombed with our ideas, and many of the soldiers belong to the Brotherhood.

"Here, in America, they have been wise enough to pay the soldiers of their standing army better salaries; and hence they do not so readily sympathize with our purposes. But we outnumber them ten to one, and do not fear them. There is, however, one great obstacle which we have not yet seen the way to overcome. More than a century ago, you know, dirigible air-ships were invented. The Oligarchy has a large force of several thousands of these, sheathed with that light but strong metal, aluminum; in popular speech they are known as The Demons. Sailing over a hostile force, they drop into its midst great bombs, loaded with the most deadly explosives, mixed with bullets; and, where one of these strikes the ground, it looks like the crater of an extinct volcano; while leveled rows of dead are strewed in every direction around it. But this is not all. Some years since a French chemist discovered a dreadful preparation, a subtle poison, which, falling upon the ground, being heavier than the air and yet expansive, rolls, 'like a slow blot that spreads,' steadily over the earth in all directions, bringing sudden death to those that breathe it. The Frenchman sold the secret of its preparation to the Oligarchy for a large sum; but he did not long enjoy his ill-gotten wealth. He was found dead in his bed the next day, poisoned by the air from a few drops of his own invention; killed, it is supposed, by the governments, so that they would possess forever the exclusive monopoly of this terrible instrument of slaughter. It is upon this that they principally rely for defense from the uprisings of the oppressed people. These air-ships, 'The Demons,' are furnished with bombs, loaded with this powerful poison; and, when an outbreak occurs, they sail, like great foul birds, dark-winged and terrible, over the insurgents; they let fall a single bomb, which inspires such terror in the multitude that those not instantaneously killed by the poison fly with the utmost speed; and the contest is at an end. We have long labored to bring the men who arm these air-ships, and who manufacture this poison, into our organization, but so far without success. The Oligarchy knows their value, and pays them well. We have, however, bribed one or two of their men, not themselves in the secret, but who have inspired the others to make demand after demand upon the government for increased pay, knowing that they held everything in their power. The Oligarchy has been constrained to yield to these demands, which have only led, under our inspiration, to still greater claims; and it is our hope that before long the rulers will refuse to go farther in that direction; and then, in the discontent that will inevitably follow, the men will yield to our approaches. It will be the old story over again—the army that was called in to defend effete Rome at last took possession of the empire and elected the emperors. This is the fate that cruelty and injustice ultimately bring upon their own heads—they are devoured by their instruments. As Manfred says:

> The spirits I have raised abandon me;
> The spells that I had recked of torture me.[3]

"You are right," I replied; "there is nothing that will insure permanent peace but universal justice; that is the only soil that grows no poisons. Universal justice means equal opportunities for all men and a repression by law of those gigantic abnormal selfishnesses which ruin millions for the benefit of thousands. In the old days selfishness took the form of conquest, and the people were reduced to serfs. Then, in a later age, it assumed the shape of individual robbery and murder. Laws were made against these crimes. Then it broke forth in the shape of subtle combinations, 'rings,' or 'trusts,' as they called them, corporations, and all the other cunning devices of the day, some of which scarcely manifested themselves on the surface, but which transferred the substance of one man into the pockets of another, and reduced the people to slavery as completely and inevitably as ever the robber barons of old did the original owners of the soil of Europe."

[3] [Mr. Donnelly has misquoted the following lines from Lord Byron's *Manfred* (1817), Act I, Scene II:

> The spirits I have raised abandon me—
> The spells which I have studied baffle me—
> The remedy I reck'd of tortured me:]

VIII

SOME LIVE QUESTIONS

JOHN P. ALTGELD[1]

INTERVIEW ON ANARCHY IN ILLINOIS[2]

Governor Altgeld, in the course of an interview on reports of recent activity among anarchists in Chicago, said:

"All talk of that kind is a malicious libel upon the great city of Chicago and the fair name of our State, and it is that kind of irresponsible talk in the past that has done incalculable injury to our good name, and it should be stopped, not only by individuals, but by the newspapers that have been indulging in it."

"Why do you say it is a libel?"

"Because it is and always has been absolutely without foundation, and has been indulged in, in part, for sensational purposes, and in part because certain individuals found that they could not only make political capital out of it, but could derive personal benefit and advantage by it."

"Why do you say that?"

"Because the man who was chief of police at the time the so-called anarchist agitation was at its height some years ago, the man who was one of the most honest and able chiefs of police Chicago ever had, has not only stated that he investigated the whole matter carefully, and watched the so-called anarchists, and that he came to the conclusion that there was

1 [John P. Altgeld, *Live Questions, Comprising His Papers, Speeches and Interviews; also His Messages to the Legislature of Illinois, and a Statement of the Facts which Influenced His Course as Governor on Several Famous Occasions* (Chicago, 1899). Chapter title supplied by editor.]

2 [This Interview appeared in the *Chicago Tribune,* August 31, 1893; *ibid.,* pp. 405-7.]

not much in the whole anarchist talk, but he has further stated that there were prominent police officials who wanted to have bogus anarchist conspiracies formed in order to get the credit of dispersing them, and who wanted to keep the conservative public in a state of alarm, in order that they themselves might derive personal advantages out of it in the way of achieving glory and promotion. Since that, the same tactics have been resorted to repeatedly by self-called detectives; and I have been informed at different times during the last seven or eight years, that some wealthy businessmen of Chicago were kept in such a state of uneasiness by this anarchistic talk, that they were induced, from time to time, to pay money to these fellows for the ostensible purpose of watching the maneuvers of a class of people who in reality had no existence.

"They have not yet found out who threw the bomb at the riot in 1886, consequently there is nothing to show that he was an anarchist. Vast sums of money have been spent and great efforts have been made to find out all about it, and if the police have any information on the subject, then the fact that they refuse to say who it was would show almost conclusively that he was not an anarchist.

Anarchy and the Election

"Now, there is an election to be held in Chicago this fall, and some of the newspapers there have again shown a readiness to slander that great city by publishing paragraphs about anarchists, in order, as they imagine, to make some political capital out of it."

"Do you think, Governor, that there are no anarchists in Chicago?"

"I have examined the whole subject carefully. I have been in communication with all classes of people, including newspapermen and others, who had previously talked much on this subject, and I am convinced that there are not and there never have been fifty anarchists in the whole State of Illinois.

I don't believe there are fifty in all America. Of course, small agitators will assert to the contrary, but that signifies nothing. We have our criminal classes, as all other States and cities have. We have our percentage of thieves, of robbers, murderers, and of swindlers, but no more than our percentage. We have discontented people, as every State and country in the world has. We have all manner of theorists, but they are law-abiding. We occasionally have serious labor troubles, as every industrial community has. Let me say now that Illinois is one of the greatest, if not the greatest, industrial State on the face of the earth, and, considering the extent of its industries, we have not the percentage of labor troubles that they have in other States. During times of strikes there are occasional collisions with the authorities, just as there are in other States, and in times of serious labor trouble, there is more or less irresponsible and wild talk, all of which subsides and is forgotten the moment the labor trouble is over. At present the outlook for laborers is bad, and we have a great many thousands of idle men.

Patriots Among Bread Rioters

"Nobody likes to starve while there is bread in sight, and we may have an occasional bread riot, but it will be by people nearly every man of whom would fight for the Stars and Stripes. There are to be found in all cities a few irresponsible agitators who talk loud and make a noise, and if the newspapers will give them space the public may be led to believe that there are many men talking. The fact is, it is time our people were developing a little more State pride. The growth of the State has been so marvelously rapid, and its development so wonderful, that our people do not yet fully understand that in everything that goes to make up a civilized and a mighty people, Illinois is the greatest State upon earth. Yet such has been the course of some of our great newspapers in the past, that an unfavorable impression has been made upon the world, and as a consequence, some of the States, that have scarcely anything left but an overweening conceit and a threadbare reminiscence, actually assume an air of superiority towards us. We can afford to smile at those pretensions, but while the people of the world are coming to us in great numbers, and are amazed at our achievements and our greatness, I hope the press will not stoop to slander the good name of our great State and of marvelous Chicago."

SECRET PROSCRIPTIVE SOCIETIES [3]

Milwaukee, January 11, 1893.

The *Catholic Citizen* of today publishes the following letter from Governor Altgeld:

Editor of the *Catholic Citizen*,
Milwaukee, Wis.:

Dear Sir—In answer to your favor of the 5th inst., asking me to give you my opinion upon the A. P. A. movement, permit me to say that I have not the time at present to enter upon a discussion of the subject, and can only give brief and off-hand answers to your specific questions:

1. "What is your opinion of secret proscriptive societies?"

Answer: Secret proscriptive societies, meeting in dark places and taking dark oaths to do dark things, have never benefited the world. They are the legitimate children of despotism and have no place in a Republic. The glory of our country is largely due to the fact that we have let sunshine in on every question and every place, and any proscriptive movement is at variance with our career and is antagonistic to free government.

2. "What do you think of the A. P. A. movement?"

Answer: The American people differ from all other people in the world in that they are composed or made up of all nationalities, representing all religions and all theories, and

[3] [*Ibid.*, pp. 407-8.]

thus constituting an entirely new people, distinct from all of its elements, and possessing an energy and enterprise such as the world has not seen before. Our marvelous achievements and great advancement are due to the fact that all of the nationalities and religionists have lived together harmoniously, have worked side by side in peace and have lent each other a helping hand. The effect of any proscriptive movement must be to entirely change this condition of affairs, to beget family feuds, to set neighbor against neighbor and townsman against townsman, to revive the spirit of fanaticism, and in the end lead to violence, riot and bloodshed. This being so, I regard the A. P. A. movement as being unpatriotic and dangerous in character, but I do not believe it can have a long life or meet with much success, because the intelligence of the American people is too great to permit this medieval spirit to take root in this country.

3. "Do you think the A. P. A. sentiment is generally diffused among Protestants?"

Answer: No, I do not; they are too intelligent for that.

4. "What is the right remedy against such movements?"

Answer: The most wide and thorough discussion possible; hold the whole subject up to the sun and it will right itself.

5. "In what respect, if any, are Catholics blamable?"

Answer: I do not know, unless it should be true that they have, in cases, been offensively aggressive, especially in the matter of securing and holding public offices, and also, perhaps, in not repudiating the sentiments of some of the priests who openly assail our public school system. The American people believe in the public schools, and are quick to resent any attack upon them.

Hoping you will excuse me from a further discussion of the subject at present, I am

Very respectfully,
JOHN P. ALTGELD
Governor of Illinois

THE PULLMAN CORRESPONDENCE [4]

Early in the summer of 1894 the employees of the Pullman Company went on a strike on account of insufficient wages. They claimed that they had long been at starvation point and could not live on the wages the company proposed to pay. Finally, the organization of the American Railway Trainmen espoused the cause of the Pullman employees and refused to handle Pullman sleeping cars. This brought on the great railway strike of that year. The Pullman employees were of a superior character. There were very few old men or men of inferior grade, the company employing only the best. Yet in a few weeks after leaving the shops, the majority had to apply for bread to a public relief committee which had been organized. But the relief that could be obtained from public charity became exhausted. The Cook County officials did what they could to furnish aid, but the demand was too great. Finally, numerous appeals were made to the Governor, when the following correspondence took place:

Kensington, Ill., August 17, 1894.

To His Excellency, the Governor of the State of Illinois: We, the people of Pullman, who, by the greed and oppression of George M. Pullman, have been brought to a condition where starvation stares us in the face, do hereby appeal to you for aid in this our hour of need. We have been refused employment and have no means of leaving this vicinity, and our families are starving. Our places have been filled with workmen from all over the United States, brought here by the Pullman Company, and the surplus were turned away to walk the streets and starve also. There are over 1,600 families here in destitution and want, and their condition is pitiful. We have exhausted all the means at our command to feed them, and we now make this appeal to you as a last resource. Trust-

[4] [*Ibid.*, pp. 420-24.]

ing that God will influence you in our behalf and that you will give this your prompt attention, we remain,

Yours in distress,

THE STARVING CITIZENS OF PULLMAN.

F. E. POLLANS, L. J. NEWELL, THEO. RODHE,
Committee.

Springfield, August 19, 1894.

To George M. Pullman, President, Pullman Palace Car Co., Chicago: Sir:—I have received numerous reports to the effect that there is great distress at Pullman. Today I received a formal appeal as Governor from a committee of the Pullman people for aid. They state that sixteen hundred families, including women and children, are starving; that they cannot get work and have not the means to go elsewhere; that your company has brought men from all over the United States to fill their places. Now, these people live in your town and were your employees. Some of them worked for your company for many years. They must be people of industry and character or you would not have kept them. Many of them have practically given their lives to you. It is claimed they struck because after years of toil their loaves were so reduced that their children went hungry. Assuming that they were wrong and foolish, they had yet served you long and well and you must feel some interest in them. They do not stand on the same footing with you, so that much must be overlooked. The State of Illinois has not the least desire to meddle in the affairs of your company, but it cannot allow a whole community within its borders to perish of hunger. The local overseer of the poor has been appealed to, but there is a limit to what he can do. I cannot help them very much at present. So unless relief comes from some other source I shall either have to call an extra session of the Legislature to make special appropriations, or else issue an appeal to the humane people of the State to give bread to your recent employees. It seems to me that you would prefer to relieve the situation yourself, especially as it has just cost the State upwards of fifty thousand dollars to protect your property, and both the State and the public have suffered enormous loss and expense on account of disturbances that grew out of the trouble between your company and its workmen. I am going to Chicago tonight to make a personal investigation before taking any official action. I will be at my office in the Unity block at 10 A.M. tomorrow, and shall be glad to hear from you if you care to make any reply.

JOHN P. ALTGELD, Governor.

(On the morning of the 20th Mr. Wickes, a vice-president of the Pullman Company, called and offered to take me in charge and show me around. I told him that I should be pleased to have him go along with me, but that I did not think it best to go under anybody's wing. I then went to Pullman where two of the company's representatives joined me, and I spent the entire day making an examination, and the next morning sent by messenger the following letter to Mr. Pullman:)

Chicago, Ill., August 21st, 1894.

Mr. George M. Pullman, President, Pullman Car Company, Chicago, Ill.: Sir:—I examined the conditions at Pullman yesterday, visited even the kitchens and bedrooms of many of the people. Two representatives of your company were with me and we found the distress as great as it was represented. The men are hungry and the women and children are actually suffering. They have been living on charity for a number of months and it is exhausted. Men who had worked for your company for more than ten years had to apply to the relief society in two weeks after the work stopped.

I learn from your manager that last spring there were 3,260 people on the payroll; yesterday there were 2,220 at work, but over 600 of these are new men, so that only about 1,600 of the old employees have been taken back, thus leaving over 1,600 of the old employees who have not been taken back. A few hundred have left; the remainder have nearly all applied for work, but were told that they were not needed. These are utterly destitute. The relief committee on last Saturday gave out two pounds of oat meal and two pounds of corn meal to each family. But even the relief committee has exhausted its resources.

Something must be done and at once. The case differs from instances of destitution found elsewhere, for generally there is somebody in the neighborhood able to give relief; this is not the case at Pullman. Even those who have gone to work are so exhausted that they cannot help their neighbors if they would. I repeat now that it seems to me your company cannot afford to have me appeal to the charity and humanity of the State to save the lives of your old employees. Four-fifths of those people are women and children. No matter what caused this distress, it must be met.

If you will allow me, I will make this suggestion: If you had shut down your works last fall when you say business was poor, you would not have expected to get any rent for your tenements. Now, while a dollar is a large sum to each of these people, all the rent now due you is a comparatively small matter to you. If you would cancel all rent to October 1st, you would be as well off as if you had shut down. This would enable those who are at work to meet their most pressing wants. Then if you cannot give work to all why [not] work some half-time so that all can at least get something to eat for their families. This will give immediate relief to the whole situation. And then by degrees assist as many to go elsewhere as desire to do so, and all to whom you cannot give work. In this way something like a normal condition could be re-established at Pullman before winter and you would not be out any more than you would have been had you shut down a year ago.

I will be at the Unity block for several hours and will be glad to see you if you care to make any reply.

Yours, respectfully,

JOHN P. ALTGELD

It should be noted that the people of Pullman were all tenants of the Pullman Company, and were charged very high rates for rent, water, etc., and when their wages were reduced these charges were not reduced.

Mr. Pullman made a short answer to the above letter, but did not offer to do anything toward relieving the situation, and he declined to abate any of the rent due from the tenants. Thereupon the following final reply was sent to him:

Chicago, August 21st, 1894.

George M. Pullman, Esq., President, Pullman Palace Car Company, City: Sir:—I have your answer to my communication of this morning. I see by it that your company refuses to do anything toward relieving the situation at Pullman. It is true that Mr. Wickes offered to take me to Pullman and show me around. I told him that I had no objections to his going, but that I doubted the wisdom of my going under anybody's wing. I was, however, met at the depot by two of your representatives, both able men, who accompanied me everywhere. I took pains to have them present in each case. I also called at your office and got what information they could give there, so that your company was represented and heard, and no man there questioned either the condition or the extent of the suffering. If you will make the round I made, go into the houses of these people, meet them face to face and talk with them, you will be convinced that none of them had $1,300, or any other sum of money only a few weeks ago.

I cannot enter into a discussion with you as to the merits of the controversy between you and your former workmen.

It is not my business to fix the moral responsibility in this case. There are nearly six thousand people suffering for the want of food—they were your employees—four-fifths of them are women and children—some of these people have worked for you for more than twelve years. I assumed that even if they were wrong and had been foolish, you would not be willing to see them perish. I also assumed that as the State had just been to a large expense to protect your property you would not want to have the public shoulder the burden of relieving distress in your town.

As you refuse to do anything to relieve the suffering in this case, I am compelled to appeal to the humanity of the people of Illinois to do so. Respectfully yours,

JOHN P. ALTGELD

Immediately after the above correspondence an appeal was made by the Governor to the humane people of the State, describing the conditions at Pullman and asking for aid. Relief of all kinds soon came and some of the old employees were enabled to move to other points.

THE DEBS CASE

United States Supreme Court in Debs Case, June 2, 1895 [5]

Governor, what have you to say on the decisions of the United States Supreme Court in the Debs Case?

The remanding of Debs to jail is in itself a matter of small consequence compared with the principle established, which is of transcendent importance. This decision marks a turning point in our history, for it establishes a new form of government never before heard of among men, that is government by injunction. Under this procedure a federal judge sitting in a rear room can on motion of some corporation lawyer issue a ukase which he calls an injunction, forbidding anything he chooses to and which the law does not forbid. Where the law forbids a thing no injunction is necessary. In other words he can legislate for himself, and having done so can then turn

[5] [*Ibid.*, pp. 459-61.]

around and arrest and imprison as many people as he pleases, not for violating any law but on the mere pretext that they had disregarded his injunction; and, mark you, they are not tried by a jury according to the forms of law, but the same judge who issued the ukase and who claims that his dignity was offended himself tries the case, and whether anything is proven or nothing is proven he can send men to prison at pleasure and there is no remedy.

The provision of the constitution "that no man shall be deprived of his liberty without a trial by an impartial jury" is practically wiped out by this decision of the United States Supreme Court and the theory that ours was exclusively a government of law is now at an end, for every community is now subject to obey any whim or caprice which any federal judge may promulgate. And if federal judges can do this then it will not be long until State judges will follow this example. The Constitution declares that our government has three departments, the legislative, judicial and executive, and that no one shall trench on the other, but under this new order of things a federal judge becomes at once a legislator, court and executioner.

For over a century our government moved along the lines of the Constitution and we became great and powerful. Life and property were protected and the law was enforced. Now we have made a departure, the bulwark of liberty has been undermined, trial by jury has been stricken down.

You know there were two separate proceedings against Debs. One was according to the established forms of law; he was indicted by a grand jury for acts alleged to have been committed during the strike, and he was regularly tried by a jury and it turned out there was absolutely no case against him. Nothing was proven. It is true the jury were not allowed to bring in a verdict because near the end of the trial one of the jurors became ill and the prosecution refused to go on. Debs' attorneys offered to proceed with the remaining eleven or to add a new man and proceed, but the railroad lawyer, who also represented the government, feeling that he had no case at all, would not consent, and he thereby prevented a verdict of acquittal and had the case postponed.

The other proceeding was by injunction. A federal judge on motion of some railroad attorneys issued a ukase against the people of all the States in that judicial circuit, in which he forbade nearly everything that the ingenuity of man could think of and which the law did not forbid, and having thus legislated he then turned around and had Debs and others arrested, not for violating any law but for failing to respect this ukase or injunction. And then this judge not only refused to give a jury trial but he himself proceeded to determine whether his own dignity had been offended, and he promptly sent the defendants to prison, the judge being legislator, court, and executioner.

Had there been a jury trial the defendants would have been discharged, because it was not proved that they had violated any law. This would have been in harmony with the Constitution, with the law of the land and with eternal justice. But the corporations wanted the Constitution brushed aside, and the federal judge kindly obliged them, and the Supreme Court has now approved his acts.

For a number of years it has been marked that the decisions of the United States courts were nearly always in favor of corporations. Then it was noticed that no man could be appointed to a federal judgeship unless he was satisfactory to those interests. Over a year ago the *New York World* talked about a packed Supreme Court, and that court has within a few days rendered two decisions which unfortunately tend to confirm this charge. A week ago it did violence to the Constitution and laws of the land by holding that the government had no power to tax the rich of this country. Now it has stricken down trial by jury and has established government by injunction.

Forty years ago the slave power predominated; today it is capitalism.

George William Curtis described the slave power of forty years ago as follows: "Slavery sat in the White House and made laws in the capitol; courts of justice were its ministers and legislatures were its lackeys. It silenced the preacher in the pulpit; it muzzled the editor at his desk and the professor in his lecture room. It set the price upon the heads of peaceful citizens; it robbed the mails and denounced the vital principles of the Declaration of Independence as treason. Even in States whose laws did not tolerate slavery it ruled the club and the drawing room, the factory and the office. It swaggered at the dinner table and scourged with scorn a cowardly society. It tore the golden rule from school books and the pictured benignity of Christ from the prayer book."

Now substitute the word "capitalism" for the word "slavery" and the above is an exact picture of our condition today. The American people crushed the slave power, they washed its stain off our flag and saved our institutions. Can they rescue them again? Many say yes, but they have not reflected that the crushing force which now confronts them is greater than was ever the slave power. Besides, slavery itself was sectional and in the end it was possible to unite the rest of the country against it. But the corrupt money power has its withering finger on every pulse in the land and is destroying the rugged manhood and love of liberty which alone can carry a people through a great crisis. What, then, is the situation today? For over twenty years foreign and domestic capitalism has dominated. "It sits in the White House and legislates in the capitol. Courts of justice are its ministers and legislatures are its lackeys." And the whole machinery of fashionable society is its handmaid.

Just see what a brood of evils has sprung from the power of capitalism since 1870.

1. The striking down of over one-third of the money of the world, thus crushing the debtor class and paralyzing industry.

2. The growing of that corrupt use of wealth which is undermining our institutions, debauching public officials, shaping legislation and creating judges who do its bidding.

3. Exemption of the rich from taxation.

4. The substitution of government by injunction for government by the Constitution and laws.

5. The striking down of trial by jury.

Never has there been so much patriotic talk as in the last twenty-five years and never were there so many influences at work strangling Republican institutions.

JOHN P. ALTGELD

IX

SPEECH CONCLUDING DEBATE ON THE CHICAGO PLATFORM[1]

WILLIAM JENNINGS BRYAN

Mr. Chairman and Gentlemen of the Convention: I would be presumptuous, indeed, to present myself against the distinguished gentlemen to whom you have listened if this were a mere measuring of abilities; but this is not a contest between persons. The humblest citizen in all the land, when clad in the armor of a righteous cause, is stronger than all the hosts of error. I come to speak to you in defense of a cause as holy as the cause of liberty—the cause of humanity.

When this debate is concluded, a motion will be made to lay upon the table the resolution offered in commendation of the administration, and also the resolution offered in condemnation of the administration. We object to bringing this question down to the level of persons. The individual is but an atom; he is born, he acts, he dies; but principles are eternal; and this has been a contest over a principle.

Never before in the history of this country has there been witnessed such a contest as that through which we have just passed. Never before in the history of American politics has a great issue been fought out as this issue has been, by the voters of a great party. On the fourth of March, 1895, a few Democrats, most of them members of Congress, issued an address to the Democrats of the nation, asserting that the money question was the paramount issue of the hour; declaring that a majority of the Democratic party had the right to control the action of the party on this paramount issue; and concluding

1 [William Jennings Bryan, *The First Battle. A Story of the Campaign of 1896* (Chicago, 1896), pp. 199-206.]

with the request that the believers in the free coinage of silver in the Democratic party should organize, take charge of, and control the policy of the Democratic party. Three months later, at Memphis, an organization was perfected, and the silver Democrats went forth openly and courageously proclaiming their belief, and declaring that, if successful, they would crystallize into a platform the declaration which they had made. Then began the conflict. With a zeal approaching the zeal which inspired the crusaders who followed Peter the Hermit, our silver Democrats went forth from victory unto victory until they are now assembled, not to discuss, not to debate, but to enter up the judgment already rendered by the plain people of this country. In this contest brother has been arrayed against brother, father against son. The warmest ties of love, acquaintance, and association have been disregarded; old leaders have been cast aside when they have refused to give expression to the sentiments of those whom they would lead, and new leaders have sprung up to give direction to this cause of truth. Thus has the contest been waged, and we have assembled here under as binding and solemn instructions as were ever imposed upon representatives of the people.

We do not come as individuals. As individuals we might have been glad to compliment the gentleman from New York (Senator Hill), but we know that the people for whom we speak would never be willing to put him in a position where he could thwart the will of the Democratic party. I say it was not a question of persons; it was a question of principle, and it is not with gladness, my friends, that we find ourselves brought into conflict with those who are now arrayed on the other side.

The gentleman who preceded me (ex-Governor Russell) spoke of the State of Massachusetts; let me assure him that not one present in all this convention entertains the least hostility to the people of the State of Massachusetts, but we stand here representing people who are the equals, before the law, of the greatest citizens in the State of Massachusetts. When you (turning to the gold delegates) come before us and tell us that we are about to disturb your business interests, we reply that you have disturbed our business interests by your course.

We say to you that you have made the definition of a businessman too limited in its application. The man who is employed for wages is as much a businessman as his employer; the attorney in a country town is as much a businessman as the corporation counsel in a great metropolis; the merchant at the crossroads store is as much a businessman as the merchant of New York; the farmer who goes forth in the morning and toils all day—who begins in the spring and toils all summer—and who by the application of brain and muscle to the natural resources of the country creates wealth, is as much a businessman as the man who goes upon the board of trade and bets upon the price of grain; the miners who go down a thousand feet into the earth, or climb two thousand feet upon the cliffs, and bring forth from their hiding places the precious metals to be poured into the channels of trade are as much businessmen as the few financial magnates who, in a back room, corner the money of the world. We come to speak for this broader class of businessmen.

Ah, my friends, we say not one word against those who live upon the Atlantic coast, but the hardy pioneers who have braved all the dangers of the wilderness, who have made the desert to blossom as the rose—the pioneers away out there (pointing to the West), who rear their children near to Nature's heart, where they can mingle their voices with the voices of the birds—out there where they have erected schoolhouses for the education of their young, churches where they praise their Creator, and cemeteries where rest the ashes of their dead—these people, we say, are as deserving of the consideration of our party as any people in this country. It is for these that we speak. We do not come as aggressors. Our war is not a war of conquest; we are fighting in the defense of our homes, our families, and posterity. We have petitioned, and our petitions have been scorned; we have entreated, and our entreaties have been disregarded; we have begged, and they have mocked when our calamity came. We beg no longer; we entreat no more; we petition no more. We defy them.

The gentleman from Wisconsin has said that he fears a Robespierre. My friends, in this land of the free you need not fear that a tyrant will spring up from among the people. What we need is an Andrew Jackson to stand, as Jackson stood, against the encroachments of organized wealth.

They tell us that this platform was made to catch votes. We reply to them that changing conditions make new issues; that the principles upon which Democracy rests are as everlasting as the hills, but that they must be applied to new conditions as they arise. Conditions have arisen, and we are here to meet those conditions. They tell us that the income tax ought not to be brought in here; that it is a new idea. They criticize us for our criticism of the Supreme Court of the United States. My friends, we have not criticized; we have simply called attention to what you already know. If you want criticisms, read the dissenting opinions of the court. There you will find criticisms. They say that we passed an unconstitutional law; we deny it. The income tax law was not unconstitutional when it was passed; it was not unconstitutional when it went before the Supreme Court for the first time; it did not become unconstitutional until one of the judges changed his mind, and we cannot be expected to know when a judge will change his mind. The income tax is just. It simply intends to put the burdens of government justly upon the backs of the people. I am in favor of an income tax. When I find a man who is not willing to bear his share of the burdens of the government which protects him, I find a man who is unworthy to enjoy the blessings of a government like ours.

They say that we are opposing national bank currency; it is true. If you will read what Thomas Benton said, you will find he said that, in searching history, he could find but one parallel to Andrew Jackson; that was Cicero, who destroyed the conspiracy of Cataline and saved Rome. Benton said that Cicero only did for Rome what Jackson did for us when he destroyed the bank conspiracy and saved America. We say in our platform that we believe that the right to coin and issue money is a function of government. We believe it. We believe that it is a part of sovereignty, and can no more with safety be delegated to private individuals than we could afford to delegate to private individuals the power to make penal statutes or levy taxes. Mr. Jefferson, who was once regarded as good Democratic authority, seems to have differed in opinion from the gentleman who has addressed us on the part of the minority. Those who are opposed to this proposition tell us that the issue of paper money is a function of the bank, and that the government ought to go out of the banking business. I stand with Jefferson rather than with them, and tell them, as he did, that the issue of money is a function of government, and that the banks ought to go out of the governing business.

They complain about the plank which declares against life tenure in office. They have tried to strain it to mean that which it does not mean. What we oppose by that plank is the life tenure which is being built up in Washington, and which excludes from participation in official benefits the humbler members of society.

Let me call your attention to two or three important things. The gentleman from New York says that he will propose an amendment to the platform providing that the proposed change in our monetary system shall not effect contracts already made. Let me remind you that there is no intention of affecting those contracts which according to present laws are made payable in gold; but if he means to say that we cannot change our monetary system without protecting those who have loaned money before the change was made, I desire to ask him where, in law or in morals, he can find justification for not protecting the debtors when the act of 1873 was passed, if he now insists that we must protect the creditors.

He says he will also propose an amendment which will provide for the suspension of free coinage if we fail to maintain the parity within a year. We reply that when we advocate a policy which we believe will be successful, we are not compelled to raise a doubt as to our own sincerity by suggesting what we shall do if we fail. I ask him, if he would apply his logic to us, why he does not apply it to himself. He says he wants this country to try to secure an international agreement. Why does he not tell us what he is going to do if he fails to secure an international agreement? There is more reason for him to do that than there is for us to provide against the failure to maintain the parity. Our opponents have tried for twenty years to secure an international agreement, and those are waiting for it most patiently who do not want it at all.

And now, my friends, let me come to the paramount issue. If they ask us why it is that we say more on the money question than we say upon the tariff question, I reply that, if protection has slain its thousands, the gold standard has slain its tens of thousands. If they ask us why we do not embody in our platform all the things that we believe in, we reply that when we have restored the money of the Constitution all other necessary reforms will be possible; but that until this is done there is no other reform that can be accomplished.

Why is it that within three months such a change has come over the country? Three months ago, when it was confidently asserted that those who believe in the gold standard would frame our platform and nominate our candidates, even the advocates of the gold standard did not think that we could elect a president. And they had good reason for their doubt, because there is scarcely a State here today asking for the gold standard which is not in the absolute control of the Republican party. But note the change. Mr. McKinley was nominated at St. Louis upon a platform which declared for the maintenance of the gold standard until it can be changed into bimetallism by international agreement. Mr. McKinley was the most popular man among the Republicans, and three months ago everybody in the Republican party prophesied his election. How is today? Why, the man who was once pleased to think that he looked like Napoleon—that man shudders today when he remembers that he was nominated on the anniversary of the battle of Waterloo. Not only that, but as he listens he can hear with ever-increasing distinctness the sound of the waves as they beat upon the lonely shores of St. Helena.

Why this change? Ah, my friends, is not the reason for the change evident to anyone who will look at the matter? No private character, however pure, no personal popularity, however great, can protect from the avenging wrath of an indignant people a man who will declare that he is in favor of fastening the gold standard upon this country, or who is willing to surrender the right of self-government and place the legislative control of our affairs in the hands of foreign potentates and powers.

We go forth confident that we shall win. Why? Because upon the paramount issue of this campaign there is not a spot of ground upon which the enemy will dare to challenge battle. If they tell us that the gold standard is a good thing, we shall point to their platform and tell them that their platform pledges the party to get rid of the gold standard and substitute bimetallism. If the gold standard is a good thing, why try to get rid of it? I call your attention to the fact that some of the very people who are in this convention today and who tell us that we ought to declare in favor of international bimetallism —thereby declaring that the gold standard is wrong and that the principle of bimetallism is better—these very people four months ago were open and avowed advocates of the gold standard, and were then telling us that we could not legislate two metals together, even with the aid of all the world. If the gold standard is a good thing, we ought to declare in favor of its retention and not in favor of abandoning it; and if the gold standard is a bad thing why should we wait until other nations are willing to help us to let go? Here is the line of battle, and we care not upon which issue they force the fight; we are prepared to meet them on either issue or on both. If they tell us that the gold standard is the standard of civilization, we reply to them that this, the most enlightened of all the nations of the earth, has never declared for a gold standard and that both the great parties this year are declaring against it. If the gold standard is the standard of civilization, why, my friends, should we not have it? If they come to meet us on that issue we can present the history of our nation. More than that; we can tell them that they will search the pages of history in vain to find a single instance where the common people of any land have ever declared themselves in favor of the gold standard. They can find where the holders of fixed investments have declared for a gold standard, but not where the masses have.

Mr. Carlisle said in 1878 that this was a struggle between "the idle holders of idle capital" and "the struggling masses, who produce the wealth and pay the taxes of the country"; and, my friends, the question we are to decide is: Upon which side will the Democratic party fight; upon the side of "the idle holders of idle capital" or upon the side of "the struggling masses"? That is the question which the party must answer first, and then it must be answered by each individual hereafter. The sympathies of the Democratic party, as shown by the platform, are on the side of the struggling masses who have ever been the foundation of the Democratic party. There are two ideas of government. There are those who believe that, if you will only legislate to make the well-to-do prosperous, their prosperity will leak through on those below. The Democratic idea, however, has been that if you legislate to make the masses prosperous, their prosperity will find its way up through every class which rests upon them.

You come to us and tell us that the great cities are in favor of the gold standard; we reply that the great cities rest upon our broad and fertile prairies. Burn down your cities and leave our farms, and your cities will spring up again as if by magic; but destroy our farms and the grass will grow in the streets of every city in the country.

My friends, we declare that this nation is able to legislate for its own people on every question, without waiting for the aid or consent of any other nation on earth; and upon that issue we expect to carry every State in the Union. I shall not slander the inhabitants of the fair State of Massachusetts nor the inhabitants of the State of New York by saying that, when they are confronted with the proposition, they will declare that this nation is not able to attend to its own business. It is the issue of 1776 over again. Our ancestors, when but three millions in number, had the courage to declare their political independence of every other nation; shall we, their descendants, when we have grown to seventy millions, declare that we are less independent than our forefathers? No, my friends, that will never be the verdict of our people. Therefore, we care not upon what lines the battle is fought. If they say bimetallism is good, but that we cannot have it until other nations help us, we reply that, instead of having a gold standard because England has, we will restore bimetallism, and then let England have bimetallism because the United States has it. If they dare to come out in the open field and defend the gold standard as a good thing, we will fight them to the uttermost. Having behind us the producing masses of this nation and the world, supported by the commercial interests, the laboring interests, and the toilers everywhere, we will answer their demand for a gold standard by saying to them: You shall not press down upon the brow of labor this crown of thorns, you shall not crucify mankind upon a cross of gold.

In view of the wide publication of this speech, I may be pardoned for making some reference to it. While a member of the Committee on Resolutions, I was prevented from attending the first sessions of the committee owing to our contest, and was not a member of the subcommittee which drafted the platform. As soon as our contest was settled, I met with the committee and took part in the final discussion and adoption of the platform. Just before the platform was reported to the convention, Senator Jones sent for me and asked me to take charge of the debate. In dividing the time I was to have twenty minutes to close, but as the minority used ten minutes more than the time originally allotted, my time was extended ten minutes. The concluding sentence of my speech was criticized both favorably and unfavorably. I had used the idea in substantially the same form in a speech in Congress, but did not recall the fact when I used it in the convention. A portion of the speech was extemporaneous, and its arrangement entirely so, but parts of it had been prepared for another occasion. Next to the conclusion, the part most quoted was the definition of the term, "businessmen." Since I became interested in the discussion of monetary questions, I have often had occasion to note and comment upon the narrowness of some of the terms used, and nowhere is this narrowness more noticeable than in the attempt to ignore the most important businessmen of the country, the real creators of wealth.

X

EQUALITY[1]

EDWIN LAWRENCE GODKIN

Equality, as everyone acknowledges, is the foundation of democracy. It means democracy when it gets itself embodied in law. When all are equal, there is no reason why all should not rule. But the equality of the French in 1792, when the revolutionary government was established, was something different from the equality of 1789. In 1789 the equality which was asked for was, in the main, simply an equality of rights and burdens between the nobility and the *tiers état*. Equality, as Montesquieu uses the term, means simply love, not of one's order, but of one's country, and as such he made it the equivalent of democracy. Democracy, he says, *is* equality. But the word "equality" for him evidently had no social signification. It meant rather equality of service to the country: that everyone was held to the same amount of public duty, according to his means, and that everyone was entitled to the same opportunities of taking part in the government. That being born of particular parents made anyone essentially of better quality than anybody else; that if one hundred babies of different conditions were brought up in the same manner, the sons of noblemen or gentlemen among them would show their superiority to the others in their character, was a doctrine which, after the Middle Ages, was probably never fully accepted even by the most ardent believers in heredity. Every generation was witness of the breakdown, if I may use the expression, of the principle of heredity. That is to say, a large number of noble or gentle families in every generation lost

1 [Edwin Lawrence Godkin, *Unforeseen Tendencies of Democracy* (Westminster, 1898), pp. 31-47.]

their position or property, because the founder did not transmit his qualities of mind or character to his descendants. The folly or extravagance or imprudence which led to this social *déchéance* was generally due to marked departures in intellect or morals from the original type. The believers in heredity were misled by the analogy of the breeding of animals. Horses transmitted speed and bottom, birds peculiar appearance, with extraordinary certainty. Therefore, it was concluded, a man was likely to have his father's wisdom, or foresight, or mental strength. But his descendants rarely inherit from a father more than one or two mental peculiarities, valuable when united with other things, but, standing alone, of little use in the battle of life—a fact which may be verified anywhere by observing the families of distinguished men. A man eminent in politics, or law, or medicine, or commerce, or finance, or war, is seldom succeeded by a son who recalls the *ensemble* of qualities which have secured the father's success, although he may have one or two of his characteristics. Heredity obtained its stronghold in the popular imagination in the Middle Ages, owing to the fact that the son was in possession of the father's power when he died, and that in a rude age, when things were mainly decided by fighting, it offered the readiest means of settling peaceably questions of succession. But as soon as the question of the right of a class to rule in virtue of heredity became a subject of discussion, heredity broke down. It was a custom which was valuable in the time of its origin, but, like most customs, found it impossible to justify itself by any better argument than that, under some circumstances, it had produced good results.

But in America, from the settlement of the colonies, the English doctrine that distinction should serve in place of heredity seems to have held its place in the popular imagination. The founding of colonies, the making of conquests, the growth of trade and commerce, and the early practice of admitting able lawyers to the House of Lords had familiarized Englishmen with the idea of a man's making his fortune by some sort of adventure, no matter what his origin. The peers, too, sapped their own power unconsciously by making legislators of young men of promise, no matter of what extraction, and giving them seats in the House of Commons. The result was that the association, in the English mind, of men of mark of some kind with office-holding and the work of government took deep root after the Revolution of 1640, and was transferred to America. It was generally leading men of prominence and character who were made governors and judges, and were sent to the legislature and to Washington. The Revolution was carried through, and the Constitution formed and its adoption brought about, by men of this kind. The idea of an obscure man, of a man who was not lifted above the crowd in some way, being fit for the transaction of public affairs was still unfamiliar. All the members of the Constitutional Convention were men of some local note, and so were the earlier administrators of the new government.

. . . .

In nothing does modern democracy differ so much from the ancient democracy as in this indifference to distinction, owing in a large degree to the size of the two communities which fully practice it, and to the great preponderance of the less instructed class in the elections. The Greek democracy, and in a less degree that of Rome, were composed of a selected body the principal occupation of which was politics, and they were brought in almost daily contact with the leading men of the community, and were consulted by them in the forum concerning both war and peace. We can hardly imagine a better education than this, touching the management of affairs and the qualities which it requires. The consequence was that the people were daily engaged in forming judgments as to the capacity of men with whom they were familiar, and the men were daily engaged in giving *viva voce* reasons for their advice, or explaining and defending their conduct, or setting forth their own claims to an office. Our democracies, on the other hand, are composed of vast bodies of men who have but small acquaintance with the machinery of public affairs, or with the capacity of individuals for managing it.

This brings me to what is probably the greatest danger of modern democracy, if, like all previous regimes, it should lose its hold on popular affections and fall into decay. The spread of democracy—that is, the participation of the whole community in the work of government—has been accompanied by a great increase in the complexity of human affairs. The interdependence of nations through the growth of trade, the increase of literature, the incessant conversation with one another kept up by the press, the greatly improved facilities of travel, has grown to a degree undreamt of even a century ago. A debate in a legislative body, the careless speech of a chief magistrate, a slight change in the system of taxation of even one nation, a small discovery by a man of science in any country, in our time produce an almost instantaneous effect over the whole civilized world; and one might say, the whole world, whether civilized or not, for civilization now asserts the dominion of its ideas everywhere. In truth, the extent to which all news, no matter whence it comes, affects or may affect the lives of most of us is present to every man when he opens his newspaper in the morning. And all private business partakes of this public complexity. The size of all undertakings, either of production or exchange or transportation, is tasking the human faculty of administration to the uttermost, and leads a great many people to suppose that individuals are no longer equal to the task, and that it must be hereafter assumed by the state. For success in any business now, an amount of knowledge is necessary which in the last century hardly one man in a million possessed; decisions must now be made on the moment, for which, a hundred years ago, a merchant might take half a year.

The result is that the government of such a world needs an increase in intellectual equipment corresponding to the increase in business. The amount of property, too, which is placed at the disposal of the modern legislator is something beyond calculation. Since the exclusion of the old landed class from the work of government, a process which began soon after the French Revolution, the growth of personal property, which to be enjoyed or increased has in some way to be displayed, and thus comes within the reach of the government, is one of the most remarkable phenomena of the modern world. When the old ruler had taxed land, his resources were well-nigh exhausted. Today the number of movables out of each of which the public treasury can extract tens of millions, in every civilized country, has made taxation one of the nicest of arts. In fact, one has but to read such a book as Mr. Wells's *Recent Economic Changes* to see that within a century we have entered a new material world, a description of which would have been deemed fantastic even in 1800. In every field of human activity we have drawn heavily on the supply of administrative talent. Whether it wishes to command a great army or a great fleet, or to conduct a great business, every state has to search its entire population to get a man fit for the work. In some things in which capacity is not easy to test, such as war, most countries remain, pending the outbreak of hostilities, in anxious uncertainty as to the capacity of their military men, by sea or by land.

. . . .

As I have already said, the really alarming feature connected with the growth of democracy is that it does not seem to make adequate provision for the government of this new world. Its chief function, like the chief function of the monarch whom it has succeeded, is to fill offices. This is the chief function of the sovereign power everywhere, no matter by what name it is called. To find the right men for the public places is almost the only work which falls, or has ever fallen, to the ruler. It is by the manner in which this is done, more than by the laws which are passed, that the goodness or badness of a government is tested. If the functionaries are honest and faithful, almost any kind of political constitution is endurable. If they are ignorant or tyrannical or corrupt, the best constitution is worthless. If we listen to the conversation of any group of men who are condemning a political system, we shall find that their talk consists mainly of reports of malfeasance in office, of officials having done things which they ought not to have done, and of their having failed to do things which they ought to have done. Government is an impalpable abstraction except as it makes itself felt through functionaries, which is about the same thing as saying that administration is even more important than legislation, that even bad laws well executed hardly work as much unhappiness as good laws badly executed.

. . . .

It is easy to see that the only way to meet this necessary growth of demand for offices was to adhere to the old system of applying to the management of state affairs the principle which reigns in business, that of securing the best talent available; and of giving the chief places, at least, to men who had already made a mark in the world by success in some field of activity. This, as I have said, was the rule of the democracies of the ancient world. To preserve for the democratic government the old respect and authority which used to surround the monarchical government, it was absolutely necessary to compete vigorously, through both money and honors, in the labor market, with private business, the demands of which on the community's store of talent became very great as soon as steam and electricity were brought into the service of commerce and manufactures. But the tendency has not run in this direction. As regards the lower offices, the duties of which are easily comprehensible by everybody, and are merely matters of routine, in which discretion or judgment plays little part, there has been in this country a decided return to the tests of ordinary business, such as character and competency, and a decided revival of confidence in such motives as security of tenure and the prospect of promotion. But as regards the higher or elective offices, such as those of legislators and governors, the tendency to discredit such qualifications as education and special experience has been marked. In the popular mind there is what may be called a disposition to believe not only that one man is as good as another, but that he knows as much on any matter of general interest. In any particular business the superiority of the man who has long followed it is freely acknowledged, but in public affairs this is not perhaps so much denied as disregarded. One of the oddest characteristics of the silver movement was the general refusal to accept the experience of any country or age as instructive, and this in a matter in which all light comes from experience. Bryan's proclamation that the opinion of all the professors in the United States would not affect his opinions in the least was an illustration of this great self-confidence of a large democracy. In a small democracy this could hardly have occurred.

All the great modern democracies have to contend almost for existence against the popular disposition to treat elective offices as representative, and to consider it of more importance that they should be filled by persons holding certain opinions or shades of opinion than by persons most competent to perform their duties. The distinction between representing and administering seems plain enough; and yet, since the French Revolution, the democratic tendency has been everywhere to obscure it. This has not unnaturally led to the idea that the offices are rewards for the persons who have done most to propagate or defend certain views, and ought to be given to them independently of their fitness. To this confusion of two different functions I must ascribe the deterioration which has been remarked so frequently in the legislatures of all democratic countries in modern times. The number of men of experience or special knowledge, as well as of conspicuous men, which they contain, seems to decline steadily, and the number of interests committed to their charge as steadily to increase.

The disregard of special fitness, combined with unwillingness to acknowledge that there can be anything special about any man, which is born of equality, constitutes the great defect of modern democracy. That large communities can be successfully administered by inferior men is a doctrine which runs directly counter not only to the experience of the race, but to the order appointed for the advance of civilization, which has been carried forward almost exclusively by the labor of the fittest, despite the resistance or reluctance of the unfit. This order of nature, too, has been recognized fully in private affairs of every description. In all of them competency on the part of administrators is the first thing sought for, and the only thing trusted. But in private affairs the penalty of any disregard of this rule comes quickly; in public affairs the operation of all causes is much slower, and their action is obscure. Nations take centuries to fall, and the catastrophe is preceded by a long period of the process called "bad government," in which there is much suffering and alarm, but not enough to make the remedy plain. France furnishes the best modern illustration of this rule. The causes of the Revolution undoubtedly began to operate at the majority of Louis XIV, but for over one hundred years their nature and certain results were not perceived, in spite of the great popular suffering which prevailed during the whole period.

The worst of the slowness of this decadence is that it affects national character to a degree which makes recovery more difficult, even after the origin and nature of the disease have become plain. Men soon get accustomed to the evils of their condition, particularly if there is nobody in particular to blame. The inaction or negligence or shortcomings of great numbers assume the appearance of a law of nature, or of repeated failures or attempts at the impossible. The apparent difficulty of reform, except by catastrophe or revolution, begets either despondency or overcheerfulness.

XI

ON A NEW PHILOSOPHY: THAT POVERTY IS THE BEST POLICY[1]

WILLIAM GRAHAM SUMNER

It is commonly asserted that there are in the United States no classes, and any allusion to classes is resented. On the other hand, we constantly read and hear discussions of social topics in which the existence of social classes is assumed as a simple fact. "The poor," "the weak," "the laborers," are expressions which are used as if they had exact and well-understood definition. Discussions are made to bear upon the assumed rights, wrongs, and misfortunes of certain social classes; and all public speaking and writing consists, in a large measure, of the discussion of general plans for meeting the wishes of classes of people who have not been able to satisfy their own desires. These classes are sometimes discontented, and sometimes not. Sometimes they do not know that anything is amiss with them until the "friends of humanity" come to them with offers of aid. Sometimes they are discontented and envious. They do not take their achievements as a fair measure of their rights. They do not blame themselves or their parents for their lot, as compared with that of other people. Sometimes they claim that they have a right to everything of which they feel the need for their happiness on earth. To make such a claim against God or Nature would, of course, be only to say that we claim a right to live on earth if we can. But God and Nature have ordained the chances and conditions of life on earth once for all. The case cannot be reopened. We cannot get a revision

1 [William Graham Sumner, *What Social Classes Owe to Each Other* (New York, 1883), pp. 13-16.]

of the laws of human life. We are absolutely shut up to the need and duty, if we would learn how to live happily, of investigating the laws of Nature, and deducing the rules of right living in the world as it is. These are very wearisome and commonplace tasks. They consist in labor and self-denial repeated over and over again in learning and doing. When the people whose claims we are considering are told to apply themselves to these tasks they become irritated and feel almost insulted. They formulate their claims as rights against society—that is, against some other men. In their view they have a right, not only to *pursue* happiness, but to *get* it; and if they fail to get it, they think they have a claim to the aid of other men—that is, to the labor and self-denial of other men—to get it for them. They find orators and poets who tell them that they have grievances so long as they have unsatisfied desires.

Now, if there are groups of people who have a claim to other people's labor and self-denial, and if there are other people whose labor and self-denial are liable to be claimed by the first groups, then there certainly are "classes," and classes of the oldest and most vicious type. For a man who can command another man's labor and self-denial for the support of his own existence is a privileged person of the highest species conceivable on earth. Princes and paupers meet on this plane, and no other men are on it at all. On the other hand, a man whose labor and self-denial may be diverted from his maintenance to that of some other man is not a free man, and approaches more or less toward the position of a slave. Therefore, we shall find that, in all the notions which we are to discuss, this elementary contradiction, that there are classes and that there are not classes, will produce repeated confusion and absurdity. We shall find that, in our efforts to eliminate the old vices of class government, we are impeded and defeated by new products of the worst class theory. We shall find that all the schemes for producing equality and obliterating the organization of society produce a new differentiation based on the worst possible distinction—the right to claim and the duty to give one man's effort for another man's satisfaction. We shall find that every effort to realize equality necessitates a sacrifice of liberty.

Under [2] the names of the poor and the weak, the negligent, shiftless, inefficient, silly, and imprudent are fastened upon the industrious and prudent as a responsibility and a duty. On the one side, the terms are extended to cover the idle, intemperate, and vicious, who, by the combination, gain credit which they do not deserve, and which they could not get if they stood alone. On the other hand, the terms are extended to include wage-receivers of the humblest rank, who are degraded by the combination. The reader who desires to guard himself against fallacies should always scrutinize the terms "poor" and "weak" as used, so as to see which or how many of these classes they are made to cover.

The humanitarians, philanthropists, and reformers, looking at the facts of life as they present themselves, find enough which is sad and unpromising in the condition of many members of society. They see wealth and poverty side by side. They note great inequality of social position and social chances. They eagerly set about the attempt to account for what they see, and to devise schemes for remedying what they do not like. In their eagerness to recommend the less fortunate classes to pity and consideration they forget all about the rights of other classes; they gloss over all the faults of the classes in question, and they exaggerate their misfortunes and their virtues. They invent new thories of property, distorting rights and perpetrating injustice, as anyone is sure to do who sets about the readjustment of social relations with the interests of one group distinctly before his mind, and the interests of all other groups thrown into the background. When I have read certain of these discussions, I have thought that it must be quite disreputable to be respectable, quite dishonest to own property, quite unjust to go one's own way and earn one's own

[2] [*Ibid.*, pp. 21-27.]

living, and that the only really admirable person was the good-for-nothing. The man who by his own effort raises himself above poverty appears, in these discussions, to be of no account. The man who has done nothing to raise himself above poverty finds that the social doctors flock about him, bringing the capital which they have collected from the other class, and promising him the aid of the state to give him what the other had to work for. In all these schemes and projects the organized intervention of society through the state is either planned or hoped for, and the state is thus made to become the protector and guardian of certain classes. The agents who are to direct the state action are, of course, the reformers and philanthropists. Their schemes, therefore, may always be reduced to this type—that A and B decide what C shall do for D. It will be interesting to inquire, at a later period of our discussion, who C is, and what the effect is upon him of all these arrangements. In all the discussions attention is concentrated on A and B, the noble social reformers, and on D, the "poor man." I call C the Forgotten Man, because I have never seen that any notice was taken of him in any of the discussions. When we have disposed of A, B, and D we can better appreciate the case of C, and I think that we shall find that he deserves our attention, for the worth of his character and the magnitude of his unmerited burdens. Here it may suffice to observe that, on the theories of the social philosophers to whom I have referred, we should get a new maxim of judicious living: Poverty is the best policy. If you get wealth, you will have to support other people; if you do not get wealth, it will be the duty of other people to support you.

No doubt one chief reason for the unclear and contradictory theories of class relations lies in the fact that our society, largely controlled in all its organization by one set of doctrines, still contains survivals of old social theories which are totally inconsistent with the former. In the Middle Ages men were united by custom and prescription into associations, ranks, guilds, and communities of various kinds. These ties endured as long as life lasted. Consequently, society was dependent, throughout all its details, on status, and the tie, or bond, was sentimental. In our modern state, and in the United States more than anywhere else, the social structure is based on contract, and status is of the least importance. Contract, however, is rational—even rationalistic. It is also realistic, cold, and matter-of-fact. A contract relation is based on a sufficient reason, not on custom or prescription. It is not permanent. It endures only so long as the reason for it endures. In a state based on contract, sentiment is out of place in any public or common affairs. It is relegated to the sphere of private and personal relations, where it depends not at all on class types, but on personal acquaintance and personal estimates. The sentimentalists among us always seize upon the survivals of the old order. They want to save them and restore them. Much of the loose thinking also which troubles us in our social discussions arises from the fact that men do not distinguish the elements of status and of contract which may be found in our society.

Whether social philosophers think it desirable or not, it is out of the question to go back to status or to the sentimental relations which once united baron and retainer, master and servant, teacher and pupil, comrade and comrade. That we have lost some grace and elegance is undeniable. That life once held more poetry and romance is true enough. But it seems impossible that anyone who has studied the matter should doubt that we have gained immeasurably, and that our farther gains lie in going forward, not in going backward. The feudal ties can never be restored. If they could be restored they would bring back personal caprice, favoritism, sycophancy, and intrigue. A society based on contract is a society of free and independent men, who form ties without favor or obligation, and co-operate without cringing or intrigue. A society based on contract, therefore, gives the utmost room and chance for individual development, and for all the self-reliance and dignity of a free man. That a society of free men, co-operating under contract, is by far the strongest society which has ever yet existed; that no such society has ever yet developed the full measure of strength of which it is capable; and that the only social improvements which are now conceivable lie in the direction of more complete realization of a society of free men united by contract, are points which cannot be controverted. It follows, however, that one man, in a free state, cannot claim help from, and cannot be charged to give help to, another. To understand the full meaning of this assertion it will be worthwhile to see what a free democracy is.

XII

THE ERA OF CHANGE[1]

CHARLES FRANCIS ADAMS, JR.

At home, too, we notice similar change [to that of Paris, London, and Rome]. The Revolution has swept away the last vestiges of colonial thoughts and persons. Who that has ever formerly lived in a New England country town does not remember its old quiet and dullness, its industry, the slow, steady growth of its prosperity, and the staidness of its inhabitants? There, also, you met a class of men now wholly gone—dull, solid, elderly men, men of some property and few ideas—the legitimate descendants of the English broadacred squires. They were the gentry—the men who went up to the General Court, and had been members of the Governor's Council; they were men of formal bearing and of formal dress—men who remembered Governor Hancock, and had a certain trace of his manners. Today this class is extinct. Railroads have abolished them and their dress and their habits—they have abolished the very houses they dwelt in. The race of hereditary gentry has gone forever, and the race of hereditary businessmen has usurped its place. They represent the railroad, as the earlier type did the stagecoach.

The same phenomena are witnessed in the regions of thought. It is bolder than of yore. It exerts its influence with a speed and force equally accelerated. The newspaper press is the great engine of modern education; and that press, obeying the laws of gravitation, is everywhere centralized—the rays of light once scattered are concentrated into one all-powerful focus. Today's metropolitan newspaper, printed by a steam

1 [Charles Francis Adams, Jr., *Chapters of Erie, and Other Essays* (Boston, 1871), pp. 344-55.]

press, is whirled three hundred miles away by a steam engine before the day's last evening edition is in the hands of the carrier. The local press is day by day fighting a losing cause with diminished strength, while the metropolitan press drives it out of circulation and filches from it its brain. Ideas are quickly exchanged, and act upon each other. Nations can no longer, except wilfully, persist in national blunders. Literatures can no longer lie hidden as did the German until so few years ago. Since 1830 the nations are woven together by the network of iron, and all thought and results of thought are in common. The same problems perplex at once the whole world, and from every quarter light floods in upon their solution. But increased communication has not alone quickened and intensified thought; it has revolutionized its process. One great feature of the future must be the rapid uprising of new communities. Of all such communities questioning is a leading characteristic. They have neither faith in, nor reverence for, that which is old. On the contrary, with them age is a strong prima facie evidence of badness, and they love novelty for novelty's sake. This mental inclination will ultimately apply the last test to truth, for error has its full chance and is sure of a trial. The burden of proof seems likely to be shifted from the innovator to the conservator.

It is in the domains of trade, however, that the revolution is the most apparent and bewildering, that the sequences of cause and effect are most innumerable and interminable. Herbert Spencer says that it would require a volume to trace through all its ramifications the contingent effects of the everyday act of lighting a fire. These effects are imperceptible, but the influence of steam locomotion as applied to trade is as apparent as it is infinite. In this respect steam has proved itself to be not only the most obedient of slaves, but likewise the most tyrannical of masters. It pulls down as well as builds up. The very forces of nature do not stand in its way. It overcomes the wind and tide, and abolishes the Mississippi River. It is as whimsical as it is powerful. The individual it carries whithersoever he will, but whole communities it carries whither they would not. It makes the grass grow in the once busy streets of small commercial centers, like Nantucket, Salem, and Charleston. It robs New Orleans of that monopoly of wealth which the Mississippi River once promised to pour into her lap. It threatens to make a solitude of the once busy wharves of Boston, and it fills New Hampshire with deserted farms. For some mysterious reasons which it will never disclose, it carries wealth and importance past one threshold that it may lay them down at another. The old channels of commerce are broken up, and the points which depended upon them are left to philosophize upon the mutability of human affairs in forgotten obscurity. Meanwhile, San Francisco and Chicago spring up like a very palace of Aladdin, and the center of population is transferred, as if by magic, to some point which existed in the school books of the present generation of men only as a howling wilderness. Meanwhile, prices seek a level; produce is exchanged; labor goes where it is needed. England and Russia exchange bread for cotton, and Iowa and Ireland, labor for corn. These countries are nearer to one another now than in 1829 were the very counties of England. Increased activity demands new centers and channels, and those phenomena result which men call railroad centers, the apparition of which on the face of the earth is confounding and puzzling all thinking men. At the time of the great plague, just before the fire of 1666, Defoe estimated the population of London at one million souls; but Macaulay places it more accurately, for about the same time, at 500,000. In the succeeding century and a half it increased about threefold, until, in 1831, it numbered 1,600,000. The new era then commenced, and from that time the growth of London was almost to be dated. During the next twenty years, its population had risen to 2,500,000; and today it contains within its limits hardly less than 4,000,000 of human beings. Between 1666 and 1821 it had a growth of three hundred per cent, and it has experienced nearly similar increase between 1821 and 1871. When Fulton steamed up the Hudson, Paris was a city of rather more than half a million of inhabitants, and it now numbers about 2,000,000. In the days of Louis XIV it had 490,000, and in 1841, 912,000—an increase of one hundred per cent in two centuries. In 1866 it had 1,825,000—an increase of one hundred per cent in twenty-five years.

The results in America have been no less extraordinary. In 1807 New York numbered a population of about 75,000. Chicago existed in 1829 only as an uninviting swamp inhabited by a dozen families, and San Francisco was hardly a name. In 1830 New York contained over 200,000 inhabitants; and today they exceed 900,000, without considering those suburbs which enter so largely into the bulk of London and Paris. Between 1829 and 1870 Chicago had increased to 300,000, and San Francisco since 1847 has become a city of 150,000 inhabitants.

Nearly twenty years ago, Macaulay called attention to the fearful human material of which this growth was composed. He then referred to the arguments used by Gibbon and Adam Smith to prove that the world would not again be flooded with barbarism; and he remarked that it had not occurred to those philosophers "that civilization itself might engender the barbarians who should destroy it. It had not occurred to them that in the very heart of great capitals, in the neighborhood of splendid palaces and churches and theatres and libraries and museums, vice and ignorance might produce a race of Huns fiercer than those who marched under Attila, and of Vandals more bent on destruction than those who followed Genseric." When Macaulay used these words in Edinburgh in 1852, he could hardly have realized that the growth of those great cities was but just begun; but since that time London has increased fifty per cent, and the "Vandals" of Paris have recently given a point to his well-balanced period which it never had before. For America, and the permanence of republican institutions, this tendency of population to concentrate at great railroad centers cannot fail to be a subject for anxious consideration. The success of popular government must depend solely upon the virtue, the intelligence, and the public spirit of the people governed. As long as the members of any community can be approached by reason, or by argument, or by considerations of the public good, there is no sound cause to despair of the safety of any republic. It is useless, however, to hope or to struggle for that safety for any length of time after one party has firmly established its power upon the basis of an ignorant, unapproachable proletariat. The tendency of all self-governed great cities is inevitably towards this political control through the agency of irresponsible masses. The history of Athens and of Rome is continually repeating itself, and never has its reproduction displayed features more closely resembling the great originals than now in the leading municipalities of America. In what respect, except in name, does the city of New York enjoy a republican form of government? Yet the difference between New York and the other great cities of the continent is simply one of degree. The same tendencies, which must inevitably lead to the same results, are manifest everywhere. The dense aggregation of mankind may be said to necessarily result in an upper class which wants to be governed, and in a lower class which has to be governed. The extreme of luxury and the extreme of misery are equally fatal to public virtues; and no one can doubt that the great cities of the future are destined infinitely to surpass, both as regards luxury and misery, anything of the kind which the world has yet seen. This must result from the mere progress of railroad development. It is no less certain that republican America is destined very shortly to be dotted all over with these centers of population. Created by railroads, the railroads lend to them a gravitating influence both moral and political which cannot be ignored. To hope for a pure government by the people at large while ignorance and corruption are the ruling forces in these centers, is as futile as it would be to look for healthy members where the vitals are diseased. This it is which really constitutes that problem of great cities which so confounds the friends of popular government.

Meanwhile, the influence of this railroad power upon the politics of America and the political theories at the base of party organizations has been very strongly defined and little considered. Paradoxical as it sounds, it has actually made that which was mistaken, right, and that which was dangerous, safe. The year 1830 was a year of political revolution in America: the friends of a strong central government went out of power, and a party hostile in theory to all concentration of governmental functions came in. It can now hardly admit of a doubt that both parties to that bitter and memorable struggle were right, and it is equally true that both were wrong. Both, however, were made right or wrong by one element which entered into the practical solution of the questions agitated with decisive consequences—an element wholly unanticipated by either side: the element of improved locomotion. It may now with safety be premised that a strong central government was a political necessity for the United States of a time anterior to 1830; that in this respect Hamilton was right and Jefferson was wrong. It may also, with equal safety, be asserted that a strong central government constitutes a continually increasing political danger for the United States of the period subsequent to 1830; that the school of Hamilton is wrong, and the school of Jefferson is right. An equally thoughtful and observant man would thus have been a Hamiltonian up to 1830, and a Jeffersonian subsequently to that date. During the first period he would have seen a country of vast dimensions and sparsely settled, without means of communication or diversified industries, full of local jealousies and destitute of any recognized center of thought or business—a country, in short, in constant danger of going to pieces from lack of cohesion, a country in which the centrifugal force continually tended to overpower the centripetal. Then the railroad system sprang into being, and all this rapidly changed; science suddenly supplied that cohesion which it had been the great study of the statesman to provide. The point from which danger was to be anticipated thus gradually passed to the other side of the circle; everything centralized of itself, all things gravitated: the unaided centripetal force was clearly overcoming the centrifugal. Thus, the error of yesterday had become the truth of today, and the only men who were hopelessly wrong were the thoroughly consistent. The world at large rarely allows for these changes of conditions; a statesman or a political party must stand or fall with the permanence of that policy with which they have identified themselves, and posterity rarely stops to consider how circumstances have altered cases. Yet it is none the less true that the inventions of Robert Fulton and George Stephenson settled, in the minds of all thinking men, those great questions of internal policy for the United States government which were so fiercely contested in the first cabinet of Washington; and the way in which they settled them was by altering every condition of the problem. The destinies of nations are, perhaps, very much more frequently decided in the workshops of mechanics than in the councils of princes.

The influence of this same power has, however, made itself felt by the people of the United States in their political capacity more recently and in another way, though the sequel of this last experience is yet to be developed. The war of the rebellion left the United States heavily burdened with debt, upon which a high rate of interest had to be paid, while its people were at once infected with a mania for speculation and debauched by an irredeemable paper currency. A system of taxation was in use calculated to excite in equal degrees the wonder and contempt of all future students of fiscal problems. Under these circumstances the shrewdest men of business were always predicting an immediate and widespread commercial catastrophe, and the more cunning politicians hastened to conciliate the spirit of repudiation, which they asserted was sure to rise up. History furnished no precedent which would lead any political economist to suppose that a currency once greatly debased would ever appreciate through a regular and healthy process; and the statesman could not but see with alarm evidences of indebtedness passing out of the country into foreign hands by the hundreds of millions. It is not too much to say that the financial history of the six years between 1865 and 1871 falsified every prediction ever made as regards it. No widespread commercial crisis, no general collapse of private credit took place in America, nor did that one which swept over England cross the Atlantic; the public debt was steadily decreased, and the interest upon it was cheerfully paid; the spirit of repudiation ruined in its early death the hopes of numerous political charlatans; the currency rapidly appreciated to its gold value, while the mass of indebtedness against the country held in foreign hands constantly increased, and showed no signs of a return for redemption.

The simple truth was that, through its energetic railroad development, the country then was producing real wealth as no country ever produced it before. Behind all the artificial inflation, which, if the experience of the past was worth anything, so clearly foreshadowed a catastrophe, there was also going on a production which exceeded all experience. This new element vitiated the best reasoned conclusions. The railroad system, acting upon undeveloped and inexhaustible natural resources, dragged the country through its difficulties in spite of itself; it actually seemed as though fraud, ignorance, and speculation combined were unable to precipitate disaster. While all of these agents were noisily at work, every mile of railroad constructed was quietly adding many times its cost to the aggregate wealth of the country; the tonnage carried over the new roads built each year was many hundreds of millions in value, while that of the old roads always increased, so that the estimated average of annual transportation, which was but eighty-five dollars for each inhabitant of the country in 1860, had, in 1870, risen to three hundred dollars.

Such an increase in actual production could alone account for the general setting aside of all the lessons of the past. Not the least instructive part of this experience was, perhaps, the complacency with which a certain class of philosophers mistook the operation of a great, quiet, natural force for the results of their own meddling. One school attributed the freedom from commercial disaster to the juggle of paper money. Another saw in the great prosperity of the day nothing but a vindication of the absurdities of protection. While sciolists talked, however, the locomotive was at work, and all the obstructions which they placed in its way could at most only check but never overcome the impetus it had given to material progress.

The same direct influences could unquestionably be traced into morals, which have been observed in other departments of life. The laws of combination and gravitation apply to ethics no less than trade. Here, however, it is far more difficult than elsewhere to strike the balance of profit and loss. Whether the world, as a whole, is better or worse than it was forty years ago is a point upon which the statistician can as yet throw little light, and concerning which the divergence of opinion between the old and the young is apt to be excessive. One thing is very clear: the golden age of purity and simplicity has always lain behind us ever since those early times when it was first created in the imagination of the earliest poets. We never realize how bad the old times were, until we come to grope amid the happily forgotten records of their filthy vices.

Such is a passing sketch of some of the disturbing influences of the new power on the general aspect of the century —influences so all-pervading in their results as to be rather revolutionizing than disturbing. Whatever affects the whole affects every part. It would therefore be mere waste of time to follow out with curious assiduity the myriad remoter ramifications, until, among larger incidents of change, we should find the possibilities of emigration modifying for a time the terrible truth of the Malthusian theory of population, and the exodus of the nations going quietly on before our eyes upon a scale which reduces to insignificance the largest of those human tides the flow of which is traced through the pages of Gibbon; or we might see the Highlander expelled from the mountain fastnesses of his clan, because the railroad has made them so accessible as a pleasure-ground to the English nobleman, and a writer like John Stuart Mill forced to declare that so wonderful are the changes, both moral and economical, taking place in our age, that, without perpetually rewriting a work like his *Elements of Political Economy,* it is impossible to keep up with them. Such would be the instances among nations and authors, and, descending, we should see the increased demand for a cheap press influencing the price of rags in a country village, and the increased use of lubricating oil compensating to the fisheries for the innovation of gas. All of these, too, are the revolutions worked in a single half-century by a force which is as yet bound up in its swaddling-clothes. Its iron arms have been stretched out in every direction; nothing has escaped their reach, and the most firmly established institutions of man have proved under their touch as plastic as clay. Everything is changing, and will change with increasing rapidity. No human power can stop it. It is useless to cast back regretful glances at the old quiet days of other years and another order of things—at the middle ages antecedent to 1807. The progressive may exult, and the conservative may repine, but the result will be all the same. We must follow out the era on which we have entered to its logical and ultimate conclusions, for it is useless for men to stand in the way of steam engines. Change is usually ugly, and the whole world, both physical and moral, is now in a period of transition. But the serpent does not cast his skin till the new one is formed beneath the old; and because the old world is now sloughing its skin, we cannot conclude that the world of the future is to exist without one.

> Today I saw the dragon-fly
> Come from the wells where he did lie.
>
> An inner impulse rent the veil
> Of his old husk; from head to tail
> Came out clear plates of sapphire-mail.
>
> He dried his wings; like gauze they grew;
> Through crofts and pastures wet with dew,
> A living flash of light he flew.

It would be simply presumptuous to try to cast the horoscope of this revolution after thus surveying the changes already wrought. If we wished to draw a few feeble inferences to reassure ourselves in regard to the future, we could best do so by falling back on the analogies of the past. The changes of the future will undoubtedly be more rapid, more complete, and more bewildering than those of the past, in the same ratio that the combined forces now at work are engines more powerful for change than the comparatively simple ones of the earlier days. Still, the past cannot but throw some light on the future. To the dwellers in it, the world doubtless seemed sufficiently lovely before the middle of the fifteenth century; but then the sloughing time came on, and the old skin was slowly shed, and, in the ripeness of time, the new was found better. The old passed away amid the fierce contortions of tortured communities—through wars and revolutions and inquisitions and anarchy. The period of change was ugly, and mankind often had cause for discouragement; but the worst times were found bearable, and the result has justified the price. Our era has just begun to work its own revolution. That its results will all be pleasant, we may not hope; that its course will be marked by fierce agonies, we have been fully taught by the events of the last few years; but that it will in the end serve to elevate and make more happy the whole race of man upon earth, we have some cause to trust. Yet, in surveying the history of the last great era just finished—the distinctive era of the printing press, with all its changes from 1441 to 1807—the imagination is bewildered and lost in the vain effort to realize those more striking changes which are to make remarkable the new era upon which we have just entered—the distinctive era of steam locomotion.

PART TWO

THE SPIRITUAL UNREST

XIII

CONSPICUOUS CONSUMPTION[1]

THORSTEIN VEBLEN

In what has been said of the evolution of the vicarious leisure class and its differentiation from the general body of the working classes, reference has been made to a further division of labor—that between different servant classes. One portion of the servant class, chiefly those persons whose occupation is vicarious leisure, come to undertake a new, subsidiary range of duties—the vicarious consumption of goods. The most obvious form in which this consumption occurs is seen in the wearing of liveries and the occupation of spacious servants' quarters. Another, scarcely less obtrusive or less effective form of vicarious consumption, and a much more widely prevalent one, is the consumption of food, clothing, dwelling, and furniture by the lady and the rest of the domestic establishment.

But already at a point in economic evolution far antedating the emergence of the lady, specialized consumption of goods as an evidence of pecuniary strength had begun to work out in a more or less elaborate system. The beginning of a differentiation in consumption even antedates the appearance of anything that can fairly be called pecuniary strength. It is traceable back to the initial phase of predatory culture, and there is even a suggestion that an incipient differentiation in this respect lies back of the beginnings of the predatory life. This most primitive differentiation in the consumption of goods is like the later differentiation with which we are all so intimately familiar, in that it is largely of a ceremonial char-

1 [Thorstein Veblen, *The Theory of the Leisure Class: An Economic Study in the Evolution of Institutions* (New York, 1899), pp. 68-77.]

acter, but unlike the latter it does not rest on a difference in accumulated wealth. The utility of consumption as an evidence of wealth is to be classed as a derivative growth. It is an adaptation to a new end, by a selective process, of a distinction previously existing and well established in men's habits of thought.

In the earlier phases of the predatory culture the only economic differentiation is a broad distinction between an honorable superior class made up of the able-bodied men on the one side, and a base inferior class of laboring women on the other. According to the ideal scheme of life in force at that time it is the office of the men to consume what the women produce. Such consumption as falls to the women is merely incidental to their work; it is a means to their continued labor, and not a consumption directed to their own comfort and fullness of life. Unproductive consumption of goods is honorable, primarily as a mark of prowess and a perquisite of human dignity; secondarily, it becomes substantially honorable in itself, especially the consumption of the more desirable things. The consumption of choice articles of food, and frequently also of rare articles of adornment, becomes taboo to the women and children; and if there is a base (servile) class of men, the taboo holds also for them. With a further advance in culture this taboo may change into simple custom of a more or less rigorous character; but whatever be the theoretical basis of the distinction which is maintained, whether it be a taboo or a larger conventionality, the features of the conventional scheme of consumption do not change easily. When the quasi-peaceable stage of industry is reached, with its fundamental institution of chattel slavery, the general principle, more or less rigorously applied, is that the base, industrious class should consume only what may be necessary to their subsistence. In the nature of things, luxuries and the comforts of life belong to the leisure class. Under the taboo, certain victuals, and more particularly certain beverages, are strictly reserved for the use of the superior class.

The ceremonial differentiation of the dietary is best seen

in the use of intoxicating beverages and narcotics. If these articles of consumption are costly, they are felt to be noble and honorific. Therefore the base classes, primarily the women, practice an enforced continence with respect to these stimulants, except in countries where they are obtainable at a very low cost. From archaic times down through all the length of the patriarchal regime it has been the office of the women to prepare and administer these luxuries, and it has been the perquisite of the men of gentle birth and breeding to consume them. Drunkenness and the other pathological consequences of the free use of stimulants therefore tend in their turn to become honorific, as being a mark, at the second remove, of the superior status of those who are able to afford the indulgence. Infirmities induced by overindulgence are among some peoples freely recognized as manly attributes. It has even happened that the name for certain diseased conditions of the body arising from such an origin has passed into everyday speech as a synonym for "noble" or "gentle." It is only at a relatively early stage of culture that the symptoms of expensive vice are conventionally accepted as marks of a superior status, and so tend to become virtues and command the deference of the community; but the reputability that attaches to certain expensive vices long retains so much of its force as to appreciably lessen the disapprobation visited upon the men of the wealthy or noble class for any excessive indulgence. The same invidious distinction adds force to the current disapproval of any indulgence of this kind on the part of women, minors, and inferiors. This invidious traditional distinction has not lost its force even among the more advanced peoples of today. Where the example set by the leisure class retains its imperative force in the regulation of the conventionalities, it is observable that the women still in great measure practice the same traditional continence with regard to stimulants.

This characterization of the greater continence in the use of stimulants practiced by the women of the reputable classes may seem an excessive refinement of logic at the expense of common sense. But facts within easy reach of anyone who cares to know them go to say that the greater abstinence of women is in some part due to an imperative conventionality; and that this conventionality is, in a general way, strongest where the patriarchal tradition—the tradition that the woman is a chattel—has retained its hold in greatest vigor. In a sense which has been greatly qualified in scope and rigor, but which has by no means lost its meaning even yet, this tradition says that the woman, being a chattel, should consume only what is necessary to her sustenance—except so far as her further consumption contributes to the comfort or the good repute of her master. The consumption of luxuries, in the true sense, is a consumption directed to the comfort of the consumer himself, and is, therefore, a mark of the master. Any such consumption by others can take place only on a basis of sufferance. In communities where the popular habits of thought have been profoundly shaped by the patriarchal tradition, we may accordingly look for survivals of the taboo on luxuries at least to the extent of a conventional deprecation of their use by the unfree and dependent class. This is more particularly true as regards certain luxuries, the use of which by the dependent class would detract sensibly from the comfort or pleasure of their masters, or which are held to be of doubtful legitimacy on other grounds. In the apprehension of the great conservative middle class of Western civilization, the use of these various stimulants is obnoxious to at least one, if not both, of these objections; and it is a fact too significant to be passed over that it is precisely among these middle classes of the Germanic culture, with their strong surviving sense of the patriarchal proprieties, that the women are to the greatest extent subject to a qualified taboo on narcotics and alcoholic beverages. With many qualifications—with more qualifications as the patriarchal tradition has gradually weakened—the general rule is felt to be right and binding that women should consume only for the benefit of their masters. The objection of course presents itself that expenditure on women's dress and household paraphernalia is an obvious exception to this rule; but it will appear in the sequel that this exception is much more obvious than substantial.

During the earlier stages of economic development, consumption of goods without stint, especially consumption of the better grades of goods—ideally all consumption in excess of the subsistence minimum—pertains normally to the leisure class. This restriction tends to disappear, at least formally, after the later peaceable stage has been reached, with private ownership of goods and an industrial system based on wage labor or on the petty household economy. But during the earlier quasi-peaceable stage, when so many of the traditions through which the institution of a leisure class has affected the economic life of later times were taking form and consistency, this principle has had the force of a conventional law. It has served as the norm to which consumption has tended to conform, and any appreciable departure from it is to be regarded as an aberrant form, sure to be eliminated sooner or later in the further course of development.

The quasi-peaceable gentleman of leisure, then, not only consumes of the staff of life beyond the minimum required for subsistence and physical efficiency, but his consumption also undergoes a specialization as regards the quality of the goods consumed. He consumes freely and of the best in food, drink, narcotics, shelter, services, ornaments, apparel, weapons and accoutrements, amusements, amulets, and idols or divinities. In the process of gradual amelioration which takes place in the articles of his consumption, the motive principle and the proximate aim of innovation is no doubt the higher efficiency of the improved and more elaborate products for personal comfort and well-being. But that does not remain the sole purpose of their consumption. The canon of reputability is at hand and seizes upon such innovations as are, according to its standard, fit to survive. Since the consumption of these more excellent goods is an evidence of wealth, it becomes honorific; and conversely, the failure to consume in due quantity and quality becomes a mark of inferiority and demerit.

This growth of punctilious discrimination as to qualitative

excellence in eating, drinking, etc., presently affects not only the manner of life, but also the training and intellectual activity of the gentleman of leisure. He is no longer simply the successful, aggressive male—the man of strength, resource, and intrepidity. In order to avoid stultification he must also cultivate his tastes, for it now becomes incumbent on him to discriminate with some nicety between the noble and the ignoble in consumable goods. He becomes a connoisseur in creditable viands of various degrees of merit, in manly beverages and trinkets, in seemly apparel and architecture, in weapons, games, dances, and the narcotics. This cultivation of the aesthetic faculty requires time and application, and the demands made upon the gentleman in this direction therefore tend to change his life of leisure into a more or less arduous application to the business of learning how to live a life of ostensible leisure in a becoming way. Closely related to the requirement that the gentleman must consume freely and of the right kind of goods, there is the requirement that he must know how to consume them in a seemly manner. His life of leisure must be conducted in due form. Hence arise good manners in the way pointed out in an earlier chapter. Highbred manners and ways of living are items of conformity to the norm of conspicuous leisure and conspicuous consumption.

Conspicuous consumption of valuable goods is a means of reputability to the gentleman of leisure. As wealth accumulates on his hands, his own unaided effort will not avail to sufficiently put his opulence in evidence by this method. The aid of friends and competitors is therefore brought in by resorting to the giving of valuable presents and expensive feasts and entertainments. Presents and feasts had probably another origin than that of naive ostentation, but they acquired their utility for this purpose very early, and they have retained that character to the present; so that their utility in this respect has now long been the substantial ground on which these usages rest. Costly entertainments, such as the potlatch or the ball, are peculiarly adapted to serve this end. The competitor with whom the entertainer wishes to institute a comparison is, by this method, made to serve as a means to the end. He consumes vicariously for his host at the same time that he is a witness to the consumption of that excess of good things which his host is unable to dispose of singlehanded, and he is also made to witness his host's facility in etiquette.

In the giving of costly entertainments other motives, of a more genial kind, are of course also present. The custom of festive gatherings probably originated in motives of conviviality and religion; these motives are also present in the later development, but they do not continue to be the sole motives. The latter-day leisure-class festivities and entertainments may continue in some slight degree to serve the religious need and in a higher degree the needs of recreation and conviviality, but they also serve an invidious purpose; and they serve it none the less effectually for having a colorable noninvidious ground in these more avowable motives. But the economic effect of these social amenities is not therefore lessened, either in the vicarious consumption of goods or in the exhibition of difficult and costly achievements in etiquette.

As wealth accumulates, the leisure class develops further in function and structure and there arises a differentiation within the class. There is a more or less elaborate system of rank and grades. This differentiation is furthered by the inheritance of wealth and the consequent inheritance of gentility. With the inheritance of gentility goes the inheritance of obligatory leisure; and gentility of a sufficient potency to entail a life of leisure may be inherited without the complement of wealth required to maintain a dignified leisure. Gentle blood may be transmitted without goods enough to afford a reputably free consumption at one's ease. Hence results a class of impecunious gentlemen of leisure, incidentally referred to already. These half-caste gentlemen of leisure fall into a system of hierarchical gradations. Those who stand near the higher and the highest grades of the wealthy leisure class, in point of birth, or in point of wealth, or both, outrank the remoter-born and the pecuniarily weaker. These lower grades, especially the impecunious, or marginal, gentlemen of leisure, affiliate themselves by a system of dependence or fealty to the great ones; by so doing they gain an increment of repute, or of the means with which to lead a life of leisure, from their patron. They become his courtiers or retainers, servants; and being fed and countenanced by their patron they are indices of his rank and vicarious consumers of his superfluous wealth. Many of these affiliated gentlemen of leisure are at the same time lesser men of substance in their own right so that some of them are scarcely at all, others only partially, to be rated as vicarious consumers. So many of them, however, as make up the retainers and hangers-on of the patron may be classed as vicarious consumers without qualification. Many of these again, and also many of the other aristocracy of less degree, have in turn attached to their persons a more or less comprehensive group of vicarious consumers in the persons of their wives and children, their servants, retainers, etc.

XIV

THREE YEARS OF THE UNIVERSITY ELEMENTARY SCHOOL[1]

JOHN DEWEY

The school was started the first week in January, three years ago. I shall try this afternoon to give a brief statement of the ideas and problems that were in mind when the experiment was started, and a sketch of the development of the work since that time. We began in a small house in Fifty-seventh Street, with fifteen children. We found ourselves the next year with twenty-five children in Kimbark Avenue, and then moved in January to Rosalie Court, the larger quarters enabling us to take forty children. The next year the number increased to sixty, the school remaining at Rosalie Court. This year we have had ninety-five on the roll at one time, and are located at 5412 Ellis Avenue, where we hope to stay till we have a building and grounds of our own.

The children during the first year of the school were between the ages of six and nine. Now their ages range between four and thirteen—the members of the oldest group being in their thirteenth year. This is the first year that we have children under six, and this has been made possible through the liberality of friends in Honolulu, H. I., who are building up there a memorial kindergarten along the same lines.

The expenses of the school during the first year, of two terms only, were between $1,300 and $1,400. The expenses this year will be about $12,000. Of this amount $5,500 will come from tuitions, $5,000 has been given by friends inter-

1 [John Dewey, *The School and Society* (Chicago, 1899), pp. 109-25.] Stenographic report of a talk by John Dewey at a meeting of the Parents' Association of the University [of Chicago] Elementary School, February, 1899; somewhat revised.

ested in the school, and there remains about $1,500 yet to be raised for the conduct of the school. This is an indication of the increase of expenses. The average expense per pupil is about the same since the start, i.e., $120 per child per school year. Relatively speaking, this year the expenses of the school took something of a jump, through the expense of moving to a new building, and the repairs and changes there necessary. An increase in the staff of teachers has also enlarged the work as well as the debits of the school. The increase in number of pupils this year is 50 per cent. Next year (1899–1900) we hope to have about 120 children, and apparently the expenses will be about $2,500 more than this. Of this amount, $2,000 will be met by the increase in tuition from the pupils. The cost of a child in the school, $120 a year, is precisely the tuition charged by the university for students. But it is not expected that the university tuition will come anywhere near meeting the expense involved there. One reason for not increasing the tuition here, even if it were advisable for other reasons, is that it is well to emphasize, from an educational point of view, that elementary as well as advanced education requires endowment. There is every reason why money should be spent freely for the organization and maintenance of foundation work in education as well as for the later stages.

The elementary school has had from the outset two sides: one, the obvious one of instruction of the children who have been entrusted to it; the other, relationship to the university, since the school is under the charge, and forms a part of the pedagogical work of the university.

When the school was started, there were certain ideas in mind—perhaps it would be better to say questions and problems—certain points which it seemed worthwhile to test. If you will permit one personal word, I would like to say that it is sometimes thought that the school started out with a number of ready-made principles and ideas which were to be put into practice at once. It has been popularly assumed that I am the author of these ready-made ideas and principles which were to go into execution. I take this opportunity to say that the educational conduct of the school, as well as the administration, the selection of subject matter, and the working out of the course of study, as well as actual instruction of children, have been almost entirely in the hands of the teachers of the school; and that there has been a gradual development of the educational principles and methods involved, not a fixed equipment. The teachers started with question marks, rather than with fixed rules, and if any answers have been reached, it is the teachers in the school who have supplied them. We started upon the whole with four such questions, or problems:

1. What can be done, and how can it be done, to bring the school into closer relation with the home and neighborhood life—instead of having the school a place where the child comes solely to learn certain lessons? What can be done to break down the barriers which have unfortunately come to separate the school life from the rest of the everyday life of the child? This does not mean, as it is sometimes, perhaps, interpreted to mean, that the child should simply take up in the school things already experienced at home and study them; but that, so far as possible, the child shall have the same attitude and point of view in the school as in the home, that he shall find the same interest in going to school, and in there doing things worth doing for their own sake, that he finds in the plays and occupations which busy him in his home and neighborhood life. It means, again, that the motives which keep the child at work and growing at home shall be used in the school, so that he shall not have to acquire another set of principles of actions belonging only to the school —separate from those of the home. It is a question of the unity of the child's experience, of its actuating motives and aims, not of amusing or even interesting the child.

2. What can be done in the way of introducing subject matter in history and science and art, that shall have a positive value and real significance in the child's own life; that shall represent, even to the youngest children, something worthy of attainment in skill or knowledge; as much so to the little pupil as are the studies of the high school or college

student to him? You know what the traditional curriculum of the first few years is, even though many modifications have been made. Some statistics have been collected showing that seventy-five or eighty per cent of the first three years of a child in school are spent upon the form—not the substance—of learning, the mastering of the symbols of reading, writing, and arithmetic. There is not much positive nutriment in this. Its purpose is important—is necessary—but it does not represent the same kind of increase in a child's intellectual and moral experience that is represented by positive truth of history and nature, or by added insight into reality and beauty. One thing, then, we wanted to find out is how much can be given a child that is really worth his while to get, in knowledge of the world about him, of the forces in the world, of historical and social growth, and in capacity to express himself in a variety of artistic forms. From the strictly educational side this has been the chief problem of the school. It is along this line that we hope to make our chief contribution to education in general; we hope, that is, to work out and publish a positive body of subject matter which may be generally available.

3. How can instruction in these formal, symbolic branches —the mastering of the ability to read, write, and use figures intelligently—be carried on with everyday experience and occupation as their background and in definite relations to other studies of more inherent content, and be carried on in such a way that the child shall feel their necessity through their connection with subjects which appeal to him on their own account? If this can be accomplished, he will have a vital motive for getting the technical capacity. It is not meant, as has been sometimes jocosely stated, that the child learn to bake and sew at school, and to read, write, and figure at home. It is intended that these formal subjects shall not be presented in such large doses at first as to be the exclusive objects of attention, and that the child shall be led by that which he is doing to feel the need for acquiring skill in the use of symbols and the immediate power they give. In any school, if the child realizes the motive for the use and application of number and

language he has taken the longest step toward securing the power, and he can realize the motive only as he has some particular—not some general and remote—use for it.

4. Individual attention. This is secured by small groupings —eight or ten in a class—and a large number of teachers supervising systematically the intellectual needs and attainments and physical well-being and growth of the child. To secure this we have now one hundred and thirty-five hours of instructors' time per week, that is, the time of nine teachers for three hours per day, or one teacher per group. It requires but little time to make this statement about attention to individual powers and needs, and yet the whole of the school's aims and methods, moral, physical, intellectual, are bound up in it.

I think these four points present a fair statement of what we have set out to discover. The school is often called an experimental school, and in one sense that is the proper name. I do not like to use it too much for fear parents will think we are experimenting on the children, and that they naturally object to. But it is an experimental school—at least I hope so—with reference to education and educational problems. We have attempted to find out by trying, by doing—not alone by discussion and theorizing—*whether* these problems may be worked out, and *how* they may be worked out.

Next, a few words about the means that have been used in the school in order to test these four questions, and to supply their answers, and first as to the place given to handwork of different kinds in the school. There are three main lines regularly pursued: (*a*) the shopwork with wood and tools, (*b*) cooking work, and (*c*) work with textiles—sewing and weaving. Of course, there is other handwork in connection with science, as science is largely of an experimental nature. It is a fact that may not have come to your attention that a large part of the best and most advanced scientific work involves a great deal of manual skill, the training of the hand and eye. It is impossible for one to be a first-class worker in science without this training in manipulation, and in handling apparatus and materials. In connection with the history work, especially with the younger children, handwork is brought in, in the way of making implements, weapons, tools, etc. Of course, the art work is another side—drawing, painting, and modeling. Logically, perhaps, the gymnasium work does not come in here, but as a means of developing moral and intellectual control through the medium of the body it certainly does. The children have one-half hour per day of this form of physical exercise. Along this line we have found that handwork, in large variety and amount, is the most easy and natural method of keeping up the same attitude of the child in and out of the school. The child gets the largest part of what he gets through his bodily activities, until he learns to work systematically with the intellect. That is the purpose of this work in the school, to direct these activities, to systematize and organize them, so that they shall not be as haphazard and as wandering as they are outside of school. The problem of making these forms of practical activity work continuously and definitely together, leading from one factor of skill to another, from one intellectual difficulty to another, has been one of the most difficult, and at the same time one in which we have been most successful. The various kinds of work—carpentry, cooking, sewing, and weaving—are selected as involving different kinds of skill and demanding different types of intellectual attitude on the part of the child, and because they represent some of the most important activities of the everyday outside world: the question of living under shelter, of daily food and clothing, of the home, of personal movement and exchange of goods. He gets also the training of sense organs, of touch, of sight, and the ability to co-ordinate eye and hand. He gets healthy exercise; for the child demands a much larger amount of physical activity than the formal program of the ordinary school permits. There is also a continual appeal to memory, to judgment, in adapting ends to means; a training in habits of order, industry, and neatness in the care of the tools and utensils, and in doing things in a systematic, instead of a haphazard, way. Then, again, these practical occupations make a background, especially in the earlier groups, for the later studies. The children get a good deal of chemistry in connection with cooking, of number work and geometrical principles in carpentry, and a good deal of geography in connection with their theoretical work in weaving and sewing. History also comes in with the origin and growth of various inventions, and their effects upon social life and political organization.

Perhaps more attention, upon the whole, has been given to our second point, that of positive subject matter, than to any one other thing. On the history side, the curriculum is now fairly well worked out. The younger children begin with the home and occupations of the home. In the sixth year the intention is that the children should study occupations outside the home, the larger social industries—farming, mining, lumber, etc.—that they may see the complex and various social industries on which life depends, while incidentally they investigate the use of the various materials—woods, metals, and the processes applied—thus getting a beginning of scientific study. The next year is given to the historical development of industry and invention—starting with man as a savage and carrying him through the typical phases of his progress upward, until the iron age is reached and man begins to enter upon a civilized career. The object of the study of primitive life is not to keep the child interested in lower and relatively savage stages, but to show him the steps of progress and development, especially along the line of invention, by which man was led into civilization. There is a certain nearness, after all, in the child to primitive forms of life. They are much more simple than existing institutions. By throwing the emphasis upon the progress of man, and upon the way advance has been made, we hope to avoid the objections that hold against paying too much attention to the crudities and distracting excitements of savage life.

The next two or three years, i.e., the fourth and fifth grades, and perhaps the sixth, will be devoted to American history. It is then that history, properly speaking, begins, as the study of primitive life can hardly be so called.

Then comes Greek history and Roman, in the regular chronological order, each year having its own work planned with reference to what has come before and after.

The science work was more difficult to arrange and systematize, because there was so little to follow—so little that has been already done in an organized way. We are now at work upon a program,[2] and I shall not speak in detail about it. The first two or three years cultivate the children's powers of observation, lead them to sympathetic interest in the habits of plants and animals, and to look at things with reference to their uses. Then the center of the work becomes geographical—the study of the earth, as the most central thing. From this almost all the work grows out, and to it the work goes back. Another standpoint in the science work is that of the application of natural forces to the service of man through machines. Last year a good deal of work was done in electricity (and will be repeated this year), based on the telegraph and telephone—taking up the things that can easily be grasped. In mechanics they have studied locks and clocks with reference to the adaptation of the various parts of the machinery. All this work makes a most excellent basis for more formal physics later on. Cooking gives opportunity for getting a great many ideas of heat and water, and of their effects. The scientific work taken up in the school differs mainly from that of other schools in having the experimental part—physics and chemistry—emphasized, and is not confined simply to nature study—the study of plants and animals. Not that the latter is less valuable, but that we find it possible to introduce the physical aspects from the first.

If I do not spend a large amount of time in speaking of the music and art work, it is not because they are not considered valuable and important—certainly as much so as any other work done in the school, not only in the development of the child's moral and aesthetic nature, but also from a strictly intellectual point of view. I know of no work in the school that better develops the power of attention, the habit of observa-

[2] This year's program has been published, and may be obtained from The University Press.

tion and of consecutiveness, of seeing parts in relation to a whole.

I shall now say a few words about the administrative side of the school. At the outset we mixed up the children of different ages and attainments as much as possible, believing there were mental advantages in the give-and-take thus secured, as well as the moral advantages in having the older assume certain responsibilities in the care of the younger. As the school grew, it became necessary to abandon the method, and to group the children with reference to their common capacities. These groupings, however, are based not on ability to read and write, but upon similarity of mental attitude and interest, and upon general intellectual capacity and mental alertness. There are ways in which we are still trying to carry out the idea of mixing up the children, that we may not build the rigid step-ladder system of the "graded" school. One step in this direction is having the children move about and come in contact with different teachers. While there are difficulties and evils connected with this, I think one of the most useful things in the school is that children come into intimate relation with a number of different personalities. The children also meet in general assemblies—for singing, and for the report of the whole school work as read by members of the different groups. The older children are also given a half-hour a week in which they join some of the younger groups, and, if possible, as in handwork, enter into the work of the younger children. In various ways we are attempting to keep a family spirit throughout the school, and not the feeling of isolated classes and grades.

The organization of the teaching force has gradually become departmental, as the needs of the work have indicated its chief branches. So we now have recognized divisions of Science, History, Domestic or Household Arts, Manual Training in the limited sense (wood and metals), Music, Art (that is, drawing, water colors, clay modeling, etc.), and Gymnasium. As the work goes on into the secondary period, the languages and mathematics will also of necessity assume a more differentiated and distinct position. As it is sometimes said that correlated or thoroughly harmonized work cannot be secured upon this basis, I am happy to say that our experience shows positively that there are no intrinsic difficulties. Through common devotion to the best development of the child, through common loyalty to the main aims and methods of the school, our teachers have demonstrated that in education, as in business, the best organization is secured through proper regard for natural divisions of labor, interest, and training. The child secures the advantages, in discipline and knowledge, of contact with experts in each line, while the individual teachers serve the common thought in diverse ways, thus multiplying and reinforcing it.

Upon the moral side, that of so-called discipline and order, where the work of the University Elementary School has perhaps suffered most from misunderstanding and misrepresentation, I shall say only that our ideal has been, and continues to be, that of the best form of family life, rather than that of a rigid, graded school. In the latter, the large number of children under the care of a single teacher, and the very limited number of modes of activity open to the pupils, have made necessary certain fixed and somewhat external forms of "keeping order." It would be very stupid to copy these, under the changed conditions of our school, its small groups permitting and requiring the most intimate personal acquaintance of child and teacher, and its great variety of forms of work, with their differing adaptations to the needs of different children. If we have permitted to our children more than the usual amount of freedom, it has not been in order to relax or decrease real discipline, but because under our particular conditions larger and less artificial responsibilities could thus be required of the children, and their entire development of body and spirit be more harmonious and complete. And I am confident that the parents who have entrusted their children to us for any length of time will agree in saying that, while the children like, or love, to come to school, yet work, and not amusement, has been the spirit and teaching of the school; and that this freedom has been granted under such conditions of intelligent and sympathetic oversight as to be a means of upbuilding and strengthening character.

At the end of three years, then, we are not afraid to say that some of our original questions have secured affirmative answers. The increase of our children from fifteen to almost one hundred, along with a practical doubling of fees, has shown that parents are ready for a form of education that makes individual growth its sole controlling aim. The presence of an organized corps of instructors demonstrates that thoroughly educated teachers are ready to bring to elementary education the same resources of training, knowledge, and skill that have long been at the command of higher education. The everyday work of the school shows that children can live in school as out of it, and yet grow daily in wisdom, kindness, and the spirit of obedience—that learning may, even with little children, lay hold upon the substance of truth that nourishes the spirit, and yet the forms of knowledge be observed and cultivated; and that growth may be genuine and thorough, and yet a delight.

XV

TRIAL OF C. B. REYNOLDS FOR BLASPHEMY. ADDRESS TO THE JURY [1]

ROBERT G. INGERSOLL

Gentlemen of the jury: I regard this as one of the most important cases that can be submitted to a jury. It is not a case that involves a little property, neither is it one that involves simply the liberty of one man. It involves the freedom of speech, the intellectual liberty of every citizen of New Jersey.

1 [Robert G. Ingersoll, *The Works of Robert G. Ingersoll* (New York, 1900), XI, 55-65.]

Within thirty miles of New York, in the city of Morristown, New Jersey, a man was put on trial yesterday for distributing a pamphlet argument against the infallibility of the Bible. The crime which the indictment alleges is blasphemy, for which the statutes of New Jersey provide a penalty of two hundred dollars fine, or twelve months imprisonment, or both. It is the first case of the kind ever tried in New Jersey, although the law dates back to colonial days. Charles B. Reynolds is the man on trial, and the State of New Jersey, through the Prosecuting Attorney of Morris County, is the prosecutor. The Circuit Court, Judge Francis Child, assisted by County Judges Munson and Quimby, sit upon the case. Prosecutor Wilder W. Cutler represents the State, and Robert G. Ingersoll appears for the defendant.

Mr. Reynolds went to Boonton last summer to hold "free-thought" meetings. Announcing his purpose without any flourish, he secured a piece of ground, pitched a tent upon it, and invited the townspeople to come and hear him. It was understood that he had been a Methodist minister; that, finding it impossible to reconcile his mind to some of the historical parts of the Bible, and unable to accept it in its entirety as a moral guide, he left the church and set out to proclaim his conclusions. The churches in Boonton arrayed themselves against him. The Catholics and Methodists were especially active. Taking this opposition as an excuse, one element of the town invaded his tent. They pelted Reynolds with ancient eggs and vegetables. They chopped away the guy ropes of the tent and slashed the canvas with their knives. When the tent collapsed, the

The question to be tried by you is whether a man has the right to express his honest thought; and for that reason there can be no case of greater importance submitted to a jury. And it may be well enough for me, at the outset, to admit that there could be no case in which I could take a greater—

---

crowd rushed for the speaker to inflict further punishment by plunging him in the duck pond. They rummaged the wrecked tent, but in vain. He had made his way out in the confusion and was no more seen in Boonton.

But what he had said did not leave Boonton with him, and the pamphlets he had distributed were read by many who probably would not have looked between their covers had his visit been attended by no unusual circumstances. Boonton was still agitated upon the subject when Mr. Reynolds appeared in Morristown. This time he did not try to hold meetings, but had his pamphlets with him.

Mr. Reynolds appeared in Morristown with the pamphlets on October thirteenth. A Boonton delegation was there, clamoring for his indictment for blasphemy. The grand jury heard of his visit and found two indictments against him: one for blasphemy at Boonton and the second for blasphemy at Morristown. He furnished a five hundred dollar bond to appear for trial. On account of Colonel Ingersoll's throat troubles the case was adjourned several times through the winter and until Monday last, when it was set peremptorily for trial yesterday.

The public feeling excited at Boonton was overshadowed by that at Morristown and the neighboring region. For six months no topic was so interesting to the public as this. It monopolized attention at the stores, and became a fruitful subject of gossip in social and church circles. Under such circumstances it was to be expected that everybody who could spare the time would go to court yesterday. Lines of people began to climb the courthouse hill early in the morning. At the hour of opening court the room set apart for the trial was packed, and distaffs had to be stationed at the foot of the stairs to keep back those who were not early enough. From nine thirty to eleven o'clock the crowd inside talked of blasphemy in all the phases suggested by this case, and the outsiders waited patiently on the lawn and steps and along the dusty approaches to the gray building.

Eleven o'clock brought the train from New York and on it Colonel Ingersoll. His arrival at the court house with his clerk opened a new chapter in the day's gossip. The event was so absorbing indeed, that the crowd failed entirely to notice an elderly man wearing a black frock suit, a silk hat, with an army badge pinned to his coat, and looking like a merchant of means, who entered the courthouse a few minutes behind the famous lawyer. The last comer was the defendant.

All was ready for the case. Within five minutes, five jurors were in the box. Then Colonel Ingersoll asked what were his rights about challenges.

a deeper interest. For my part, I would not wish to live in a world where I could not express my honest opinions. Men who deny to others the right of speech are not fit to live with honest men.

I deny the right of any man, of any number of men, of any church, of any state, to put a padlock on the lips—to make

---

He was informed that he might make six peremptory challenges and must challenge before the jurors took their seats. The only disqualification the Court would recognize would be the inability of a juror to change his opinion in spite of evidence. Colonel Ingersoll induced the Court to let him examine the five in the box and promptly ejected two Presbyterians.

Thereafter Colonel Ingersoll examined every juror as soon as presented. He asked particularly about the nature of each man's prejudice, if he had one. To a juror who did not know that he understood the word, the Colonel replied: "I may not define the word legally, but my own idea is that a man is prejudiced when he has made up his mind on a case without knowing anything about it." This juror thought that he came under that category.

Presbyterians had a rather hard time with the examiner. After twenty men had been examined and the defense had exercised five of its peremptory challenges, the following were sworn as jurymen. . . .

The jury having been sworn, Prosecutor Cutler announced that he would try only the indictment for the offense in Morristown. He said that Reynolds was charged with distributing pamphlets containing matter claimed to be blasphemous under the law. If the charge could be proved he asked a verdict of guilty. Then he called sixteen townspeople, to most of whom Reynolds had given a pamphlet.

Colonel Ingersoll tried to get the Presbyterian witnesses to say that they had read the pamphlet. Not one of them admitted it. Further than this he attempted no cross-examination.

"I do not know that I shall have any witnesses one way or the other," Colonel Ingersoll said, rising to suggest a recess. "Perhaps after dinner I may feel like making a few remarks."

"There will be great disappointment if you do not," Judge Child responded, in a tone that meant a word for himself as well as for the other listeners. The spectators nodded approval to this sentiment. At 4:20 o'clock, Colonel Ingersoll having spoken since 2 o'clock, Judge Child adjourned until this morning.

As Colonel Ingersoll left the room a throng pressed after him to offer congratulations. One old man said: "Colonel Ingersoll, I am a Presbyterian pastor, but I must say that was the noblest speech in defense of liberty I ever heard! Your hand, sir; your hand."—*The* [*New York*] *Times*, May 20, 1887.

the tongue a convict. I passionately deny the right of the Herod of authority to kill the children of the brain.

A man has a right to work with his hands, to plow the earth, to sow the seed, and that man has a right to reap the harvest. If we have not that right, then all are slaves except those who take these rights from their fellow men. If you have the right to work with your hands and to gather the harvest for yourself and your children, have you not a right to cultivate your brain? Have you not the right to read, to observe, to investigate—and when you have so read and so investigated, have you not the right to reap that field? And what is it to reap that field? It is simply to express what you have ascertained—simply to give your thoughts to your fellow men.

If there is one subject in this world worthy of being discussed, worthy of being understood, it is the question of intellectual liberty. Without that, we are simply painted clay; without that, we are poor, miserable serfs and slaves. If you have not the right to express your opinions, if the defendant has not this right, then no man ever walked beneath the blue of heaven that had the right to express his thought. If others claim the right, where did they get it? How did they happen to have it, and how did you happen to be deprived of it? Where did a church or a nation get that right?

Are we not all children of the same Mother? Are we not all compelled to think, whether we wish to or not? Can you help thinking as you do? When you look out upon the woods, the fields—when you look at the solemn splendors of the night—these things produce certain thoughts in your mind, and they produce them necessarily. No man can think as he desires. No man controls the action of his brain, any more than he controls the action of his heart. The blood pursues its old accustomed ways in spite of you. The eyes see, if you open them, in spite of you. The ears hear, if they are unstopped, without asking your permission. And the brain thinks in spite of you. Should you express that thought? Certainly you should, if others express theirs. You have exactly the same right. He who takes it from you is a robber.

For thousands of years people have been trying to force other people to think their way. Did they succeed? No. Will they succeed? No. Why? Because brute force is not an argument. You can stand with the lash over a man, or you can stand by the prison door, or beneath the gallows, or by the stake, and say to this man: "Recant, or the lash descends, the prison door is locked upon you, the rope is put about your neck, or the torch is given to the fagot." And so the man recants. Is he convinced? Not at all. Have you produced a new argument? Not the slightest. And yet the ignorant bigots of this world have been trying for thousands of years to rule the minds of men by brute force. They have endeavored to improve the mind by torturing the flesh—to spread religion with the sword and torch. They have tried to convince their brothers by putting their feet in iron boots, by putting fathers, mothers, patriots, philosophers, and philanthropists in dungeons. And what has been the result? Are we any nearer thinking alike today than we were then?

No orthodox church ever had power that it did not endeavor to make people think its way by force and flame. And yet every church that ever was established commenced in the minority, and while it was in the minority advocated free speech—every one. John Calvin, the founder of the Presbyterian Church, while he lived in France, wrote a book on religious toleration in order to show that all men had an equal right to think; and yet that man afterward, clothed in a little authority, forgot all his sentiments about religious liberty, and had poor Servetus [2] burned at the stake, for differing with him on a question that neither of them knew anything about. In the minority, Calvin advocated toleration—in the majority, he practiced murder.

I want you to understand what has been done in the world

2 [Refers to Michael Servetus (Miguel Serveto, 1511-1553), a Spanish physician and polemic writer who sent to Calvin in 1545 or 1546 a copy of the ms. of his theological tracts. After his tracts were published in a volume, Servetus was arrested and incriminated through material furnished by Calvin. Servetus was sentenced to be burned alive.]

to force men to think alike. It seems to me that if there is some infinite being who wants us to think alike, he would have made us alike. Why did he not do so? Why did he make your brain so that you could not by any possibility be a Methodist? Why did he make yours so that you could not be a Catholic? And why did he make the brain of another so that he is an unbeliever—why the brain of another so that he became a Mohammedan—if he wanted us all to believe alike?

After all, maybe Nature is good enough and grand enough and broad enough to give us the diversity born of liberty. Maybe, after all, it would not be best for us all to be just the same. What a stupid world, if everybody said yes to everything that everybody else might say.

The most important thing in this world is liberty. More important than food or clothes—more important than gold or houses or lands—more important than art or science—more important than all religions, is the liberty of man.

If civilization tends to do away with liberty, then I agree with Mr. Buckle that civilization is a curse. Gladly would I give up the splendors of the nineteenth century—gladly would I forget every invention that has leaped from the brain of man—gladly would I see all books ashes, all works of art destroyed, all statues broken, and all the triumphs of the world lost—gladly, joyously would I go back to the abodes and dens of savagery, if that were necessary to preserve the inestimable gem of human liberty. So would every man who has a heart and brain.

How has the church in every age, when in authority, defended itself? Always by a statute against blasphemy, against argument, against free speech. And there never was such a statute that did not stain the book that it was in, and that did not certify to the savagery of the men who passed it. Never. By making a statute and by defining blasphemy, the church sought to prevent discussion—sought to prevent argument—sought to prevent a man giving his honest opinion. Certainly a tenet, a dogma, a doctrine, is safe when hedged about by a statute that prevents your speaking against it. In the silence of slavery it exists. It lives because lips are locked. It lives because men are slaves.

If I understand myself, I advocate only the doctrines that in my judgment will make this world happier and better. If I know myself, I advocate only those things that will make a man a better citizen, a better father, a kinder husband—that will make a woman a better wife, a better mother—doctrines that will fill every home with sunshine and with joy. And if I believed that anything I should say today would have any other possible tendency, I would stop. I am a believer in liberty. That is my religion—to give to every other human being every right that I claim for myself; and I grant to every other human being, not the right—because it is his right—but instead of granting, I declare that it is his right to attack every doctrine that I maintain, to answer every argument that I may urge—in other words, he must have absolute freedom of speech.

I am a believer in what I call "intellectual hospitality." A man comes to your door. If you are a gentleman and he appears to be a good man, you receive him with a smile. You ask after his health. You say: "Take a chair; are you thirsty, are you hungry, will you not break bread with me?" That is what a hospitable, good man does—he does not set the dog on him. Now, how should we treat a new thought? I say that the brain should be hospitable and say to the new thought: "Come in; sit down; I want to cross-examine you; I want to find whether you are good or bad; if good, stay; if bad, I don't want to hurt you—probably you think you are all right —but your room is better than your company, and I will take another idea in your place." Why not? Can any man have the egotism to say that he has found it all out? No. Every man who has thought, knows not only how little he knows, but how little every other human being knows, and how ignorant, after all, the world must be.

There was a time in Europe when the Catholic Church had power. And I want it distinctly understood with this jury, that while I am opposed to Catholicism I am not opposed to Catholics—while I am opposed to Presbyterianism I am not opposed to Presbyterians. I do not fight people—I fight ideas, I fight principles, and I never go into personalities. As I said, I do not hate Presbyterians, but Presbyterianism—that is, I am opposed to their doctrine. I do not hate a man that has the rheumatism—I hate the rheumatism when it has a man. So I attack certain principles because I think they are wrong, but I always want it understood that I have nothing against persons—nothing against victims.

There was a time when the Catholic Church was in power in the Old World. All at once there arose a man called Martin Luther, and what did the dear old Catholics think? "Oh," they said, "that man and his followers are going to hell." But they did not go. They were very good people. They may have been mistaken—I do not know. I think they were right in their opposition to Catholicism—but I have just as much objection to the religion they founded as I have to the church they left. But they thought they were right, and they made very good citizens, and it turned out that their differing from the Mother Church did not hurt them. And then after awhile they began to divide, and there arose Baptists; and the other gentlemen, who believed in this law that is now in New Jersey, began cutting off their ears so that they could hear better; they began putting them in prison so that they would have a chance to think. But the Baptists turned out to be good folks—first rate—good husbands, good fathers, good citizens. And in a little while, in England, the people turned to Episcopalians, on account of a little war that Henry VIII had with the Pope—and I always sided with the Pope in that war—but it made no difference; and in a little while the Episcopalians turned out to be just about like other folks—no worse—and, as I know of, no better.

After awhile arose the Puritan, and the Episcopalian said, "We don't want anything of him—he is a bad man," and they finally drove some of them away and they settled in New England; and there were among them Quakers, than whom there never were better people on the earth—industrious, frugal, gentle, kind and loving—and yet these Puritans began hanging them. They said: "They are corrupting our children; if this thing goes on, everybody will believe in being kind and gentle and good, and what will become of us?" They were honest about it. So they went to cutting off ears. But the Quakers were good people and none of the prophecies were fulfilled.

In a little while there came some Unitarians and they said, "The world is going to ruin, sure"; but the world went on as usual, and the Unitarians produced men like Channing—one of the tenderest spirits that ever lived—they produced men like Theodore Parker—one of the greatest-brained and greatest-hearted men produced upon this continent—a good man—and yet they thought he was a blasphemer—they even prayed for his death—on their bended knees they asked their God to take time to kill him. Well, they were mistaken. Honest, probably.

After awhile came the Universalists, who said: "God is good. He will not damn anybody always, just for a little mistake he made here. This is a very short life; the path we travel is very dim, and a great many shadows fall in the way, and if a man happens to stub his toe, God will not burn him forever." And then all the rest of the sects cried out, "Why, if you do away with hell, everybody will murder just for pastime—everybody will go to stealing just to enjoy themselves." But they did not. The Universalists were good people—just as good as any others. Most of them much better. None of the prophecies were fulfilled, and yet the differences existed.

And so we go on until we find people who do not believe the Bible at all, and when they say they do not, they come within this statute.

Now, gentlemen, I am going to try to show you, first, that this statute under which Mr. Reynolds is being tried is unconstitutional—that it is not in harmony with the constitution of New Jersey; and I am going to try to show you in addition to that, that it was passed hundreds of years ago, by men who believed it was right to burn heretics and tie Quakers to the end of a cart, men and even modest women—stripped naked—and lash them from town to town. They were the men who originally passed that statute; and I want to show you that it has slept all this time, and I am informed—I do not know how it is—that there never has been a prosecution in this State for blasphemy.

Now, gentlemen, what is blasphemy? Of course nobody knows what it is, unless he takes into consideration where he is. What is blasphemy in one country would be a religious exhortation in another. It is owing to where you are and who is in authority. And let me call your attention to the impudence and bigotry of the American Christians. We send missionaries to other countries. What for? To tell them that their religion is false, that their gods are myths and monsters, that their saviors and apostles were impostors, and that our religion is true. You send a man from Morristown—a Presbyterian—over to Turkey. He goes there, and he tells the Mohammedans—and he has it in a pamphlet and he distributes it—that the Koran is a lie, that Mohammed was not a prophet of God, that the angel Gabriel is not so large that it is four hundred leagues between his eyes—that it is all a mistake—there never was an angel so large as that. Then what would the Turks do? Suppose the Turks had a law like this statute in New Jersey. They would put the Morristown missionary in jail, and he would send home word, and then what would the people of Morristown say? Honestly—what do you think they would say? They would say, "Why, look at those poor, heathen wretches. We sent a man over there armed with the truth, and yet they were so blinded by their idolatrous religion, so steeped in superstition, that they actually put that man in prison." Gentlemen, does not that show the need of more missionaries? I would say, yes.

Now, let us turn the tables. A gentleman comes from Turkey to Morristown. He has got a pamphlet. He says, "The Koran is the inspired book, Mohammed is the real prophet, your Bible is false and your Savior simply a myth." Thereupon the Morristown people put him in jail. Then what would the Turks say? They would say, "Morristown needs more missionaries," and I would agree with them.

In other words, what we want is intellectual hospitality. Let the world talk. And see how foolish this trial is. I have no doubt that the prosecuting attorney agrees with me today, that whether this law is good or bad, this trial should not have taken place. And let me tell you why. Here comes a man into your town and circulates a pamphlet. Now, if they had just kept still, very few would ever have heard of it. That would have been the end. The diameter of the echo would have been a few thousand feet. But in order to stop the discussion of that question, they indicted this man, and that question has been more discussed in this country since this indictment than all the discussions put together since New Jersey was first granted to Charles II's dearest brother James, the Duke of York. And what else? A trial here that is to be reported and published all over the United States, a trial that will give Mr. Reynolds a congregation of fifty millions of people. And yet this was done for the purpose of stopping a discussion of this subject. I want to show you that the thing is in itself almost idiotic—that it defeats itself, and that you cannot crush out these things by force. Not only so, but Mr. Reynolds has the right to be defended, and his counsel has the right to give his opinions on this subject.

Suppose that we put Mr. Reynolds in jail. The argument has not been sent to jail. That is still going the rounds, free as the winds. Suppose you keep him at hard labor a year—all the time he is there, hundreds and thousands of people will be reading some account, or some fragment, of this trial. There is the trouble. If you could only imprison a thought, then intellectual tyranny might succeed. If you could only take an argument and put a striped suit of clothes on it—if you could only take a good, splendid, shining fact and lock it up in some dungeon of ignorance, so that its light would never again enter the mind of man, then you might succeed in stopping human progress. Otherwise, no.

Liberty [3] is the condition of progress. Without Liberty, there remains only barbarism. Without Liberty, there can be no civilization.

If another man has not the right to think, you have not even the right to think that he thinks wrong. If every man has not the right to think, the people of New Jersey had no right to make a statute, or to adopt a constitution—no jury has the right to render a verdict, and no court to pass its sentence.

In other words, without liberty of thought, no human being has the right to form a judgment. It is impossible that there should be such a thing as real religion without Liberty. Without Liberty there can be no such thing as conscience, no such word as justice. All human actions—all good, all bad—have for a foundation the idea of human liberty, and without Liberty there can be no vice, and there can be no virtue.

Without Liberty there can be no worship, no blasphemy—no love, no hatred, no justice, no progress.

Take the word Liberty from human speech and all the other words become poor, withered, meaningless sounds—but with that word realized—with that word understood, the world becomes a paradise.

Understand me. I am not blaming the people. I am not blaming the prosecution, or the prosecuting attorney. The officers of the court are simply doing what they feel to be their duty. They did not find the indictment. That was found by the grand jury. The grand jury did not find the indictment of its own motion. Certain people came before the grand jury and made their complaint—gave their testimony; and upon that testimony, under this statute, the indictment was found.

3 [*Ibid.*, pp. 116-17.]

While I do not blame these people—they not being on trial —I do ask you to stand on the side of right.

I cannot conceive of much greater happiness than to discharge a public duty, than to be absolutely true to conscience, true to judgment, no matter what authority may say, no matter what public opinion may demand. A man who stands by the right, against the world, cannot help applauding himself, and saying: "I am an honest man."

I want your verdict—a verdict born of manhood, of courage; and I want to send a dispatch today to a woman who is lying sick. I wish you to furnish the words of this dispatch—only two words—and these two words will fill an anxious heart with joy. They will fill a soul with light. It is a very short message —only two words—and I ask you to furnish them: "Not guilty."

You are expected to do this, because I believe you will be true to your consciences, true to your best judgment, true to the best interests of the people of New Jersey, true to the great cause of Liberty.

I sincerely hope that it will never be necessary again, under the flag of the United States—that flag for which has been shed the bravest and best blood of the world—under that flag maintained by Washington, by Jefferson, by Franklin and by Lincoln—under that flag in defense of which New Jersey poured out her best and bravest blood—I hope it will never be necessary again for a man to stand before a jury and plead for the Liberty of Speech.[4]

[4] [C. P. Farrell, publisher of Ingersoll's *Works,* adds here the following note: "The jury in this case brought in a verdict of guilty. The Judge imposed a fine of twenty-five dollars and costs amounting in all to seventy-five dollars, which Colonel Ingersoll paid, giving his services free."]

XVI

UNCONSECRATED SERVICE [1]

GEORGE D. HERRON

The time has come when the church must be started upon a new career—a career that will give back Christianity to Christendom, and restore the faith of the apostles to a waiting and expectant world. From the prison house of churchly selfishness, from the bonds of dogmatic theology, the gospel must be set free, or there will arise a new Protestantism. In the problems of our day Christ comes to call the church to a more comprehensive mission. Except the church be born again, and a heart of flesh take the place of its heart of pride, it cannot see the kingdom of God, which is pressing in upon it from the future. To this work God now calls the church to consecrate, yea, perhaps to sacrifice, its freshest thought, its most passionate devotion, its bravest hearts, its strongest lives, that the unsearchable riches of Christ may be poured afresh upon an impoverished world, and all men be made to see what is the dispensation of the mystery which from all ages hath been hid in God, waiting for the manifestation of his Son and the preparation of the earth for a regenerated society, a heavenly civilization. To this end must these be dedicated, or the church will perish like the temple, or be rent like Rome. The Spirit calls upon the church to furnish prophetic souls who will feel the anger of the Infinite Love against the covetousness which has betrayed Christ to be crucified at the hands of mammon. There is a divine inconsistency that drives the prophets of larger truth beyond the realm of logic and opinion into the sphere of infinite liberty, where the Spirit

[1] [George D. Herron, *A Plea for the Gospel* (New York, 1892), pp. 20-31.]

utters through them the thoughts of God—these the church needs, for these the churchless multitudes wait, to lead them through the trial hour that is coming upon the whole earth. The church must raise up men who will obey the Spirit's voice, or it must get out of God's way. For what cares God for churches, if they obstruct the march of the divine purposes?

Do not think I would detract any honor from the innumerable company of saints and martyrs, scholars and missionaries, who by their heroic lives of service have gathered the glory of God about our Protestant Christianity, and have made the race rich with their sacrifices. These cannot be too highly honored. But we truly honor the brave and good who have been faithful in the great crises of the past, and broken the old bonds, and pioneered the race's way into larger futures, by being ourselves true and fearless in welcoming the new life and meeting the fateful crises of our day of opportunity. We never dishonor the truth and faith of the past so much as when we try to make them the defense of our own stupidity and cowardice.

We know, when we consider the matter intelligently and honestly, that Christianity is not fulfilling its mission of establishing the righteousness of God, as it is defined in the Sermon on the Mount and revealed in the incarnation, and by the cross, as the basis of human society. The world is conquering the church, at this moment, as truly as the church is conquering the world. The church itself would regard the attempt to realize the prophetic and apostolic vision of a new earth as not only hopeless lunacy, but a dangerous and disreputable movement towards the disruption of society. There is nothing which the vested interests of conservative Protestantism resent so much as the kingdom of God, which is the brotherhood of man. The world knows the church is failing, that it has become a secular more than a Christian institution. The divine common sense of man discerns a difference between the Christianity of Christ and the Christianity of the modern church which cannot be reconciled. The world of doubt believes that the gospel, if emancipated from philosophy and actually practiced, would cure all the ills and solve all the problems of society. There is more vital faith in much of the skepticism and heresy of our day than in a great deal of what we call orthodoxy. There is more hunger for righteousness in the unrest that is slowly gathering into mighty storms on the horizon of human hope than in the self-satisfaction and religious complacency of the church. The children of darkness are seeing the signs of the times more clearly than the children of light. Again is God hiding his mighty purposes from the wise and prudent, and revealing them unto babes. We need to ask ourselves earnestly whether the Son of man, if he should suddenly come into our churches, would find among us the faith that overcometh the world.

We point to our costly and beautiful temples of worship, to the crosses crowning the village hilltops, and the crosses the church spires lift above the city's smoke and strife. We count our great missionary benefactions, and hold mammoth religious conventions. We are perfecting and unifying our great ecclesiastical organizations, and forming new societies, and appointing countless committees. We have revised creeds, and progressive theologies, and renowned preachers. But all the while the church is getting farther and farther away from the lost sheep it was sent to save. The covetousness that fattens on the flesh of toiling boys and girls, the greed that wrecks the hopes and fortunes of less cunning rivals, the fashion whose fatuous arrogance fans the flame of judgment that is kindling in the skies, the luxury that is content to enjoy, while men with dark thoughts beg for work, and hopeless women slave in sweaters' dens, and the life withers out of starved babes—all these smile and bow and pray in the church, while the great, sad, suspicious world impatiently waits to see whether God be living or dead. This is not Christianity. This is not according to the gospel of Jesus Christ. Much of what we call Christianity is no less than an aristocratic and shameless pauperism, thriving on the wealth of sacrifice inherited from the past; resting in high-priced pews and fashionable residences; cunningly squeezing a luxurious living out of humanity, and superciliously labelling as charity the appeals made to serve the humanity that supports it. It is the victorious forces of time the church worships—prudence, thrift, respectability, reputation, culture—while it is practically infidel to the Christian gospel. We hear wise men, indeed, "preaching up truth and preaching down error" from the pulpit; but it is nearly always theological error, while a refined brutality practices, under the church's protection, a conscienceless and defiant atheism. Religious papers deplore the influence of money in politics, but seem innocent of the fact that money has no less influence, if not more, in securing certain kinds of ecclesiastical prominence, in obtaining positions of trust in religious corporations, than in securing seats in our national legislature. *Our social system, even where it is churchly, is not Christian, but respectable paganism, galvanized with Christianity.* The church does not dream of practicing the gospel; rather, it has practically abandoned the gospel as the law of life, putting opinion and money in its place, rearing the throne of mammon in the place of the changeless cross of the slain Christ, taking to itself the attitude of the scribes and Pharisees, instead of following the Son of God with the divine sorrow which alone can cleanse the race of sin. Unconsecrated men, who lie, and rob, and destroy, who outrage all humanities and gorge themselves with blood-red gold, may yet pass for men of integrity and conspicuous Christian philanthropy, whose self-satisfaction it seems cruel and unjust to disturb with the social impoliteness of the Sermon on the Mount. The church as an institution is saying, "Lord, Lord"; but its leaders are not doing, nor have they any faith in the practicability of doing, the things the Lord tells them. And I sadly fear it to be true—would God that I might be wrong!—that the most unmoving obstacle which the coming Christ confronts in the redemption of human society is the raw unbelief in righteousness, the nice and delicate yet no less blind and hateful infidelity to the gospel, which permeates our conservative Christianity, making the church the antagonist of the righteousness of Christ. For that church which worships Christ, and yet rejects his way of living, is the Judas Iscariot of modern Christendom.

The church must have a new career. There must be a resurrection of the gospel. An emancipated gospel is the hope of human society. For this the world prays and waits. To deliver the gospel from the weight of heathen theology, which has well-nigh smothered its life, to wrest Christianity from the distorting grasp of human selfishness, to preach the gospel in its divine simplicity and regal authority, to Christianize the church which bears Christ's name—this is the work which calls all the sons of God who are ready to make themselves of no reputation in the eyes of the Pharisees, and be despised and rejected by the self-indulgent worshippers of mammon. That faith which tries to be a substitute for life is the self-willed infidelity, the incurable unbelief, which an apostolic faith must scourge from the church, before the Son of man can lead it forth in the victory of righteousness which shall bring in the thousand years of peace. The church which, under the cover of dogma, disbelieves in the power of Christ to lead us out of actual selfishness; which believes that men can be saved from sin by holding certain opinions about God, without ceasing from sin; which impugns the honesty of God by assuming that he never intended us to do as his Eternal Son tells us; which presumes that God would promulgate a divine gospel which is unnatural law, and which man cannot practice; which puts forth Christ's righteousness as something to take the place of our own, so that we can go on enjoying the world's comforts, and gaining its profits according to its covetous customs—not by such a church will God convert the race. God will never permit a church which does not itself believe the gospel, or pretend to obey it, to carry the gospel to every creature. Nor will the divine intelligence of humanity receive a theology that teaches a salvation from sin without ceasing from sin; for, however needful and progressive such a theology may once have been, it has done its work; and, in the increasing light of the grace that shines from the face of the healing Christ, is naught but an unholy superstition. No revision of creeds, no holding of conventions, no flaunting of banners, no missionary enthusiasm can evade the supreme and epochal issue which now confronts the church, in this the beginning of the most revolutionary period of Christian history. The question the church must answer, the question which converges all gone and coming historic crises, carrying in itself the solution of all human problems, is this: Is the gospel practicable? does God mean it? is redemption a reality? has Christ overcome the world? is the Christ who is in us greater than the devil of selfishness without us? Until the church—I trust not at the point of death—enters upon a searching self-examination, and decides whether it really believes in this gospel, whether it accepts or rejects it, the conversion of the world to Christianity is the very vanity of our moral imbecility. If the church tries to evade this supreme moment of its history, persisting in preaching the gospel of theology instead of the living Christ; if it revels in the glory of the past, and rejoices in its heritage in the present, without presenting itself as a living and unblemished sacrifice unto God; if it continues to hide from the world, in the interests of social selfishness and dogmatic theology, what Christianity really is; if it persists in a wordy loyalty to its creeds, and infidelity to the Sermon on the Mount; then God will meet it upon the way upon which he sent it, in its palaces of vain worship, and leave not one stone of its goodly temples upon another.

I have said all this, my brothers, because I am an optimist, because I believe in the divine life in man, because I see that the kingdom of heaven is at hand. If I were a pessimist I should glorify what is, rather than herald the better that is to be. The world is redeemed. Our Redeemer lives, and his Spirit reigns, and there is no more excuse for our abiding in unrighteousness. This is God's world, and the laws of God are more practicable than the laws of the devil. This was the faith of the apostles. It is the faith which the Spirit of God has wrung from the agony of apostolic souls since the rapt John saw the Christ of judgment moving in the progress of the ages toward their divine consummation in the new earth of righteousness, resting in the eternal Sabbath of God, communistic with the ensphering love of the new heaven.

PART THREE

THE SOCIAL QUESTION

XVII

THE EIGHT-HOUR PROBLEM[1]

TERENCE V. POWDERLY

On Washington's birthday, 1885, a number of papers throughout the country contained communications on the short-hour subject, and the fact that so many papers had opened up their columns to the discussion of the question brought out a number of very able editorials from several leading papers on the necessity for shorter hours of toil for the laborer and mechanic. The agitation was continued during the spring and summer of 1885, and interest in the movement was not centered in the workingmen alone. Manufacturers began to discuss the question and study its possibilities. A "healthy public opinion" was being created, and the tendency toward a reduction of hours was becoming quite rapid when the annual conventions of the labor organizations of the country were held. The Federation of Trades, at its annual session in 1885, named May 1, 1886, as the day on which to put the eight-hour system into operation, but the convention made no provision for the enforcement of the order. It was left to the discretion of each subordinate union to adopt its own plan of operations. Those who passed the resolution did but little to secure its enforcement, and from the very first the movement, so far as its operations on May 1, 1886, were concerned, was doomed to defeat.

When the General Assembly of the Knights of Labor met in Hamilton, Ontario, in October, 1885, the General Master Workman [Terence V. Powderly] touched upon the subject in his address in the following words:

1 [Terence V. Powderly, *Thirty Years of Labor, 1859 to 1889* . . . (Columbus, Ohio, 1890), pp. 492-502. Interspersed subheadings have been joined with the sentences from which they were separated.]

> When the Secret Circular was issued on the 15th of last December, fixing Washington's birthday as the date on which to begin an agitation on the eight-hour question, which is a political one, the answer which came from all parts of the country was astonishing. In the Dominion of Canada, and in every State of the Union, the papers gave special prominence to the question, and the agitation has continued unabated since that time. The short-hour movement has received more attention since the first of last January than it did in the ten years preceding that date. While speaking on the eight-hour question, let me say that the proposition to inaugurate a general strike for the establishment of the short-hour plan on the first of May, 1886, should be discountenanced by this body. The people most interested in the project are not as yet educated in the movement, and a strike under such conditions must prove abortive. The date fixed is not a suitable one; the plan suggested to establish the system is not the proper one.

The convention took no action on the matter. There was no discussion on the subject. That part of the address was not considered, and the convention adjourned without action. Soon after the adjournment of the General Assembly, the street car strike of St. Louis, Mo., attracted the attention of the country toward the order, and inquiring minds began to investigate the aims and methods of the organization. Public attention once fastened upon the society, the press devoted much space to reports of labor meetings, and reporters were instructed to gather "labor news" wherever they could get it.

A reporter of the New York *Sun* was delegated to get up a story of the strength and purposes of the Knights of Labor, and he performed his mission in sending forth one of the most sensational and wonderful narratives that ever appeared concerning the order. The article started out with a falsehood, and in so misleading a manner that much harm was done, not only to the organization, but to the whole country. The introduction to the *Sun* article was in the following language:

> Five men in this country control the chief interests of five hundred thousand workingmen, and can at any moment take the means of livelihood from two and a half millions of souls. These men compose the executive board of the noble

order of the Knights of Labor of America. The ability of the president and cabinet to turn out all the men in the civil service, and to shift from one post or ship to another the duties of the men in the army and navy, is a petty authority compared with that of these five Knights. The authority of the late cardinal was, and that of the bishops of the Methodist Church is, narrow and prescribed, so far as material affairs are concerned, in comparison with that of these five rulers.

They can stay the nimble touch of almost every telegraph operator; can shut up most of the mills and factories, and can disable the railroads. They can issue an edict against any manufactured goods so as to make their subjects cease buying them, and the tradesmen stop selling them.

They can array labor against capital, putting labor on the offensive or the defensive, for quiet and stubborn self-protection, or for angry, organized assault, as they will.

The publication of that introduction did incalculable mischief. The correspondent for the *Sun* never obtained his information from a reliable source. He gathered it from those who felt that to tell a wonderful story was the best means of booming the organization. The organization began to boom, but those who sought its shelter were led to believe that they could secure the co-operation of the "five hundred thousand workingmen," referred to in the *Sun* article, in the shutting off of the railroads, and in stopping the "nimble touch" of the telegraph operators of America.

When that story was written, the order of the Knights of Labor was scarcely one hundred thousand strong, but in a few months, after the labor journals, the western press, and papers generally, had copied the sensational romance of the *Sun,* the number doubled, and the majority of the newcomers was not of the quality the order had sought for in the past.

In the early part of 1886 many of the new local assemblies began to pass resolutions favoring the "action of the General Assembly in fixing the first of May, 1886, as the day on which to strike for eight hours." They sent them to the General Master Workman, who saw at once that a grave danger threatened the order through the ignorance of the members who had been so hurriedly gathered into the assemblies. They were induced to come in by a false statement. Many organizers assisted in keeping up the delusion for the purpose of making "big returns" to the general office. In order to avert the danger which threatened the order, and to place facts before the membership, the General Master Workman issued a secret circular on March 13, 1886, in which the following occurs:

> It is evident that our members are not properly instructed, else we would not find them passing resolutions "approving of the action of our executive officers in fixing the first of May as the day to strike for eight hours." The executive officers of the Knights of Labor have never fixed upon the first of May for a strike of any kind, and they will not do so until the proper time arrives and the word goes forth from the General Assembly. No assembly of the Knights of Labor must strike for the eight-hour system on May first under the impression that they are obeying orders from headquarters, for such an order was not, and will not, be given. Neither employer or employee are educated to the needs and necessities for the short-hour plan. If one branch of trade or one assembly is in such a condition, remember that there are many who are in total ignorance of the movement. Out of the sixty millions of people in the United States and Canada, our order has possibly three hundred thousand. Can we mould the sentiment of the millions in favor of the short-hour plan before May first? It is nonsense to think of it. Let us learn why our hours of labor should be reduced, and then teach others.

Many persons, who blindly believed every statement made through the press or by interested parties that it was the aim of the Knights of Labor to strike for eight hours on May first, grew indignant to think that the General Master Workman should issue such an order since the General Assembly had resolved to act on May first. In the discussion of the proposed movement no prominence was given to any other organization, and the greater part of the reading public believed that the Federation of Trades was but a part of the Knights of Labor. Many members of the last-named society were impressed with the same belief, and the General Master Workman felt that those who were so blind to their surroundings as not to know the name of the organization they belonged to, or the difference between it and other societies, could not be trusted to go very far, or act intelligently in an undertaking of such magnitude as the establishment of the eight-hour system must necessarily be. There never was a time when the Knights of Labor were so flagrantly misrepresented, or the aims and purposes of the order so misunderstood. Designing and unscrupulous persons flocked into the order in all parts of the country. The time-serving politician, the trader in votes, the seeker for office, the spoils-hunter, who sought for a following that he might appear to have influence, and the sharp, shrewd shopkeeper, with an eye to business, all thronged into the assemblies during the spasmodic growth of the order. Each one anxious to further his own interests, and to stand well in the favor of those who surrounded him, encouraged the belief that it was the order of Knights of Labor which issued the eight-hour order for May first.

The silence and indifference of the organization which did issue the order gave rise to the impression that the whole affair must have been appropriated by the Knights of Labor. The anarchist element, ever busy in meddling with the affairs of the organization, and particularly interested at that time in the attempt to gain control of the machinery of the labor movement, availed themselves of every opportunity to spread discord and distrust because of the alleged lack of support of the General Master Workman of the Knights of Labor. That officer wished to see the eight-hour movement succeed. It was due to his efforts, as much as to those of any other one man, that the agitation of 1885 was begun and continued. While he sincerely wished to have the system established, he regarded the plan of operations to be inaugurated May first as being rash, shortsighted, and lacking in system; he could not conscientiously lend his sanction to the scheme and felt it to be his duty to warn those whose interests he had in his keeping against entering into the struggle under a disadvantage and while laboring under a false impression that it was the order of the Knights of Labor that named May 1, 1886, as the day on which to establish the eight-hour system.

The officers of the Federation of Trades did not hold any communication with those of the Knights of Labor. They imparted to them no part of their plans, nor did they in any way seek the co-operation of the order of Knights of Labor. As a consequence the general officers of the Knights of Labor knew absolutely nothing of the strength, wishes, or intentions of the other society until they were demonstrated in the strike for eight hours on May 1, 1886.

When the convention of the Federation of Trades met in Washington, D. C., in December, 1885, the Furniture Workers' International Union introduced a series of resolutions bearing on the question of inaugurating the eight-hour system on May first. They appear in the proceedings of that session as follows:

> WHEREAS, The last annual Congress of the Federation approved of the opinion expressed by Secretary Frank K. Foster, in his annual report, that it would be in vain to expect the introduction of the eight-hour rule through legislative measures, and that a united demand to reduce the hours of labor, supported by a firmly established and determined organization, would be far more effective than a thousand laws whose execution depends upon the good will of aspiring politicians or sycophantic department officials.
>
> WHEREAS, The congress has adopted the following:
>
> *Resolved,* By the Federation of organized Trades and Labor Unions of the United States and Canada, that eight hours shall constitute a legal day's labor from and after May 1, 1886, and that we recommend to labor organizations throughout this jurisdiction that they so direct their laws as to conform to this resolution by the time named.
>
> WHEREAS, This resolution, and the views upon which it is based, namely, that the workmen in their endeavor to reform the prevailing economic conditions must rely upon themselves and their own power exclusively, have found an echo in the hearts of all those organized workmen of this country, who are fighting for a principle and are willing to make sacrifices in order to secure an improvement of the condition of themselves and their fellow workers, and as

there is in many parts of this country a strong movement going on for the purpose of carrying out this resolution.

WHEREAS, It is a well-known truism that the success of workmen contending against capitalistic oppression is due to their policy of concentrating their forces whenever they desire to gain a point.

WHEREAS, The workmen of this country interested in the reduction of the hours of labor are considering the Federation of Trades and Labor Unions as a medium through which that concentration of forces can be accomplished, and to which belongs the leadership in this movement; and,

WHEREAS, The Federation has taken upon itself a great responsibility in regard to the movement inaugurated by this organization, as a failure of the same would be detrimental to all organizations, and would throw back the movement for the reduction of the hours of labor for many years to come; therefore be it

Resolved, That the Legislative Committee be hereby instructed to again appeal to the workmen of this country for the purpose of pointing out to them the necessity of them acting on their own account, and to call upon them to unite the different trades in their respective cities that they may be able to more thoroughly assist each other morally and financially.

Resolved, That all organizations under the jurisdiction of the Federation be called upon to report to the Legislative Committee on or before March 1, 1886, whether or not they have resolved to introduce the eight-hour work day; and if so, what steps they have taken in that respect, how they are organized throughout the country, etc., whereupon the Legislative Committee shall request all of those organizations having not yet determined to join in introducing the reduction of the hours of labor to assist such organizations with all the power at their command; *Provided, That, together with the reduction of the hours of labor, they do not ask for an increase of wages.*

Resolved, That all organizations intending to reduce the hours of labor on May first shall give an opportunity to the respective manufacturers and employers to give their consent by submitting a document to be signed by them to that effect, the contents of the said document to be prepared by the Legislative Committee, and the same to be forwarded to all organizations.

To these resolutions two amendments were added, one by Mr. Edmonston and the other by Mr. Gompers. That offered by the former stands upon the record in the following words:

> We recommend to all labor organizations a thorough canvass in their respective trades for the purpose of securing the co-operation of as many as possible to effect this object.

The amendment of Mr. Gompers was:

> *Resolved,* That the trades and labor unions be and they are hereby requested to forward to the secretary of the Legislative Committee on the evening of the first day of May, 1886, or as soon thereafter as possible, what results have been attained in the establishment of the eight-hour law.

The resolutions and amendments were referred to the committee on resolutions; the result was the presentation of the following recommendation by that committee:

> Your committee recommend the adoption of the eight-hour resolution presented by the furniture workers' delegation, with the amendments of Messrs. Edmonston and Gompers.

The report of the committee was adopted by the convention, and no further action was taken at that session. That organization, as such, never again held a convention. When the trades unions met in annual congress in December, 1886, they met under the name of "The American Federation of Labor," and have been known by that name ever since. It was not generally known that the Federation did not advocate the retention of the same rate of wages for eight, as that which prevailed under the ten-hour system, and manufacturers universally regarded the movement as having for its object a strike for ten-hour pay for eight-hour work. The mistake of the Federation was to assume that the workmen of the country regarded it as the only medium through which the eight-hour system would be brought into effect, and that the leadership in the movement belonged to the Federation. Had the resolutions been published to the world, and presented to other labor organizations for approval, a far better feeling would have prevailed, for the impression which pervaded the masses was that the resolutions of the Federation counselled a strike as the means by which to bring about the desired result. Why the Federation allowed this erroneous impression to prevail has never been explained.

XVIII

EXPEDIENCY OF THE CO-OPERATIVE COMMONWEALTH[1]

LAURENCE GRONLUND

"The relations of structures are actually such, that, by the help of a central regulative system, each organ is supplied with blood in proportion to the work it does."—HERBERT SPENCER.

"No thinking man will controvert, that associated industry is the most powerful agent of production, and that the principle of association is susceptible of further and beneficial development."—J. S. MILL.

"All human interests, combined human endeavors and social growths in this world, have at a certain stage of their development required organizing; and work, the grandest of human interests, does now require it."—CARLYLE.

We now have reached our objective point: the Co-operative Commonwealth.

The previous chapters were mere steppingstones, leading us to where we are, but as such indispensable, for it is their reasoning, rather than its own reasonableness, which will determine whether the Socialist System is to be, like Thomas More's imaginary island, a "Utopia": an *unreality,* or not.

The observation in our Declaration of Independence "that mankind are more disposed to suffer while evils are sufferable than to right themselves by abolishing the forms to which they are accustomed" is true of changes in forms of govern-

1 Laurence Gronlund, *Modern Socialism: The Coöperative Commonwealth* (Boston, 1884), pp. 100-106.]

ment, but much more true of alterations in the structure of society. To these, in fact, nations must be *driven* by an inward necessity.

For this reason we had to show that the present chaotic system, with all instruments of labor in private hands, will soon become unbearable and renders a change of some kind inevitably impending. For this reason, further, we had to point out the significance of the recent factory and educational legislation and state action in regard to railroads and telegraphs, accomplished or proposed, in our country and Great Britain, and to show that this extension of the state's activity was a sign that society is approaching a crisis in its development; an indication that this transitory state in which we are living, after having lasted about as long as that other transitory state between paganism and Christianity, is on the point of crystallizing into another enduring social order.

These reflections will make it clear—and we cannot lay too much stress upon it—that modern socialists do not pretend to be *architects* of the new order. That is to say, they do not propose to demolish the present order of things, as we tear down an old building, and then compel humanity to rear a new edifice according to any plan that they have drawn. They have no such absurd idea, just because they know that society is *not* an edifice at all, but an organism; and men are not in the habit of "planning" the development of a dog or a rosebush.

Right here is the radical distinction between us, socialists of the German school, and such socialists as St. Simon and Fourier. These had the same faults to find with the present social order as we have; they were, indeed, capital critics, but as reformers they were miserable failures simply because they wanted to be architects—inventors. They entirely ignored all social and political conditions and wanted mankind to don their ready-made systems as men do ready-made clothes. Fourier fancied that he had only to publish his system and all classes of Frenchmen would eagerly embrace it and in the twinkling of an eye transform all France into "phalansteries."

St. Simon went even to the length of having his first scheme patented.

They and all the old-style socialists represent the childhood of our movement, stand in the same relation to it as astrology and alchemy do to physical science. All great changes that have taken place in the world have had to pass through a "Utopian" phase. These primitive socialists were true "Utopists": they invented systems; we are intent on discovering the laws of development. They framed universal precepts; we ascertain universal sequences.

For what is "the Co-operative Commonwealth?"

Extend in your mind division of labor and all the other factors that increase the productivity of labor; apply them to *all* human pursuits as far as can be; imagine manufactures, transportation, and commerce conducted on the grandest possible scale, and in the most effective manner; then add to division of labor its *complement:* "concert"; introduce *adjustment* everywhere where now there is anarchy; add that *central regulative system* which Spencer says distinguishes all highly organized structures, and which supplies "each organ with blood in proportion to the work it does" and—behold the *co-operative commonwealth!*

The co-operative commonwealth, then, is that future social order—the natural heir of the present one—in which all important instruments of production have been taken under collective control; in which the citizens are consciously public functionaries, and in which their labors are rewarded according to results.

A definition is an argument.

It shows that our critics, when they style socialism a utopia, do not know about what they are talking. We can imagine a caterpillar, more knowing than its fellows, predicting to another that some day they both will be butterflies, and the other sneeringly replying: "What utopian nonsense you are talking there!" Our censors are just as ignorant of the groundwork of socialism. For our definition makes it evident that the co-operative commonwealth is not to be regarded as a product of personal conceit, but as *an historical product,* as a product in which our whole people are unconscious partakers. When the times are ripe for social co-operation, it will be just as expedient as feudalism was, or as private enterprise was, when each, respectively, made its appearance. It will prove its right to control by virtue of its own superior fitness.

Or is there anything utopian in predicting that division of labor will go on increasing? Has not wholesale production already vindicated its right to be the ruling system, and is it utopian to assert that private ownership of capital, so far from being necessary to production in wholesale, will prove a greater and greater obstruction to its inevitable development? Is it utopian to expect that all enterprises will become more and more centralized, until in the fullness of time they all end in *one* monopoly, that of society? Are not, indeed, *anti*monopolists—as far as they believe that they can crush the big establishments or even prevent their growth—the real utopists?

But that is by no means all. We have not yet sufficiently emphasized the *central* fact of society of *today.* Not alone is the necessity which we claim will drive the nations into socialism steadily growing, *but all civilized societies are being driven into socialism under our very eyes*—if we may apply the word "driven" to an inward impulse. Not alone are the conditions for the establishment of the new order fast ripening, but the new order is amongst us and asserting itself vigorously. Not only is the social organism growing from the circumference by society multiplying and subdividing its activities and again concentrating them, but the central regulative system *has* silently put in an appearance and *is* irresistibly organizing one social activity after another. This is a *fact,* of *transcendent significance;* and yet our politicians, the gentlemen of our "editorial staffs," our would-be-wise leaders and statesmen, all, indeed, except socialists, seem not to have the smallest inkling of it. They all look upon the factory legislation across the ocean and here and the agitation for nationalization of the land and national control of the telegraphs as isolated, rash expedients, and those who have adopted the accepted theories forthwith condemn this legislation and agitation and loudly proclaim that society—is going astray!

But the fact is, that our modern civilization mainly consists in this: that the state—that is, society in its organized form—has of late been constantly expanding its jurisdiction and has more and more contracted the sphere of individual ownership and control. Why, nearly everything the state now manages for us was once entrusted to private individuals.

Consider, criminal jurisprudence was once in private hands, and was the first in time to be taken in charge by the state. There was a time when the customs and national finances were farmed out to private persons, but that time is long passed by. Then the state turned its attention to postal affairs, and they are now everywhere under national control. The world has entirely forgotten that these affairs once were private enterprises, simply because the state has managed them so much better than was [formerly] [2] done. The whole struggle between state and church is also here in point; the principal consequence of that struggle has been that nearly all civilized states have taken charge of education, which undoubtedly will also soon in our country be a matter of national concern. There are still other matters, in which the older states of Europe in this development are ahead of us: national control of railroads and telegraphs. And in proposing that the state shall insure workingmen against accidents and against want in their old age, Bismarck is virtually impelled by the same spirit, rather than by any concern for the welfare of the working classes.

This fact of "the centralization of power in the national government," as it is called, is the central fact of society everywhere *now*. You may deny everything else, but you cannot deny that. You cannot look at a democratic paper without seeing a lament over the fact. The Democrats, though, are giving undue credit to the Republicans in charging it to their account, for they were but humble instruments in the hands of

[2] [The 1884 ed. reads "formally."]

the laws of the universe; if the Democrats should come into power, they would have to be "centralizers" to the same extent. The social organism has once for all got the impetus in that direction, and the movement is gathering greater momentum. That is why it is now everywhere in the air. That is why this fact is *the true rationale of socialism.*

The cry: "Beware, it is *socialistic!*" will have absolutely no effect. The state will go on expanding its jurisdiction, hurry on to its destiny, without asking or caring if it is "socialistic." The workingmen and grangers will continue to importune the state to come to their relief, without knowing anything about socialism. Henry George has written a book [3] that has enticed very many persons very far out on the road to socialism, protesting all the time that he is not a socialist. Frederic Harrison abominates socialism, and yet preaches: "Look to the State! From *that* you can expect the highest experience and skill, publicity, concentration of power, real and efficient control, a national aim and spirit and far more true responsibility."

But it is evident that the process of placing all industries and all instruments of labor under collective control will be carried on with far more energy and directness, when once the true leaders learn that the state is not some power outside of the people, but that it is the social organism itself; and that, as an organism, it is destined to grow until it embraces all social activities. Hitherto the state has acted from impulse, in opposition to accepted theories. But a logical foundation of some sort is necessary to all great movements. Rousseau's theory of a "social contract," though false, did in that way a great service to humanity.

The new social order to which we look forward is thus, certainly, the very reverse of utopian. As a historical product from every point of view we consider it, it will be a *natural* product, hence *rational.* "Whatever is, is rational," Hegel said; that is, it necessarily conforms to the innermost nature of things; and so: whatever is to be is rational. As soon as the

[3] [Reference is apparently to *Progress and Poverty.*]

people learn not to be scared by the word "socialism"; as soon as they learn the true nature of the state and see whither they are drifting, the co-operative commonwealth will be the only *expedient* system. But it certainly was not expedient when Plato wrote his *Republic;* it was not expedient, but it *was* a "Utopia" in the times of Thomas More; it was not expedient when St. Simon "invented" his system, for private enterprise, with the steam engine and other inventions, had first to increase the productive capacity of man a thousand times, and thus to prepare the way for it. And when it becomes expedient, it will be so for the first time in human history.

When the co-operative commonwealth becomes an accomplished fact we shall have the full-grown society: the *normal* state. That commonwealth—whose citizens will, *consciously* and avowedly, be public functionaries—will not know of a particle of distinction between the terms "state" and "society"; the two ideas will come to cover each other, will become synonymous. It will be a social order that will endure as long as society itself, for no higher evolution is thinkable, except organized humanity, and that is but social co-operation extended to the whole human race. It will effect a complete regeneration of society: in its economic, politic, and juridic relations; in the condition of women and in the education of youth (indeed its chief concern, its true starting point); in morals and, we may add, in religion and philosophy. The remainder of this treatise will draw in barest outline this normal state in these various relations, in the order above named, for the economic features are the foundation of every social system, out of which grow all the others, morals and religion last of all. It is, as we once observed, at the top, in morals and philosophy, that all changes from one social order to another commence, from whence they insinuate themselves down to the material conditions; *there the change of base takes place* and the new superstructure is then gradually built up. Therefore, also, we defined our system in economic terms alone.

XIX

THE CO-OPERATIVE MOVEMENT[1]

HENRY DEMAREST LLOYD

When democratic thought sought expression in democratic action in Europe, the Continental workingmen began kicking over thrones and slicing off the heads of kings and queens. The English workingmen saved their tuppences for flour and tea and fustian clubs to buy social regeneration for themselves out of what they could save by this self-help. Penny by penny and sacrifice by sacrifice they have gone on building, tolerated as enthusiasts, until the conventional world wakens to see a very great fact.

This co-operative movement, after fifty years of struggle, has had fifty years of living prosperity, and a greater prosperity is coming into plain view.

It has achieved an economic footing of a hundred millions of property.

Some of the best men and best thinkers have given it leadership.

At least one-seventh of the population of Great Britain have been enlisted in its ranks—the pick of the working classes of the greatest of European nations.

A program has been evolved looking to thoroughgoing social reconstruction.

It is an established religion; for co-operation is not a method of business merely, but an ideal of conduct and a theory of human relations. Without cathedrals, creeds, ritual, or priests, it has not only openly professed, but has successfully institutionalized the Golden Rule in business.

As significant as its cold facts and figures are its recognition of conscience and sentiment as business factors of the first

1 [Henry Demarest Lloyd, *Labor Copartnership* . . . (New York, 1899), pp. 326-30. Chapter title supplied by editor.]

force, and its success in establishing among men a new method of union. A movement like this of self-help, growing of itself, already big and getting bigger, with a clear and high purpose to do great things, even the greatest, with so broad a constitution that it may fairly be said to be of the people, is a fact with which no one who wishes to be well informed will neglect to acquaint himself, and no one who wishes to help on the coming of human brotherhood but will work for its extension. In contrast with the unscientific individualism which preaches that selfish interest is the only actual and practical motive in the world of values, we have in co-operation the individualism of millions of men and women organizing millions of capital into successful business under the ethics and economics of each-other-help and all-the-world-help as well as self-help. Here is applied brotherhood; here, the Golden Rule realized; here, a political economy of the kind that seeks wealth for itself by creating wealth for others.

Co-operation has won the right to be accounted the most important social movement of our times outside of politics. It is, of course, only a half-truth. It is the voluntary or domestic expression of the same resurgent spirit of self-help by each-other-help of which the republic, democracy, and the hopes of socialism are the political or public expression. Each of these —the private or voluntary, the public or political—is a half-truth; but the world needs half-truths to make up its whole truth.

The trades-unions have organization, local and federal; the German Socialist Labor Party has votes; but co-operation has organization, federation, votes whenever it shall choose to use them, and—what none of the others have—an economic foothold wide enough to give it a sure place from which to work its lever to move the world. No other social movement of our times surpasses it in radicalism; no other has as many members; no other approaches it in achievements nor solidity of resources in men and money. Labor copartnership is its most advanced element; it has the historic prestige of all the great names of co-operation, the crusading spirit with its accumulating momentum of moral enthusiasm. It is growing as the distributive movement, once fairly started, grew, by leaps and bounds; and it speaks the democratic invitation to all, which in human history has been the only thing that has never been turned back, nor overcome, nor silenced. It is a law of social dynamics that leadership in any movement passes steadily into the hands of its radicals. If this proves true in co-operation, the head of the column will be taken by labor copartnership.

The British co-operative movement is a living reality, and is in the flooding tide of growth, success, and confidence. This tide is not yet at the full. It is still rising. Between the time of making my notes in England and correcting my proofs a few months later, the returns which came in made it necessary to increase nearly all my figures. Both in England and Scotland, the productive and distributive concerns, with very few exceptions—like those of Walsall and Burnley—are making new records of success. The English Wholesale passes, for the first time in its history, the $15,000,000 mark of business in one quarter, and the annual turnover of its bank becomes $200,000,000. The Scottish Wholesale shows a gain of nearly sixty per cent in its workshops. The Leicester Equity boot and shoe works add to their capacity seventy-five per cent. In Ireland in the year the number of creameries rises from ninety-four to one hundred and thirty-one, and of people's banks from three to thirteen. The statistics in the appendix show the march.[2] The movement is pressing forward into fresh enterprises in old fields and ventures in new worlds like farming. The renaissance of the labor copartnership ideas of the founders evidences that there is a moral expansion as well as a material.

We [3] are a different people from the English, and our circumstances are different. When the English co-operative move-

[2] [The appendix has been omitted in this edition.]

[3] [*Ibid.*, pp. 333-36.]

ment struck its present roots, the consolidation of industry had hardly begun; while today, in America, it does not seem to have much further to go to bring us to the consummation of an industrial feudalism which will make impossible any individual, or even co-operative initiative or independence. Many of the American students and workers feel faintheartedly that the development of the trusts makes it hopeless for co-operation to obtain that foothold here which the English workmen succeeded in obtaining a generation ago. There is, too, the feeling among many of us that Americans are not a co-operative people; that, as has been said, our genius is more for co-talking than for co-working. But this is the greatest of mistakes. America has been doing a co-operative work even more remarkable than that of England. Each nation has followed its genius on the lines of greatest need and least resistance. English co-operation has been industrial; ours has been political. The achievement of America in uniting in one common life and one co-operative citizenship the African and European, and even Asiatic types, which elsewhere glare at each other with hatred across frontiers of bayonets, is the greatest triumph of co-operation which the history of civilization has yet shown. Compared with this, the English task of getting the men of one trade and one locality to unite in so simple a social function as purchasing or making commodities was easy. As America advances from political co-operation to industrial, its accomplishment is likely to be as much grander than that of Great Britain as the task is more difficult on account of extent of territory, racial variance, and the newness of social life. There is some reason to expect that the American evolution in co-operation will be partly along the lines of colonization and the establishment of new communities. The American is a colonizer. All Americans are colonists from abroad. The West was colonized from the East. We colonized California, and are now colonizing Alaska. One hears colonies. That aptitude for political co-operation which has today in every direction in America of plans for co-operative been forced upon us by the necessity of amalgamating so many nationalities fits us specially for community building. Village communities so placed as to have an easy command of the necessities of life can achieve an independence of the railroads and trusts and an opportunity for the members for production and exchange with each other which would be out of reach if they remained disconnected individuals, lost in the meshes of the highly complicated and centralized economic system of the American business world. The English co-operators, I found, look with great hope to America. Thomas Hughes, in one of the letters which I saw, said in 1887: "I should not be surprised if America took the lead out of our hands." Mr. E. O. Greening, one of the closest of living students of the co-operative movement, said to me: "Co-operation will be slow to take root in America, but once started, it will develop into forms far greater than anything here." Mr. George Jacob Holyoake made an interesting suggestion: "The churches," he said, "may make co-operation go in the United States." Rev. F. D. Maurice pointed out to the workingmen of Great Britain that the one indispensability for the success of co-operation was mutual confidence. Certain is it that co-operation in America must progress along lines where the people know each other, in their trades-unions or some other organizations—perhaps, as Mr. Holyoake has said, in the churches—or where they will be forced together as in village communities. There is hardly, as yet, anywhere in America that neighborhood life which made it easy for the weavers of Rochdale or the shoemakers of Kettering, who had known each other almost from childhood, to get together. In London, where the population is nearly as shifting as in America, it has been found almost impossible to acclimatize co-operation. Co-operation can go on in America as in Great Britain and on the Continent, only by the help of men of means, culture, and good will—men well-to-do in good deeds as well as title deeds; men like Horace Plunkett, who is leading the Irish in co-operation to-day, and like Holyoake, Ludlow, Hughes, Neale, Kingsley, Maurice, Owen, Godin, Leclaire, Van Marken, Schultze-Delitzsch, Raffeisen, and Luzzatti, who have been leading European workingmen. What co-operation needs here, as elsewhere, is not philanthropy, but leadership; not endowment but initative.

XX

THE BEND[1]

JACOB A. RIIS

Where Mulberry Street crooks like an elbow within hail of the old depravity of the Five Points, is "the Bend," foul core of New York's slums. Long years ago, the cows coming home from the pasture trod a path over this hill. Echoes of tinkling bells linger there still, but they do not call up memories of green meadows and summer fields; they proclaim the home-coming of the ragpicker's cart. In the memory of man the old cowpath has never been other than a vast human pigsty. There is but one Bend in the world, and it is enough. The city authorities, moved by the angry protests of ten years of sanitary reform effort, have decided that it is too much and must come down. Another Paradise Park will take its place and let in sunlight and air to work such transformation as at the Five Points, around the corner of the next block. Never was change more urgently needed. Around the Bend cluster the bulk of the tenements that are stamped as altogether bad, even by the optimists of the Health Department. Incessant raids cannot keep down the crowds that make them their home. In the scores of back alleys, of stable lanes, and hidden byways, of which the rent collector alone can keep track, they share such shelter as the ramshackle structures afford with every kind of abomination rifled from the dumps and ash barrels of the city. Here, too, shunning the light, skulks the unclean beast of dishonest idleness. The Bend is the home of the tramp as well as the ragpicker.

1 [Jacob A. Riis, *How the Other Half Lives. Studies Among the Tenements of New York* (New York, 1925 ed.), pp. 55-70. The illustrations of this section have been omitted in this edition.]

It is not much more than twenty years since a census of the Bend district returned only twenty-four of the six hundred and nine tenements as in decent condition. Three-fourths of the population of the "Bloody Sixth" Ward were then Irish. The army of tramps that grew up after the disbandment of the armies in the field, and has kept up its muster roll, together with the inrush of the Italian tide, have ever since opposed a stubborn barrier to all efforts at permanent improvement. The more that has been done, the less it has seemed to accomplish in the way of real relief, until it has at last become clear that nothing short of entire demolition will ever prove of radical benefit. Corruption could not have chosen ground for its stand with better promise of success. The whole district is a maze of narrow, often unsuspected passageways—necessarily, for there is scarce a lot that has not two, three, or four tenements upon it, swarming with unwholesome crowds. What a bird's-eye view of the Bend would be like is a matter of bewildering conjecture. Its everyday appearance, as seen from the corner of Bayard Street on a sunny day, is one of the sights of New York.

Bayard Street is the high road to Jewtown across the Bowery, picketed from end to end with the outposts of Israel. Hebrew faces, Hebrew signs, and incessant chatter in the queer lingo that passes for Hebrew on the East Side attend the curious wanderer to the very corner of Mulberry Street. But the moment he turns the corner the scene changes abruptly. Before him lies spread out what might better be the market place in some town in Southern Italy than a street in New York—all but the houses; they are still the same old tenements of the unromantic type. But for once they do not make the foreground in a slum picture from the American metropolis. The interest centers not in them, but in the crowd they shelter only when the street is not preferable, and that with the Italian is only when it rains or he is sick. When the sun shines, the entire population seeks the street, carrying on its household work, its bargaining, its love-making on street or sidewalk, or idling there when it has nothing better to do, with the reverse of the impulse that makes the Polish Jew coop himself up in his den with the thermometer at stewing heat. Along the curb women sit in rows, young and old alike, with the odd head covering, pad or turban, that is their badge of servitude—hers to bear the burden as long as she lives—haggling over baskets of frowsy weeds, some sort of salad probably, stale tomatoes, and oranges not above suspicion. Ash barrels serve them as counters, and not infrequently does the arrival of the official cart en route for the dump cause a temporary suspension of trade until the barrels have been emptied and restored. Hucksters' and peddlers' carts make two rows of booths in the street itself, and along the houses is still another—a perpetual market doing a very lively trade in its own queer staples, found nowhere on American ground save in the Bend. Two old hags, camping on the pavement, are dispensing stale bread, baked not in loaves, but in the shape of big wreaths like exaggerated crullers, out of bags of dirty bedtick. There is no use disguising the fact: they look like and they probably are old mattresses mustered into service under the pressure of a rush of trade. Stale bread was the one article the health officers, after a raid on the market, once reported as "not unwholesome." It was only disgusting. Here is a brawny butcher, sleeves rolled up above the elbows and clay pipe in mouth, skinning a kid that hangs from his hook. They will tell you with a laugh at the Elizabeth Street police station that only a few days ago when a dead goat had been reported lying in Pell Street it was mysteriously missing by the time the offal-cart came to take it away. It turned out that an Italian had carried it off in his sack to a wake or feast of some sort in one of the back alleys.

On either side of the narrow entrance to Bandits' Roost, one of the most notorious of these, is a shop that is a fair sample of the sort of invention necessity is the mother of in the Bend. It is not enough that trucks and ash barrels have provided four distinct lines of shops that are not down on the insurance maps, to accommodate the crowds. Here have the very hallways been made into shops. Three feet wide by four deep, they have just room for one, the shopkeeper, who, himself within, does his business outside, his wares displayed on a board hung across what was once the hall door. Back of the rear wall of this unique shop a hole has been punched from the hall into the alley and the tenants go that way. One of the shops is a "tobacco bureau," presided over by an unknown saint, done in yellow and red—there is not a shop, a stand, or an ash barrel doing duty for a counter, that has not its patron saint—the other is a fishstand full of slimy, odd-looking creatures, fish that never swam in American waters, or if they did, were never seen on an American fishstand, and snails. Big, awkward sausages, anything but appetizing, hang in the grocer's doorway, knocking against the customer's head as if to remind him that they are there waiting to be bought. What they are, I never had the courage to ask. Down the street comes a file of women carrying enormous bundles of firewood on their heads, loads of decaying vegetables from the market wagons in their aprons, and each a baby at the breast supported by a sort of sling that prevents it from tumbling down. The women do all the carrying, all the work one sees going on in the Bend. The men sit or stand in the streets, on trucks, or in the open doors of the saloons smoking black clay pipes, talking and gesticulating as if forever on the point of coming to blows. Near a particularly boisterous group, a really pretty girl with a string of amber beads twisted artlessly in the knot of her raven hair has been bargaining long and earnestly with an old granny, who presides over a wheelbarrow load of secondhand stockings and faded cotton yarn, industriously darning the biggest holes while she extols the virtues of her stock. One of the rude swains, with patched overalls tucked into his boots, to whom the girl's eyes have strayed more than once, steps up and gallantly offers to pick her out the handsomest pair, whereat she laughs and pushes him away with a gesture which he interprets as an invitation to stay; and he does, evidently to the satisfaction of the beldame, who forthwith raises her prices fifty per cent without being detected by the girl.

Red bandannas and yellow kerchiefs are everywhere; so is the Italian tongue, infinitely sweeter than the harsh gutturals of the Russian Jew around the corner. So are the *ristorantes* of innumerable Pasquales; half of the people in the Bend are christened Pasquale, or get the name in some other way. When the police do not know the name of an escaped murderer, they guess at Pasquale and send the name out on alarm; in nine cases out of ten it fits. So are the "banks" that hang out their shingle as tempting bait on every hand. There are half a dozen in the single block, steamship agencies, employment offices, and savings banks, all in one. So are the toddling youngsters, bowlegged half of them, and so are no end of mothers, present and prospective, some of them scarce yet in their teens. Those who are not in the street are hanging halfway out of the windows, shouting at someone below. All the Bend must be, if not altogether, at least half out of doors when the sun shines.

In the street, where the city wields the broom, there is at least an effort at cleaning up. There has to be, or it would be swamped in filth overrunning from the courts and alleys where the ragpickers live. It requires more than ordinary courage to explore these on a hot day. The undertaker has to do it then, the police always. Right here, in this tenement on the east side of the street, they found little Antonia Candia, victim of fiendish cruelty, "covered," says the account found in the records of the Society for the Prevention of Cruelty to Children, "with sores, and her hair matted with dried blood." Abuse is the normal condition of the Bend, murder its everyday crop, with the tenants not always the criminals. In this block between Bayard, Park, Mulberry, and Baxter Streets, the Bend proper, the late Tenement House Commission counted 155 deaths of children [2] in a specimen year (1882). Their percentage of the total mortality in the block was 68.28, while for the whole city the proportion was only 46.20. The infant mortality in any city or place as compared with the whole number of deaths is justly considered a good barometer of its general sanitary condition. Here, in this tenement, No. 59½, next to

[2] The term child means in the mortality tables a person under five years of age. Children five years old and over figure in the tables as adults.

Bandits' Roost, fourteen persons died that year, and eleven of them were children; in No. 61 eleven, and eight of them not yet five years old. According to the records in the Bureau of Vital Statistics only thirty-nine people lived in No. 59½ in the year 1888, nine of them little children. There were five baby funerals in that house the same year. Out of the alley itself, No. 59, nine dead were carried in 1888, five in baby coffins. Here is the record of the year for the whole block, as furnished by the Registrar of Vital Statistics, Dr. Roger S. Tracy:

Deaths and Death Rates in 1888 *in Baxter and Mulberry Streets, between Park and Bayard Streets.*

	Population			Deaths			Death rate		
	Five years old and over	Under five years	Total	Five years old and over	Under five years	Total	Five years old and over	Under five years	General
Baxter Street ..	1,918	315	2,233	26	46	72	13.56	146.02	32.24
Mulberry Street	2,788	629	3,417	44	86	130	15.78	136.70	38.05
Total	4,706	944	5,650	70	132	202	14.87	139.83	35.75

The general death rate for the whole city that year was 26.27.

These figures speak for themselves, when it is shown that in the model tenement across the way at Nos. 48 and 50, where the same class of people live in greater swarms (161, according to the record), but under good management, and in decent quarters, the hearse called that year only twice, once for a baby. The agent of the Christian people who built that tenement will tell you that Italians are good tenants, while the owner of the alley will oppose every order to put his property in repair with the claim that they are the worst of a bad lot. Both are right, from their different standpoints. It is the standpoint that makes the difference—and the tenant.

What if I were to tell you that this alley, and more tenement property in the Bend, all of it notorious for years as the vilest and worst to be found anywhere, stood associated on the tax books all through the long struggle to make its owners responsible, which has at last resulted in a qualified victory for the law, with the name of an honored family, one of the "oldest and best," rich in possessions and in influence, and high in the councils of the city's government? It would be but the plain truth. Nor would it be the only instance by very many that stand recorded on the Health Department's books of a kind that has come near to making the name of landlord as odious in New York as it has become in Ireland.

Bottle Alley is around the corner in Baxter Street, but it is a fair specimen of its kind, wherever found. Look into any of these houses, everywhere the same piles of rags, of malodorous bones and musty paper, all of which the sanitary police flatter themselves they have banished to the dumps and the warehouses. Here is a "flat" of "parlor" and two pitch-dark coops called bedrooms. Truly, the bed is all there is room for. The family teakettle is on the stove, doing duty for the time being as a wash boiler. By night it will have returned to its proper use again, a practical illustration of how poverty in the Bend makes both ends meet. One, two, three beds are there, if the old boxes and heaps of foul straw can be called by that name; a broken stove with crazy pipe from which the smoke leaks at every joint, a table of rough boards propped up on boxes, piles of rubbish in the corner. The closeness and smell are appalling. How many people sleep here? The woman with the red bandanna shakes her head sullenly, but the bare-legged girl with the bright face counts on her fingers—five, six!

"Six, sir!" Six grown people and five children.

"Only five," she says with a smile, swathing the little one on her lap in its cruel bandage. There is another in the cradle—actually a cradle. And how much the rent?

Nine and a half, and "please, sir! he won't put the paper on."

"He" is the landlord. The "paper" hangs in musty shreds on the wall.

Well do I recollect the visit of a health inspector to one of these tenements on a July day when the thermometer outside was climbing high in the nineties; but inside, in that awful room, with half a dozen persons washing, cooking, and sorting rags, lay the dying baby alongside the stove, where the doctor's thermometer ran up to 115°! Perishing for the want of a breath of fresh air in this city of untold charities! Did not the manager of the Fresh Air Fund write to the pastor of an Italian church only last year [3] that "no one asked for Italian children," and hence he could not send any to the country?

Half a dozen blocks up Mulberry Street there is a ragpicker's settlement, a sort of overflow from the Bend, that exists today in all its pristine nastiness. Something like forty families are packed into five old two-story and attic houses that were built to hold five, and out in the yards additional crowds are, or were until very recently, accommodated in sheds built of all sorts of old boards and used as drying racks for the Italian tenants' "stock." I found them empty when I visited the settlement while writing this. The last two tenants had just left. Their fate was characteristic. The "old man," who lived in the corner coop, with barely room to crouch beside the stove —there would not have been room for him to sleep had not age crooked his frame to fit his house—had been taken to the "crazy house," and the woman who was his neighbor and had lived in her shed for years had simply disappeared. The agent and the other tenants "guessed," doubtless correctly, that she might be found on the "island," but she was decrepit anyhow from rheumatism, and "not much good," and no one took the trouble to inquire for her. They had all they could do attending to their own business and raising the rent. No wonder; I found that, for one front room and two "bedrooms" in the shameful old wrecks of buildings, the tenant was paying ten dollars a month, for the back-room and one bedroom nine dollars, and for the attic rooms, according to size, from three seventy-five to five fifty.

There is a standing quarrel between the professional—I

[3] See *City Mission Report,* February, 1890, p. 77.

mean now the official—sanitarian and the unsalaried agitator for sanitary reform over the question of overcrowded tenements. The one puts the number a little vaguely at four or five hundred, while the other asserts that there are thirty-two thousand, the whole number of houses classed as tenements at the census of two years ago, taking no account of the better kind of flats. It depends on the angle from which one sees it which is right. At best, the term "overcrowding" is a relative one, and the scale of official measurement conveniently sliding. Under the pressure of the Italian influx the standard of breathing space required for an adult by the health officers has been cut down from six to four hundred cubic feet. The "needs of the situation" is their plea, and no more perfect argument could be advanced for the reformer's position.

It is in the Bend the sanitary policeman locates the bulk of his four hundred, and the sanitary reformer gives up the task in despair. Of its vast homeless crowds the census takes no account. It is their instinct to shun the light, and they cannot be corralled in one place long enough to be counted. But the houses can, and the last count showed that in the Bend district, between Broadway and the Bowery and Canal and Chatham Streets, in a total of four thousand three hundred and sixty-seven "apartments" only nine were for the moment vacant, while in the old "Africa," west of Broadway, that receives the overflow from Mulberry Street and is rapidly changing its character, the notice "standing room only" is up. Not a single vacant room was found there. Nearly a hundred and fifty "lodgers" were driven out of two adjoining Mulberry Street tenements, one of them aptly named "the House of Blazes," during that census. What squalor and degradation inhabit these dens the health officers know. Through the long summer days their carts patrol the Bend, scattering disinfectants in streets and lanes, in sinks and cellars, and hidden hovels where the tramp burrows. From midnight till far into the small hours of the morning the policeman's thundering rap on closed doors is heard, with his stern command, "Apri port'!" on his rounds gathering evidence of illegal overcrowding. The doors are opened unwillingly enough—but the order means business, and the tenant knows it even if he understands no word of English—upon such scenes as the one presented in the picture [here omitted]. It was photographed by flashlight on just such a visit. In a room not thirteen feet either way slept twelve men and women, two or three in bunks set in a sort of alcove, the rest on the floor. A kerosene lamp burned dimly in the fearful atmosphere, probably to guide other and later arrivals to their "beds," for it was only just past midnight. A baby's fretful wail came from an adjoining hall-room, where, in the semi-darkness, three recumbent figures could be made out. The "apartment" was one of three in two adjoining buildings we had found, within half an hour, similarly crowded. Most of the men were lodgers, who slept there for five cents a spot.

Another room on the top floor, that had been examined a few nights before, was comparatively empty. There were only four persons in it, two men, an old woman, and a young girl. The landlord opened the door with alacrity, and exhibited with a proud sweep of his hand the sacrifice he had made of his personal interests to satisfy the law. Our visit had been anticipated. The policeman's back was probably no sooner turned than the room was reopened for business.

XXI

CHILD WORKERS IN NEW YORK[1]

HELEN CAMPBELL

Political economists in general, with the additional number of those who for one purpose and another turn over statistics of labor, nodded approvingly as they gazed upon the figures of the last general census for the state of New York, which showed that among the myriad of workers in factory and other occupations, but twenty-four thousand children were included.

> Fifty-six million and more inhabitants, and all faring so well that only one fortieth part of one of these millions is employed too early in this Empire State. Civilization could hardly do more. See how America leads among all civilized countries as the protector of the feeble, the guarantee of strength for the weakest. No other country guards its children so well. There have been errors, of course; such enlightenment is not reached at a bound; but the last Legislature made further ones impossible, for it fixed the minimum limit at which a child may be employed in factories at thirteen years of age. By thirteen a child isn't likely to be stunted or hurt by overwork. We protect all classes and the weakest most.

Thus the political economist who stops at figures and considers any further dealing with the question unnecessary. And if the law were of stringent application; if parents told the truth as to age, and if the two inspectors who are supposed to suffice for the thousands of factories in the state of New York were multiplied by fifty, there might be some chance of carrying out the provisions of this law. As it is, it is a mere

[1] [Helen Campbell, *Prisoners of Poverty. Women Wage-Workers, Their Trades and Their Lives* (Boston, 1889), pp. 199-209.]

form of words, evaded daily; a bit of legislation which, like much else bearing with it apparent benefit, proves when analyzed to be not much more than sham. The law applies to factories only. It does not touch mercantile establishments or trades that are carried on in tenement houses, and it is with these two latter forms of labor that we deal today. In factory labor in the city of New York nine thousand children under twelve years of age are doing their part toward swelling the accumulation of wealth, each adding their tiny contribution to the great stream of what we call the prosperity of the nineteenth century. Thus far their share in the trades we have considered has been ignored. Let us see in what fashion they make part of the system.

For a large proportion of the women visited, among whom all forms of the clothing industry were the occupation, children under ten, and more often from four to eight, were valuable assistants. In a small room on Hester Street, a woman on work on overalls—for the making of which she received one dollar a dozen—said:

"I couldn't do as well if it wasn't for Jinny and Mame there. Mame has learned to sew on buttons first-rate, and Jinny is doing almost as well. I'm alone today, but most days three of us sew together here, and Jinny keeps right along. We'll do better yet when Mame gets a bit older."

As she spoke the door opened and a woman with an enormous bundle of overalls entered and sat down on the nearest chair with a gasp.

"Them stairs is killin'," she said. "It's lucky I've not to climb 'em often."

Something crept forward as the bundle slid to the floor, and busied itself with the string that bound it.

"Here you, Jinny," said the woman, "don't you be foolin'. What do you want anyhow?"

The something shook back a mat of thick hair and rose to its feet—a tiny child who in size seemed no more than three, but whose countenance indicated the experience of three hundred.

"It's the string I want," the small voice said. "Me an' Mame was goin' to play with it."

"There's small time for play," said the mother; "there'll be two pair more in a minute or two, an' you're to see how Mame does one an' do it good too, or I'll find out why not."

Mame had come forward and stood holding to the one thin garment which but partly covered Jinny's little bones. She too looked out from a wild thatch of black hair, and with the same expression of deep experience, the pallid, hungry little faces lighting suddenly as some cheap cakes were produced. Both of them sat down on the floor and ate their portion silently.

"Mame's seven and Jinny's going on six," said the mother, "but Jinny's the smartest. She could sew on buttons when she wasn't but much over four. I had five then, but the Lord's took 'em all but these two. I couldn't get on if it wasn't for Mame."

Mame looked up but said no word, and as I left the room settled herself with her back against the wall, Jinny at her side, laying the coveted string near at hand for use if any minute for play arrived. In the next room, half-lighted like the last, and if possible even dirtier, a Jewish tailor sat at work on a coat, and by him on the floor a child of five picking threads from another.

"Netta is good help," he said after a word or two. "So fast as I finish, she pick all the threads. She care not to go away—she stay by me always to help."

"Is she the only one?"

"But one that sells papers. Last year is five, but mother and dree are gone with fever. It is many that die. What will you? It is the will of God."

On the floor below two children of seven and eight were found also sewing on buttons—in this case for four women who had their machines in one room and were making the cheapest order of corset cover, for which they received fifty cents a dozen, each one having five buttons. It could not be called oppressive work, yet the children were held there to be ready for each one as completed, and sat as such children most often do, silent and half asleep waiting for the next demand.

"It's hard on 'em," one of the women said. "We work till ten and sometimes later, but then they sleep between and we can't; and they get the change of running out for a loaf of bread or whatever's wanted, and we don't stir from the machine from morning till night. I've got two o' me own, but they're out peddling matches."

On the lower floor back of the small grocery in which the people of the house bought their food supply—wilted or half-decayed vegetables, meat of the cheapest order, broken eggs and stale fish—a tailor and two helpers were at work. A girl of nine or ten sat among them and picked threads or sewed on buttons as needed; a haggard, wretched-looking child who did not look up as the door opened. A women who had come down the stairs behind me stopped a moment, and as I passed out said:

"If there was a law for him I'd have him up. It's his own sister's child, and he workin' her ten hours a day an' many a day into the night, an' she with an open sore on her neck, an' crying many's the time when she draws out a long needleful an' so gives it a jerk. She's sewed on millions of buttons, that child has, an' she but a little past ten. May there be a hot place waitin' for him!"

A block or two beyond, the house entered proved to be given over chiefly to cigar making. It is to this trade that women and girls turn during the dull season, and one finds in it representatives from every trade in which women are engaged. The sewing women employed in suit and clothing manufactories during the busy season have no resource save this, and thus prices are kept down and the regular cigar makers constantly reinforced by the irregular. In the present case it was chiefly with regular makers that the house was filled, one room a little less than twelve by fourteen feet holding a family of seven persons, three of them children under ten, all girls. Tobacco lay in piles on the floor and under the long table at one end where the cigars were rolled, its rank smell dominating that from the sinks and from the general filth, not only of this room but of the house as a whole. Two of the children sat on the floor stripping the leaves, and another on a small stool. A girl of twenty sat near them, and all alike had sores on lips and cheeks and on the hands. Children from five or six years up can be taught to strip and thus add to the week's income, which is far less for the tenement house manufacture than for regular factory work, the latter averaging from eight to twelve dollars a week. But the work if done at home can be made to include the entire family, and some four thousand women are engaged in it, an almost equal but unregistered number of young children sharing it with them. As in sewing, a number of women often club together, using one room, and in such case their babies crawl about in the filth on the wet floors, playing with the damp tobacco and breathing the poison with which the room is saturated.

Here, as in tobacco factories, women and girls of every age become speedily the victims of nervous and hysterical complaints, the direct result of nicotine poisoning; while succeeding these come consumption and throat diseases resulting from the dust. Canker is one of the most frequent difficulties, and sores of many orders, the trade involving more dangers than any that can be chosen. Yet because an entire family can find occupation in it, with no necessity for leaving home, it is often preferred to easier employment. It is the children who suffer most, growth being stunted, nervous disease developed and ending often in St. Vitus's dance, and skin diseases of every order being the rule, the causes being not only tobacco, but the filth in which they live.

It is doubtful if the most inveterate smoker would feel much relish for the cigar manufactured under such conditions; yet hundreds of thousands go out yearly from these houses, bearing in every leaf the poison of their preparation. In this one house nearly thirty children of all ages and sizes, babies predominating, rolled in the tobacco which covered the floor and was piled in every direction; and of these children under ten thirteen were strippers and did their day's work of ten hours and more. Physical degeneration in its worst forms becomes inevitable. Even the factory child worker fares better, for in the factory there is exercise and the going to and from work; while in the tenement house cigar-making, the worn-out little creatures crawl to the bed, often only a pile of rags in the corner, or lie down on a heap of the tobacco itself, breathing this poison day and night uninterruptedly. Vices of every order flourish in such air, and morality in this trade is at lowest ebb. Nervous excitement is so intense that necessarily nothing but immorality can result, and the child of eight or ten is as gross and confirmed an offender as the full-grown man or woman. Diligent search discovers few exceptions to this rule, and the whole matter has reached a stage where legislative interference is absolutely indispensable. Only in forbidding tenement house manufacture absolutely can there be any safety for either consumer or producer.

Following in the same line of inquiry, I take here the facts furnished to Professor Adler by a lady physician whose work has long lain among the poor. During the eighteen months prior to February 1, 1886, she found among the people with whom she came in contact five hundred and thirty-five children under twelve years old—most of them between ten and twelve—who either worked in shops or stores or helped their mothers in some kind of work at home. Of these five hundred and thirty-five children, but sixty were healthy. In one family a child at three years old had infantile paralysis, easily curable. The mother had no time to attend to it. At five years old the child was taught to sew buttons on trousers. She is now at thirteen a hopeless cripple; but she finishes a dozen pair of trousers a day, and her family are thus twenty cents the richer. In another family she found twin girls four and a half years old sewing on buttons from six in the morning till ten at night; and near them was a family of three

—a woman who did the same work and whose old father of eighty and little girl of six were her co-workers.

There is a compulsory education law, but it demands only fourteen weeks of the year, and the poorer class work from early morning till eight A.M. and after school hours from four till late in the night. With such energy as is left they take their fourteen weeks of education, but even in these many methods of evasion are practiced. It is easy to swear that the child is over fourteen, but small of its age, and this is constantly done. It is sometimes done deliberately by thinking workmen, who deny that the common school as it at present exists can give any training that they desire for their children, or that it will ever do so till manual training forms part of the course. But for most it is not intelligent dissatisfaction, but the absorbing press of getting a living that compels the employment of child labor, and thus brings physical and moral degeneration, not only for this generation but for many to come. It is not alone the nine thousand in factories that we must deal with, but many hundred thousands uncounted and unrecognized, the same spirit dominating all.

In one of the better class of tenement houses a woman, a polisher in a jewelry manufactory, said the other day:

"I'm willing to work hard, I don't care how hard; but it's awful to me to see my little boy and the way he goes on. He's a cashboy at D——'s, and they don't pay by the week, they pay by checks, so every cashboy is on the keen jump after a call. They're so worried and anxious and afraid they won't get enough; and Johnny cries and says, 'O mamma, I do try, but there's one boy that always gets ahead of me.' I think it's an awful system, even if it does make them smart."

An awful system, yet in its ranks march more and more thousands every year. It would seem as if every force in modern civilization bent toward this one end of money-getting, and the child of days and the old man of years alike shared the passion and ran the same mad race. It is the passion itself that has outgrown all bounds and that faces us today—the modern

Medusa on which he who looks has no more heart of flesh and blood but forever heart of stone, insensible to any sorrow, unmoved by any cry of child or woman. It is with this shape that the battle must be, and no man has yet told us its issue. Nay, save here and there one, who counts that battle is needed, or sees the shadow of the terror walking not only in darkness but before all men's eyes, who is there that has not chosen blindness and will not hear the voice that pleads: "Let my people go free"?

XXII

THE SETTLEMENT AS A FACTOR IN THE LABOR MOVEMENT[1]

JANE ADDAMS

One man or group of men sometimes reveal to their contemporaries a higher conscience by simply incorporating into the deed what has been before but a philosophic proposition. By this deed the common code of ethics is stretched to a higher point.

Such an act of moral significance, for instance, was John Burns's loyalty to the dockers' strike of East London. "The injury to one" did at last actually "become the concern of all"; and henceforth the man who does not share that concern drops below the standard ethics of his day. The proposition which workingmen had long quoted was at last incarnated by a mechanic, who took his position so intelligently that he carried with him the best men in England, and set the public conscience. Other men became ashamed of a wrong to which before they had been easily indifferent.

When the social conscience, if one may use the expression, has been thus strikingly formulated, it is not so hard for others to follow. They do it weakly and stumblingly perhaps; but they yet see a glimmer of light of which the first man could not be sure, and they have a code of ethics upon which the first man was vague. They are also conscious of the backing of a large share of the community, who before this expression knew not the compunction of their own hearts. A settlement accepts the ethics of its contemporaries that the sharing of the life of the poor is essential to the understand-

[1] [Jane Addams, *Hull-House Maps and Papers. . . . Comments and Essays on Problems Growing Out of the Social Conditions by Residents of Hull-House, a Social Settlement* (New York, 1895), pp. 183-86.]

ing and bettering of that life; but by its very existence it adopts this modern code somewhat formally. The social injury of the meanest man not only becomes its concern, but by virtue of its very locality it has put itself into a position to see, as no one but a neighbor can see, the stress and need of those who bear the brunt of the social injury. A settlement has not only taken a pledge towards those thus injured, but it is placed where the motive power for the fulfillment of such a pledge is constantly renewed. Propinquity is an unceasing factor in its existence.

A review of the sewing trades, as seen from a settlement, will be sufficient to illustrate this position.

Hull-House is situated in the midst of the sweaters' district of Chicago. The residents came to the district with the general belief that organization for working people was a necessity. They would doubtless have said that the discovery of the power to combine was the distinguishing discovery of our time; that we are using this force somewhat awkwardly, as men use that which is newly discovered. In social and political affairs the power to combine often works harm; but it is already operating to such an extent in commercial affairs, that the manufacturer who does not combine with others of his branch is in constant danger of failure; that a railroad cannot be successfully projected unless the interests of parallel roads are consulted; and that working people likewise cannot be successful until they, too, learn skillfully to avail themselves of this power.

This was to the residents, as to many people, an accepted proposition, but not a working formula. It had not the driving force of a conviction. The residents have lived for five years in a neighborhood largely given over to the sewing trades, which is an industry totally disorganized. Having observed the workers in this trade as compared to those in organized trades, they have gradually discovered that lack of organization in a trade tends to the industrial helplessness of the workers in that trade. If in all departments of social, political, and commercial life, isolation is a blunder, and results in dreariness and apathy, then in industrial affairs isolation is a social crime; for it there tends to extermination.

This process of extermination entails starvation and suffering, and the desperate moral disintegration which inevitably follows in their train, until the need of organization in industry gradually assumes a moral aspect. The conviction arrived at entails a social obligation.

No trades are so overcrowded as the sewing trades, for the needle has ever been the refuge of the unskilled woman. The wages paid throughout the manufacture of clothing are less than those in any other trade. In order to meet the requirements of the workers, lack of skill and absence of orderly life, the work has been so subdivided that almost no skill is required after the garment leaves the cutter. It is given practically to the one who is at hand when it is ready, and who does it for the least money. This subdivision and low wage have gone so far that the woman who does home finishing alone cannot possibly gain by it a living wage. The residents of Hull-House have carefully investigated many cases, and are ready to assert that the Italian widow who finishes the cheapest goods, although she sews from six in the morning until eleven at night, can only get enough to keep her children clothed and fed; while for her rent and fuel she must always depend upon charity or the hospitality of her countrymen. If the American sewing woman, supporting herself alone, lives on bread and butter and tea, she finds a Bohemian woman next door whose diet of black bread and coffee enables her to undercut. She competes with a wife who is eager to have home finishing that she may add something to the family comfort; or with a daughter who takes it that she may buy a wedding outfit.

The [2] trades-unions say to each workingman, "Associate yourself with the fellow workers in your trade. Let your trade

2 [*Ibid.*, pp. 188-92.]

organization federate with the allied trades, and they, in turn, with the National and International Federation, until working people become a solid body, ready for concerted action. It is the only possible way to prevent cuts in the rate of wages, and to regulate the hours of work. Capital is organized, and has influence with which to secure legislation in its behalf. We are scattered and feeble because we do not work together."

Trades-unionism, in spite of the many pits into which it has fallen, has the ring of altruism about it. It is clearly the duty of the settlement to keep it to its best ideal and to bring into it something of the spirit which has of late characterized the unions in England. This keeping to the ideal is not so easy as the more practical work of increasing unions, although that is difficult enough. Of the two women's unions organized at Hull-House, and of the four which have regularly held their meetings there, as well as those that come to us during strikes at various times, I should venture to say of only one of them that it is filled with the new spirit, although they all have glimpses of it, and even during times of stress and disturbance strive for it.

It was perhaps natural, from the situation, that the unions organized at Hull-House should have been those in the sewing trades. The shirtmakers were organized in the spring of 1891. The immediate cause was a cut in a large factory from twenty-five cents a dozen for the making of collars and cuffs to twelve cents. The factory was a model in regard to its sanitary arrangements, and the sole complaint of the girls was of the long hours and low rate of wages. The strike which followed the formation of the union was wholly unsuccessful; but the union formed then has thriven ever since, and has lately grown so strong that it has recently succeeded in securing the adoption of the national labels.

The cloakmakers were organized at Hull-House in the spring of 1892. Wages had been steadily falling, and there was great depression among the workers of the trade. The number of employees in the inside shops was being rapidly reduced, and the work of the entire trade handed over to the sweaters. The union among the men numbered two hundred; but the skilled workers were being rapidly supplanted by untrained women, who had no conscience in regard to the wages they accepted. The men had urged organization for several years, but were unable to secure it among the women. One apparently insurmountable obstacle had been the impossibility of securing any room, save one over a saloon, that was large enough and cheap enough for a general meeting. To a saloon hall the women had steadfastly refused to go, save once, when, under the pressure of a strike the girls in a certain shop had met with the men from the same shop, over one of the more decent saloons, only to be upbraided by their families upon their return home. They of course refused ever to go again. The first meeting at Hull-House was composed of men and girls and two or three of the residents. The meeting was a revelation to all present. The men, perhaps forty in number, were Russian-Jewish tailors, many of whom could command not even broken English. They were ill-dressed and grimy, suspicious that Hull-House was a spy in the service of the capitalists. They were skilled workers, easily superior to the girls when sewing on a cloak, but shamefaced and constrained in meeting with them. The American-Irish girls were well-dressed, and comparatively at ease. They felt chaperoned by the presence of the residents, and talked volubly among themselves. These two sets of people were held together only by the pressure upon their trade. They were separated by strong racial differences, by language, by nationality, by religion, by mode of life, by every possible social distinction. The interpreter stood between the two sides of the room, somewhat helpless. He was clear upon the economic necessity for combination; he realized the mutual interdependence; but he was baffled by the social aspect of the situation. The residents felt that between these men and girls was a deeper gulf than the much talked of "chasm" between the favored and unfavored classes. The working girls before them, who were being forced to cross such a gulf, had a positive advantage over the cultivated girl who consciously, and sometimes heroically, crosses the "chasm" to join hands with her working sisters.

There was much less difference of any sort between the residents and working girls than between the men and girls of the same trade. It was a spectacle only to be found in an American city under the latest conditions of trade life. Working people among themselves are being forced into a social democracy from the pressure of the economic situation. It presents an educating and broadening aspect of no small value.

The Woman's Cloakmakers' Union has never been large, but it always has been characterized by the spirit of generosity which marked its organization. It feels a strong sense of obligation toward the most ill-paid and ignorant of the sweaters' victims, and no working people of Chicago have done more for abolition of the sweating-system than this handful of women.

But the labor movement is by no means so simple as trades-unionism. A settlement finds in the movement devoted men, who feel keenly the need for better industrial organization, but who insist that industrial organization must be part of the general reorganization of society. The individualists, for instance, insist that we will never secure equal distribution until we have equality of opportunity; that all state and city franchises, all privilege of railroad, bank, and corporation, must be removed before competition will be absolutely free, and the man with his labor alone to offer will have a fair chance with the man who offers anything else; that the sole function of the state is to secure the freedom of each, guarded by the like freedom of all, and that each man free to work for his own existence and advantage will by this formula work out our industrial development. The individualist, then, works constantly for the recall of franchise and of special privilege, and for the untrammelled play of each man's force. There is much in our inheritance that responds to this, and he has followers among workingmen and among capitalists; those who fear to weaken the incentive to individual exertion, and those who believe that any interference would work injuriously. The residents of a settlement hear the individualist pleading in many trades assemblies. Opposite to him, springing up in discussion every time he speaks, is the socialist in all varieties. The scientific socialist reads his Karl Marx, and sees a gradual and inevitable absorption of all the means of production and of all capital by one entity, called the community. He makes out a strong case because he is usually a German or a Russian, with a turn for economic discussion, and widely read. He sees in the present tendency towards the concentration of capital, and in the growth of trusts and monopolies, an inevitable transition to the socialistic state. Every concentration of capital into fewer hands but increases the mass of those whose interests are opposed to the maintenance of its power, and vastly simplifies the final absorption. He contends that we have already had the transformation of scattered private property into capitalistic property, and that it is inevitable that it should be turned into collective property. In the former cases we had the expropriation of the mass of the people by a few usurpers; in the latter we have the expropriation of a few usurpers by the mass of people. He points with pride to the strong tendency toward state regulation of the means of transportation, and of many industries, and he urges legislative check and control at every point.

Between these two divergent points of view we find many shades of opinion and many modifications of philosophy; but perhaps a presentation of these two, as heard many times from earnest workingmen, will illustrate how difficult a settlement finds it to be liberal in tone, and to decide what immediate measures are in the line of advantage to the labor movement and which ones are against it.

A [3] century ago there was an irresistible impulse, an upward movement, among the mass of people to have their

[3] [*Ibid.*, pp. 196-201.]

share in political life—hitherto the life of the privileged. The universal franchise was demanded, not only as a holy right, but as a means of entrance into the sunshine of liberty and equality. There is a similar demand at the close of this century on the part of working people, but this time it is for a share in the results of industry.

It is an impulse to come out into the sunshine of prosperity. As the leaders of political democracy overestimated the possession of the franchise, and believed it would obtain blessings for the working people which it has not done, so, doubtless, the leaders of the labor movement are overestimating the possession of wealth and leisure. Mazzini was the inspired prophet of the political democracy, preaching duties and responsibilities rather than rights and franchises; and we might call Arnold Toynbee the prophet of the second development when we contend that the task of the labor movement is the interpretation of democracy into industrial affairs. In that remarkable exposition called "Industry and Democracy," Toynbee sets forth the struggle between the masters and men during the industrial revolution. Two ideals in regard to the relationship between employer and employee were then developed. Carlyle represented one, pleading passionately for it. He declared that the rich millowner's duty did not end with the "cash nexus"; that after he had paid his men he should still cherish them in sickness, protect them in misfortune, and not dismiss them when trade was bad. In one word, he would have the rich govern and protect the poor. But the workers themselves, the mass of the people, had caught another ideal; they dreamed of a time when they should have no need of protection, but when each workman should stand by the side of his employer—the free citizen of a free state. Each workingman demanded, not class protection, but political rights. He wished to be a unit; not that he might be isolated, but that he might unite in a fuller union, first with his fellow workers, and then with the entire people. Toynbee asks who was right, Carlyle or the people. And replies that the people were right—"The people who, sick with hunger and deformed with toil, dreamed that democracy would bring deliverance." And democracy did save industry. It transformed disputes about wages from social feuds into business bargains. It swept away the estranging class elements of suspicion and arrogance. "It gradually did away with the feudal notion among the masters that they would deal with their men one at a time, denying to them the advantages of association." It is singular that in America, where government is founded upon the principle of representation, the capitalist should have been so slow to accord this right to workingmen; that he should refuse so steadily to treat with a "walking delegate," and so long maintain that no "outsider" could represent the men in his shop.

We must learn to trust our democracy, giant-like and threatening as it may appear in its uncouth strength and untried applications. When the English people were demanding the charter, the English nobility predicted that the franchise would be used to inaugurate all sorts of wild measures, to overturn long-established customs, as the capitalist now sometimes assumes that higher wages will be spent only in the saloons. In both cases there is a failure to count the sobering effect of responsibilities in the education and development which attend the entrance into a wider life.

The effort to keep the movement to some consciousness of its historic value in the race development is perhaps no more difficult than to keep before its view the larger ethical aims. There is doubtless a tendency among the workingmen who reach leadership in the movement to yield to individual ambition, as there is among capitalists to regard class interests, and yield only that which must be yielded. This tendency on one side to yield to ambition, and on the other to give in to threats, may be further illustrated.

The poor man has proverbially been the tyrant of poor men when he has become rich. But while such a man was yet poor, his heart was closed to his fellows, and his eyes were blinded to the exploitation of them and himself, because in his heart he hoped one day to be rich, and to do the exploiting; because he secretly approved the action of his master, and said, "I would do the same if I were he."

Workingmen say, sometimes, that the rich will not hear the complaint of the poor until it rises into a threat and carries a suggestion of ruin with it; that they then throw the laborers a portion of the product, to save the remainder.

As the tendency to warfare shows the primitive state of the labor movement, so also this division on class lines reveals its present undeveloped condition. The organization of society into huge battalions with syndicates and corporations on the side of capital, and trades-unions and federations on the side of labor, is to divide the world into two hostile camps, and to turn us back into class warfare and class limitations. All our experience tells us that no question of civilization is so simple as that, nor can we any longer settle our perplexities by mere good fighting. One is reminded of one's childish conception of life—that Right and Wrong were drawn up in battle array into two distinct armies, and that to join the army of Right and fight bravely would be to settle all problems.

But life itself teaches us nothing more inevitable than that right and wrong are most confusedly mixed; that the blackest wrong is by our side and within our own motives; that right does not dazzle our eyes with its radiant shining, but has to be found by exerting patience, discrimination, and impartiality. We cease to listen for the bugle note of victory our childish imagination anticipated, and learn that our finest victories are attained in the midst of self-distrust, and that the waving banner of triumph is sooner or later trailed to the dust by the weight of self-righteousness. It may be that as the labor movement grows older and riper, it will cease to divide all men so sharply into capitalists and proletarians, into exploiter and exploited.

We may live to remind its leaders in later years, as George Eliot has so skillfully reminded us, that the path we all like when we first set out in our youth is the path of martyrdom and endurance, where the palm branches grow; but that later we learn to take the steep highway of tolerance, just allowance, and self-blame, where there are no leafy honors to be gathered and worn. As the labor movement grows older, its leaders may catch the larger ethical view which genuine experience always gives; they may have a chance to act, free from the pressure of threat or ambition. They should have nothing to gain or lose, save as they rise or fall with their fellows. In raising the mass, men could have a motive power as much greater than the motive for individual success, as the force which sends the sun above the horizon is greater than the force engendered by the powder behind the rocket.

Is it too much to hope that as the better organized and older trades-unions are fast recognizing a solidarity of labor, and acting upon the literal notion of brotherhood, that they will later perceive the larger solidarity which includes labor and capital, and act upon the notion of universal kinship? That before this larger vision of life there can be no perception of "sides" and no "battle array"? In the light of the developed social conscience the "sympathetic strike" may be criticized, not because it is too broad, but because it is too narrow, and because the strike is but a wasteful and negative demonstration of ethical fellowship. In the summer of 1894 the Chicago unions of Russian-Jewish cloakmakers, German compositors, and Bohemian and Polish butchers, struck in sympathy with the cause of the American Railway Union, whom they believed to be standing for a principle. Does an event such as this, clumsy and unsatisfactory as its results are, prefigure the time when no factory child in Chicago can be overworked and underpaid without a protest from all good citizens, capitalist and proletarian? Such a protest would be founded upon an ethical sense so strong that it would easily override business interests and class prejudices.

XXIII

THE PLIGHT OF THE INDIAN[1]

HELEN HUNT JACKSON

There are within the limits of the United States between two hundred and fifty and three hundred thousand Indians, exclusive of those in Alaska. The names of the different tribes and bands, as entered in the statistical tables of the Indian Office Reports, number nearly three hundred. One of the most careful estimates which have been made of their numbers and localities gives them as follows: "In Minnesota and States east of the Mississippi, about 32,500; in Nebraska, Kansas, and the Indian Territory, 70,650; in the Territories of Dakota, Montana, Wyoming, and Idaho, 65,000; in Nevada and the Territories of Colorado, New Mexico, Utah, and Arizona, 84,000; and on the Pacific slope, 48,000."

Of these, one hundred and thirty thousand are self-supporting on their own reservations, "receiving nothing from the Government except interest on their own moneys, or annuities granted them in consideration of the cession of their lands to the United States."[2]

This fact alone would seem sufficient to dispose forever of the accusation, so persistently brought against the Indian, that he will not work.

Of the remainder, eighty-four thousand are partially supported by the government—the interest money due them and their annuities, as provided by treaty, being inadequate to their subsistence on the reservations where they are confined.

1 [Helen Hunt Jackson. *A Century of Dishonor. A Sketch of the United States Government's Dealings with Some of the Indian Tribes . . .* (Boston, 1895 ed.), pp. 336-42. Chapter title supplied by editor.]

2 Annual Report of Indian Commissioner for 1872.

In many cases, however, these Indians furnish a large part of their support—the White River Utes, for instance, who are reported by the Indian Bureau as getting sixty-six per cent of their living by "root-digging, hunting, and fishing"; the Squaxin band, in Washington Territory, as earning seventy-five per cent, and the Chippewas of Lake Superior as earning fifty per cent in the same way. These facts also would seem to dispose of the accusation that the Indian will not work.

There are about fifty-five thousand who never visit an agency, over whom the government does not pretend to have either control or care. These fifty-five thousand "subsist by hunting, fishing, on roots, nuts, berries, etc., and by begging and stealing"; and this also seems to dispose of the accusation that the Indian will not "work for a living." There remains a small portion, about thirty-one thousand, that are entirely subsisted by the government.

There is not among these three hundred bands of Indians one which has not suffered cruelly at the hands either of the government or of white settlers. The poorer, the more insignificant, the more helpless the band, the more certain the cruelty and outrage to which they have been subjected. This is especially true of the bands on the Pacific slope. These Indians found themselves of a sudden surrounded by and caught up in the great influx of gold-seeking settlers, as helpless creatures on a shore are caught up in a tidal wave. There was not time for the government to make treaties; not even time for communities to make laws. The tale of the wrongs, the oppressions, the murders of the Pacific-slope Indians in the last thirty years would be a volume by itself, and is too monstrous to be believed.

It makes little difference, however, where one opens the record of the history of the Indians; every page and every year has its dark stain. The story of one tribe is the story of all, varied only by differences of time and place; but neither time nor place makes any difference in the main facts. Colorado is as greedy and unjust in 1880 as was Georgia in 1830, and Ohio in 1795; and the United States government breaks promises now as deftly as then, and with an added ingenuity from long practice.

One of its strongest supports in so doing is the widespread sentiment among the people of dislike to the Indian, of impatience with his presence as a "barrier to civilization," and distrust of it as a possible danger. The old tales of the frontier life, with its horrors of Indian warfare, have gradually, by two or three generations' telling, produced in the average mind something like a hereditary instinct of unquestioning and unreasoning aversion which it is almost impossible to dislodge or soften.

There are hundreds of pages of unimpeachable testimony on the side of the Indian; but it goes for nothing, is set down as sentimentalism or partisanship, tossed aside and forgotten.

President after president has appointed commission after commission to inquire into and report upon Indian affairs, and to make suggestions as to the best methods of managing them. The reports are filled with eloquent statements of wrongs done to the Indians, of perfidies on the part of the government; they counsel, as earnestly as words can, a trial of the simple and unperplexing expedients of telling truth, keeping promises, making fair bargains, dealing justly in all ways and all things. These reports are bound up with the government's Annual Reports, and that is the end of them. It would probably be no exaggeration to say that not one American citizen out of ten thousand ever sees them or knows that they exist, and yet any one of them, circulated throughout the country, read by the right-thinking, right-feeling men and women of this land, would be of itself a "campaign document" that would initiate a revolution which would not subside until the Indians' wrongs were, so far as is now left possible, righted.

In 1869 President Grant appointed a commission of nine men, representing the influence and philanthropy of six leading states, to visit the different Indian reservations, and to "examine all matters appertaining to Indian affairs."

In the report of this commission are such paragraphs as the following:

To assert that "the Indian will not work" is as true as it would be to say that the white man will not work.

Why should the Indian be expected to plant corn, fence lands, build houses, or do anything but get food from day to day, when experience has taught him that the product of his labor will be seized by the white man tomorrow? The most industrious white man would become a drone under similar circumstances. Nevertheless, many of the Indians [the commissioners might more forcibly have said 130,000 of the Indians] are already at work, and furnish ample refutation of the assertion that "the Indian will not work." There is no escape from the inexorable logic of facts.

The history of the Government connections with the Indians is a shameful record of broken treaties and unfulfilled promises. The history of the border white man's connection with the Indians is a sickening record of murder, outrage, robbery, and wrongs committed by the former, as the rule, and occasional savage outbreaks and unspeakably barbarous deeds of retaliation by the latter, as the exception.

Taught by the Government that they had rights entitled to respect, when those rights have been assailed by the rapacity of the white man, the arm which should have been raised to protect them has ever been ready to sustain the aggressor.

The testimony of some of the highest military officers of the United States is on record to the effect that, in our Indian wars, almost without exception, the first aggressions have been made by the white man; and the assertion is supported by every civilian of reputation who has studied the subject. In addition to the class of robbers and outlaws who find impunity in their nefarious pursuits on the frontiers, there is a large class of professedly reputable men who use every means in their power to bring on Indian wars for the sake of the profit to be realized from the presence of troops and the expenditure of Government funds in their midst. They proclaim death to the Indians at all times in words and publications, making no distinction between the innocent and the guilty. They irate [!] the lowest class of men to the perpetration of the darkest deeds against their victims, and as judges and jurymen shield them from the justice due to their crimes. Every crime committed by a white man against an Indian is concealed

> or palliated. Every offense committed by an Indian against a white man is borne on the wings of the post or the telegraph to the remotest corner of the land, clothed with all the horrors which the reality or imagination can throw around it. Against such influences as these the people of the United States need to be warned.

To assume that it would be easy, or by any one sudden stroke of legislative policy possible, to undo the mischief and hurt of the long past, set the Indian policy of the country right for the future, and make the Indians at once safe and happy, is the blunder of a hasty and uninformed judgment. The notion which seems to be growing more prevalent, that simply to make all Indians at once citizens of the United States would be a sovereign and instantaneous panacea for all their ills and all the government's perplexities, is a very inconsiderate one. To administer complete citizenship of a sudden, all round, to all Indians, barbarous and civilized alike, would be as grotesque a blunder as to dose them all round with any one medicine, irrespective of the symptoms and needs of their diseases. It would kill more than it would cure. Nevertheless, it is true, as was well stated by one of the superintendents of Indian Affairs in 1857, that, "so long as they are not citizens of the United States, their rights of property must remain insecure against invasion. The doors of the federal tribunals being barred against them while wards and dependents, they can only partially exercise the rights of free government, or give to those who make, execute, and construe the few laws they are allowed to enact, dignity sufficient to make them respectable. While they continue individually to gather the crumbs that fall from the table of the United States, idleness, improvidence, and indebtedness will be the rule, and industry, thrift, and freedom from debt the exception. The utter absence of individual title to particular lands deprives every one among them of the chief incentive to labor and exertion—the very mainspring on which the prosperity of a people depends."

All judicious plans and measures for their safety and salvation must embody provisions for their becoming citizens as fast as they are fit, and must protect them till then in every right and particular in which our laws protect other "persons" who are not citizens.

There is a disposition in a certain class of minds to be impatient with any protestation against wrong which is unaccompanied or unprepared with a quick and exact scheme of remedy. This is illogical. When pioneers in a new country find a tract of poisonous and swampy wilderness to be reclaimed, they do not withhold their hands from fire and axe till they see clearly which way roads should run, where good water will spring, and what crops will best grow on the redeemed land. They first clear the swamp. So with this poisonous and baffling part of the domain of our national affairs—let us first "clear the swamp."

However great perplexity and difficulty there may be in the details of any and every plan possible for doing at this late day anything like justice to the Indian, however hard it may be for good statesmen and good men to agree upon the things that ought to be done, there certainly is, or ought to be, no perplexity whatever, no difficulty whatever, in agreeing upon certain things that ought not to be done, and which must cease to be done before the first steps can be taken toward righting the wrongs, curing the ills, and wiping out the disgrace to us of the present condition of our Indians.

Cheating, robbing, breaking promises—these three are clearly things which must cease to be done. One more thing, also, and that is the refusal of the protection of the law to the Indian's rights of property, "of life, liberty, and the pursuit of happiness."

When these four things have ceased to be done, time, statesmanship, philanthropy, and Christianity can slowly and surely do the rest. Till these four things have ceased to be done, statesmanship and philanthropy alike must work in vain, and even Christianity can reap but small harvest.

XXIV

THE ATLANTA EXPOSITION ADDRESS[1]

BOOKER T. WASHINGTON

Mr. President and Gentleman of the Board of Directors and Citizens:

One third of the population of the South is of the Negro race. No enterprise seeking the material, civil, or moral welfare of this section can disregard this element of our population and reach the highest success. I but convey to you, Mr. President and Directors, the sentiment of the masses of my race when I say that in no way have the value and manhood of the American Negro been more fittingly and generously recognized than by the managers of this magnificent Exposition at every stage of its progress. It is a recognition that will do more to cement the friendship of the two races than any occurrence since the dawn of our freedom.

Not only this, but the opportunity here afforded will awaken among us a new era of industrial progress. Ignorant and inexperienced, it is not strange that in the first years of our new life we began at the top instead of at the bottom; that a seat in congress or the state legislature was more sought than real estate or industrial skill; that the political convention of stump speaking had more attractions than starting a dairy farm or truck garden.

A ship lost at sea for many days suddenly sighted a friendly vessel. From the mast of the unfortunate vessel was seen a signal, "Water, water; we die of thirst!" The answer from the friendly vessel at once came back, "Cast down your bucket

1 [Booker T. Washington, *Up from Slavery: An Autobiography* (New York, 1926 ed.), pp. 218-25.]

where you are." A second time the signal, "Water, water; send us water!" ran up from the distressed vessel, and was answered, "Cast down your bucket where you are." And, a third and fourth signal for water was answered, "Cast down your bucket where you are." The captain of the distressed vessel, at last heeding the injunction, cast down his bucket, and it came up full of fresh, sparkling water from the mouth of the Amazon River. To those of my race who depend on bettering their condition in a foreign land or who underestimate the importance of cultivating friendly relations with the Southern white man, who is their next door neighbor, I would say: "Cast down your bucket where you are"—cast it down in making friends in every manly way of the people of all races by whom we are surrounded.

Cast it down in agriculture, mechanics, in commerce, in domestic service, and in the professions. And in this connection it is well to bear in mind that whatever other sins the South may be called to bear, when it comes to business, pure and simple, it is in the South that the Negro is given a man's chance in the commercial world, and in nothing is this Exposition more eloquent than in emphasizing this chance. Our greatest danger is that in the great leap from slavery to freedom we may overlook the fact that the masses of us are to live by the productions of our hands, and fail to keep in mind that we shall prosper in proportion as we learn to dignify and glorify common labor and put brains and skill into the common occupations of life; shall prosper in proportion as we learn to draw the line between the superficial and the substantial, the ornamental gewgaws of life and the useful. No race can prosper till it learns that there is as much dignity in tilling a field as in writing a poem. It is at the bottom of life we must begin, and not at the top. Nor should we permit our grievances to overshadow our opportunities.

To those of the white race who look to the incoming of those of foreign birth and strange tongue and habits for the prosperity of the South, were I permitted I would repeat what I say to my own race, "Cast down your bucket where you are." Cast it down among the eight millions of Negroes whose habits you know, whose fidelity and love you have tested in days when to have proved treacherous meant the ruin of your firesides. Cast down your bucket among these people who have, without strikes and labor wars, tilled your fields, cleared your forests, builded your railroads and cities, and brought forth treasures from the bowels of the earth, and helped make possible this magnificent representation of the progress of the South. Casting down your bucket among my people, helping and encouraging them as you are doing on these grounds, and to education of head, hand, and heart, you will find that they will buy your surplus land, make blossom the waste places in your fields, and run your factories. While doing this, you can be sure in the future, as in the past, that you and your families will be surrounded by the most patient, faithful, law-abiding, and unresentful people that the world has seen. As we have proved our loyalty to you in the past, in nursing your children, watching by the sickbed of your mothers and fathers, and often following them with tear-dimmed eyes to their graves, so in the future, in our humble way, we shall stand by you with a devotion that no foreigner can approach, ready to lay down our lives, if need be, in defense of yours, interlacing our industrial, commercial, civil, and religious life with yours in a way that shall make the interests of both races one. In all things that are purely social we can be as separate as the fingers, yet one as the hand in all things essential to mutual progress.

There is no defense or security for any of us except in the highest intelligence and development of all. If anywhere there are efforts tending to curtail the fullest growth of the Negro, let these efforts be turned into stimulating, encouraging, and making him the most useful and intelligent citizen. Effort or means so invested will pay a thousand per cent interest. These efforts will be twice blessed—"blessing him that gives and him that takes."

There is no escape through law of man or God from the inevitable:

The laws of changeless justice bind
Oppressor with oppressed;
And close as sin and suffering joined
We march to fate abreast.

Nearly sixteen millions of hands will aid you in pulling the load upward, or they will pull against you the load downward. We shall constitute one-third and more of the ignorance and crime of the South, or one-third its intelligence and progress; we shall contribute one-third to the business and industrial prosperity of the South, or we shall prove a veritable body of death, stagnating, depressing, retarding every effort to advance the body politic.

Gentlemen of the Exposition, as we present to you our humble effort at an exhibition of our progress, you must not expect overmuch. Starting thirty years ago with ownership here and there in a few quilts and pumpkins and chickens (gathered from miscellaneous sources), remember the path that has led from these to the inventions and production of agricultural implements, buggies, steam engines, newspapers, books, statuary, carving, paintings, the management of drugstores and banks, has not been trodden without contact with thorns and thistles. While we take pride in what we exhibit as a result of our independent efforts, we do not for a moment forget that our part in this exhibition would fall far short of your expectations but for the constant help that has come to our educational life, not only from the Southern states, but especially from Northern philanthropists, who have made their gifts a constant stream of blessing and encouragement.

The wisest among my race understand that the agitation of questions of social equality is the extremest folly, and that progress in the enjoyment of all the privileges that will come to us must be the result of severe and constant struggle rather than of artificial forcing. No race that has anything to contribute to the markets of the world is long in any degree ostracized. It is important and right that all privileges of the law be ours, but it is vastly more important that we be prepared for the exercises of these privileges. The opportunity to earn a dollar in a factory just now is worth infinitely more than the opportunity to spend a dollar in an opera house.

In conclusion, may I repeat that nothing in thirty years has given us more hope and encouragement, and drawn us so near to you of the white race, as this opportunity offered by the Exposition; and here bending, as it were, over the altar that represents the results of the struggles of your race and mine, both starting practically empty-handed three decades ago, I pledge that in your effort to work out the great and intricate problem which God has laid at the doors of the South, you shall have at all times the patient, sympathetic help of my race; only let this be constantly in mind, that, while from representations in these buildings of the product of field, of forest, of mine, of factory, letters, and art, much good will come, yet far above and beyond material benefits will be that higher good, that, let us pray God, will come, in a blotting out of sectional differences and racial animosities and suspicions, in a determination to administer absolute justice, in a willing obedience among all classes to the mandates of law. This, this, coupled with our material prosperity, will bring into our beloved South a new heaven and a new earth.

XXV

JUSTICE FOR THE NEGRO[1]

GEORGE W. CABLE

The case is before the reader. The points of fact made in our earlier paper—the privations suffered by the colored people in their matters of civil rights—have been met with feeble half-denials equivalent to admissions by opponents in controversy too engrossed with counter statements and arguments that crumble at the touch, to attend to a statement of facts. In the end they stand thus: As to churches, there is probably not a dozen in the land, if one, "colored" or "white," where a white person is not at least professedly welcome to its best accommodations; while the colored man, though he be seven-eighths white, is shut up, on the ground that "his race" prefers it, to the poor and often unprofitable appointments of the "African" church, whether he like it best or not, unless he is ready to accept without a murmur distinctions that mark him, in the sight of the whole people, as one of a despised caste and that follow him through the very sacraments. As to schooling, despite the fact that he is today showing his eager willingness to accept separate schools for his children wherever the white man demands the separation, yet both his children and the white man's are being consigned to illiteracy wherever they are too few and poor to form separate schools. In some mountainous parts of Kentucky there is but one colored school district in a *county*. In railway travel the colored people's rights are tossed from pillar to post with an ever-varying and therefore more utterly indefensible and intolerable capricious-

1 [George W. Cable, *The Silent South, Together with the Freedman's Case in Equity and the Convict Lease System* (New York, 1885), pp. 82-94. Chapter title supplied by editor.]

ness. In Virginia they may ride exactly as white people do and in the same cars. In a neighboring State, a white man may ride in the "ladies' car," while a colored man of exactly the same dress and manners—nay, his wife or daughter—must ride in the notorious "Jim Crow car," unprotected from smokers and dram drinkers and lovers of vile language. "In South Carolina," says the Charleston *News and Courier,* on the other hand, "respectable colored persons who buy first-class tickets on any railroad ride in the first-class cars as a right, and their presence excites no comment on the part of their white fellow passengers. It is a great deal pleasanter to travel with respectable and well-behaved colored people than with unmannerly and ruffianly white men." In Alabama the majority of the people have not made this discovery, at least if we are to believe their newspapers. In Tennessee the law *requires* the separation of all first-class passengers by race with equal accommodations for both; thus waiving the old plea of decency's exigencies and forcing upon American citizens adjudged to be first-class passengers an alienism that has thrown away its last shadow of an excuse. But this is only the law, and the history of the very case alluded to by our traditionist friends, in which a colored woman gained damages for being compelled to accept inferior accommodation or none for a first-class ticket, is the history of an outrage so glaring that only a person blinded to the simplest rights of human beings could cite it in such a defense.

A certain daily railway train was supplied, according to the law, with a smoking car, and two first-class cars, one for colored and one for whites. The two first-class cars were so nearly of a kind that they were exchangeable. They generally kept their relative positions on the track; but the "ladies' car" of the morning trip became the "colored car" of the return, afternoon, trip, and vice versa. But the rules of the colored car were little regarded. Men, white and black, were sometimes forbidden, sometimes allowed, to smoke and drink there. Says the court, "The evidence is abundant to show that the rule excluding smoking from that car was but a nominal one, that it was often disregarded, that white passengers understood it to be a nominal rule, and that adequate means were not adopted to secure the same first-class and orderly passage to the colored passengers occupying that car as was accorded to the passengers in the rear car. Nor was the separation of the classes of the passengers complete. There is no evidence tending to show that the white passengers were excluded from the car assigned to colored passengers, and it appears that whenever the train was unusually crowded it was expected that the excess of white passengers would ride, as they then did ride, in the forward one of the two first-class cars. So, too, it appeared that persons of color, of whom the plaintiff was one, had several times occupied seats in the rear car." A certain "person of ladylike appearance and deportment," one day in September, 1883, got aboard this train with a first-class ticket. She knew the train, and that, as the court states it, "in the rear car . . . quiet and good order were to so great an extent the rule that it was rarely if ever that any passenger gave annoyance by his conduct to his fellow passengers." In the colored car there was at least one colored man smoking, and one white man whom she saw to be drunk. She entered the rear car and sat down, no one objecting. She was the only colored person there. The conductor, collecting his tickets, came to her. He was not disconcerted. Not long previously he had forbidden another colored person to ride in that car, who must also have been "of ladylike appearance and deportment," for when he saw this one he "supposed her to be the same person . . . intentionally violating the defendant's (Railroad's) rules and *seeking to annoy his other passengers.*" Twice they exchanged polite request and refusal to leave the car; and then, in full presence of all those "other passengers" whom this person of ladylike appearance and deportment was erroneously suspected of seeking to annoy, there occurred a thing that ought to make the nation blush. The conductor laid hands upon this defenseless woman, whose infraction of a rule was interfering neither with the running of the road, the collection of fares, nor the comfort of passengers, and "by force removed her from her seat and carried her out of the car. When near the door of the car the plaintiff promised that she would then, if permitted, leave the car rather than be forcibly ejected; but the conductor, as he says, told her that her consent came too late, and continued to remove her forcibly. On reaching the platform of the car, plaintiff left the train." Judgment was given for the plaintiff. But the point was carefully made that she would have been without any grievance if the "colored car" had only been kept in first-class. In other words, for not providing separate first-class accommodations, five hundred dollars damages; for laying violent hands upon a peaceable, ladylike, and unprotected woman, nothing; and nothing for requiring such a one publicly to sit apart from passengers of the same grade under a purely ignominious distinction. What! not ignominious? Fancy the passenger a white lady, choosing, for reasons of her own, to sit in a first class "colored car"; infringing, if you please, some rule; but paying her way, and causing no one any inconvenience, unsafety, or delay. Imagine her, on insisting upon her wish to stay, drawn from her seat by force, and lifted and carried out by a black conductor, telling her as he goes that her offer to walk out comes too late. If this is not ignominy, what is it? To the commission and palliation of such unmanly deeds are we driven by our attempts to hold under our own arbitrary dictation others' rights that we have no moral right to touch, rights that in ourselves we count more sacred than property and dearer than life.

But we must not tarry. If we turn to the matter of roadside refreshment what do we see? Scarcely a dozen railroad refreshment rooms from the Rio Grande to the Potomac—is there one?—where the weary and hungry colored passenger, be he ever so perfect in dress and behavior, can snatch a hasty meal in the presence of white guests of any class whatever, though in any or every one of them he or she can get the same food, and eat with the same knife, fork, and plate that are furnished to white strangers, if only he or she will take a menial's attitude and accept them in the kitchen. Tennessee has formally "abrogated the rule of the common law" in order to make final end of "any right in favor of any such person so refused admission" to the enjoyment of an obvious civil right which no public host need ever permit any guest to mistake for a social liberty. As to places of public amusement, the gentlemen who say that "each [race] gets the same accommodations for the same money," simply—forget. The statement comes from Atlanta. But, in fact, in Atlanta, in Georgia, in the whole South, there is scarcely a place of public amusement—except the cheap museums, where there are no seated audiences—in which a colored man or woman, however unobjectionable personally, can buy, at any price, any but a second—sometimes any but a third- or fourth-class accommodation. During a day's stay in Atlanta lately, the present writer saw many things greatly to admire; many inspiring signs of thrift, stability, virtue, and culture. Indeed, where can he say that he has not seen them, in ten Southern States lately visited? And it is in contemplation of these evidences of greatness, prosperity, safety, and the desire to be just, that he feels constrained to ask whether it must be that in the principal depot of such a city the hopeless excommunication of every person of African tincture from the civil rewards of gentility must be advertised by three signs at the entrances of three separate rooms, one for "Ladies," one for "Gentlemen," and the third a "Colored waiting room"? Visiting the principal library of the city, he was eagerly assured, in response to inquiry, that no person of color would be allowed to draw out books; and when a colored female, not particularly tidy in dress, came forward to return a book and draw another, it was quickly explained that she was merely a servant and messenger for some white person. Are these things necessary to—are they consistent with—an exalted civilization founded on equal rights and the elevation of the masses?

And the freedman's rights in the courts. It is regarding this part of our subject that our friends on the other side make a mistake too common everywhere and very common among us of the South. That is, they assume the state of affairs in more distant localities to be the same as that immediately around them. A statement concerning certain matters in Florida or Maryland is indignantly denied in Tennessee or Texas because it is not true of those regions; and so throughout. It is in this spirit that one of these gentlemen explains that in Georgia Negroes are not excluded from the jury lists except for actual incompetency, and thereupon "*assumes* that Georgia does not materially differ from the other States." But really, in Tennessee they may not sit in the jury box at all, except that in a few counties they may sit in judgment on the case of a colored person. While in Texas, at the very time of the gentleman's writing, the suggestion of one of her distinguished citizens to accord the right of jury duty to the colored people was being flouted by the press as an "innovation upon established usage," and a "sentimental and utterly impracticable idea." This in the face of a State constitution and laws that give no warrant for the race distinction. So much for assumption.

The same mistake is repeated by the same writer in discussing the question of the freedmen's criminal sentences. No fact or person is brought forward to prove or disprove anything except for Georgia. And even the prosecuting attorney for the Atlanta circuit, brought in to testify, says, for the State's cities and towns, that the Negro gets there "equal and exact justice before the courts"; but he is not willing to deny "a lingering prejudice and occasional injustice" in remote counties. Why, with nearly 6,000,000 freed people getting "full and exact justice in the courts whether the jury is white or black," why could there not be found *among them* two or three trustworthy witnesses to testify to this fact? Their testimony would have been important, for these lines are written within hand's reach of many letters from colored men denying that such is the case.

The present writer does not charge, and never did, that our Southern white people consciously and maliciously rendered oppressive verdicts against the freedman. On the contrary, it is plainly stated by him that they acted "not so maliciously as unreflecting," and "ignorant of the awful condition of the penitentiaries." His only printed utterance on the subject is on record in "The Freedman's Case in Equity," and is too long to quote; but he cited the *official reports* of our Southern State prisons themselves, and asked how with their facts before us we are to escape the conviction that the popular mind had been seduced—as every student of American prison statistics knows it has—by the glittering temptations of our Southern convict lease system; and not one word of reply have we had, except the assertion, which nobody would think of denying, that the black man, often in Georgia, and sometimes elsewhere, gets an evenhanded and noble justice from white juries.

Have our opponents observed the workings of this convict lease system? To put such a system as a rod of punishment into the hands of a powerful race sitting in judgment upon the misdemeanors of a feebler and despised caste would warp the verdicts of the most righteous people under the sun. Examine our Southern penitentiary reports. What shall we say to such sentences inflicted for larceny alone, as twelve, fourteen, fifteen, twenty, and in one case forty years of a penal service whose brutal tasks and whippings kill in an average of five years? Larceny is the peculiar crime of the poorest classes everywhere. In all penitentiaries out of the South the convicts for this offense always exceed and generally double the number of convicts for burglary. Larceny has long been called the favorite crime of the Negro criminal. What, then, shall we say to the facts, deduced from official records, that in the Georgia penitentiary and convict camps there were in 1882 twice as many colored convicts for burglary as for larceny, and that they were, moreover, serving sentences averaging nearly twice the average of the white convicts in the same places for the same crime? This, too, notwithstanding a very large number of short sentences to colored men, and a difference between their longest and shortest terms twice as great as in the case of the whites. For larceny the difference is five times as great.[2] Shall we from these facts draw hasty conclusions? We draw none. If anyone can explain them away, in the name of humanity let us rejoice to see him do so. We are far from charging anyone with deliberately prostituting justice. We are far from overlooking "the depravity of the Negro." But those who rest on this cheap explanation are bound to tell us which shows the greater maliciousness: for one man to be guilty of hog-stealing or for twelve jurors to send him to the coal mines for twenty years for doing it? In Georgia, outside her prisons there are eight whites to every seven blacks. Inside, there are eight whites to every eighty blacks. The depravity of the Negro may explain away much, but we cannot know how much while there also remain in force the seductions of our atrocious convict lease system, and our attitude of domination over the blacks, so subtly dangerous to our own integrity. Here is a rough, easy test that may go for what it is worth: These crimes of larceny and burglary are just the sort—since they are neither the most trivial nor the most horrible—to incur excessive verdicts and sentences, if the prejudices of one class against another come into the account. Now, what is the fact in the prisons we have mentioned? Of all the inmates under sentence for these crimes nineteen-twentieths are classed as of that race which we "dominate" both out of and in the jury box. We ask no opinion on these points from the stupid or vicious of either whites or blacks; but is it wise for us not to consider what may be their effect upon the minds of the property-holding, intelligent, and virtuous portion of the "dominated" race? Is it right?

[2] Without counting the exceptional forty years' sentence mentioned.

THE CONVICT LEASE SYSTEM [3]

Its features vary in different regions. In some, the State retains the penitentiary in charge of its officers, and leases out the convicts in gangs of scores or hundreds to persons who use them anywhere within the State boundaries in the execution of private enterprises or public or semi-public works. In a few cases the penitentiary itself, its appliances and its inmates, all and entire, are leased, sometimes annually or biennially, sometimes for five and sometimes for ten or even twenty years, and the convicts worked within or without the prison walls, and near to or distant from them, as various circumstances may regulate, being transferred from place to place in companies under military or semi-military guard, and quartered in camps or herded in stockades convenient to their fields of labor. In two or three States the government's abandonment of its trust is still more nearly complete, the terms of the lease going so far as to assign to the lessees the entire custody and discipline of the convicts, and even their medical and surgical care. But a clause common to all these prison leases is that which allows a portion, at least, and sometimes all of the prisoners to be worked in parts of the State remote from the prison. The fitness of some lessees to hold such a trust may be estimated from the spirit of the following letters:

Office of Lessee Arkansas State Penitentiary,
Little Rock, Arkansas, January 12, 1882.

Dear Sir: Your postal of request to hand; sorry to say cannot send you report, as there are none given. The business of the Arkansas State Penitentiary is of a private nature, and no report is made to the public. Any private information relative to the men will be furnished upon application for same.

Very respectfully,
ZEB WARD, Lessee
Z. J.

[3] [*Ibid.*, pp. 122-26.]

Office of Lessee Arkansas State Penitentiary,
Little Rock, Arkansas, July 2, 1882.

Dear Sir: Yours of —— date to hand and fully noted. Your inquiries, if answered, would require much time and labor. I am sole lessee, and work all the convicts, and of course the business of the prison is my private business. My book-keeper is kept quite busy with my business, and no time to make out all the queries you ask for. Similar information is given to the Legislature once in two years.

Respectfully,
ZEB. WARD.

The wonder is that such a scheme should not, upon its face, be instantly rejected by any but the most sordid and shortsighted minds. It is difficult to call its propositions less than an insult to the intelligence and humanity of any enlightened community. It was a Governor of Kentucky who, in 1873, justly said to his State Legislature: "I cannot but regard the present system under which the State penitentiary is leased and managed as a reproach to the commonwealth. . . . It is the system, not the officer acting under it, with which I find fault." [4]

This system springs primarily from the idea that the possession of a convict's person is an opportunity for the State to make money; that the amount to be made is whatever can be wrung from him; that for the officers of the State to waive this opportunity is to impose upon the clemency of a taxpaying public; and that, without regard to moral or mortal consequences, the penitentiary whose annual report shows the largest cash balance paid into the State's treasury is the best penitentiary. The mitigations that arise in its practice through the humane or semi-humane sentiments of keepers and guards, and through the meagerest of legislation, are few, scanty, and rare; and in the main the notion is clearly set forth and followed that a convict, whether pilferer or mur-

[4] Quoted in *Transactions of the National Prison Congress* (St. Louis, 1874), p. 325.

derer, man, woman, or child, has almost no human right that the State is bound to be at any expense to protect.

It hardly need be said that the system is not in operation by reason of any malicious public intention. On the part of lessees there is a most unadmirable spirit of enterprise. On the part of State officials there is a very natural eagerness to report themselves as putting money into the treasury, and a low estimate of public sentiment and intelligence. In the people at large there is little more than a listless oblivion that may be reprehensible, but is not intentional, unless they are to be judged by the acts of their elected legislators, a rule by which few communities would stand unaccused. At any rate, to fall into the error is easy. Outlays for the maintenance of police and courts are followed with a jealous eye. Expense and danger keep the public on the alert. Since neither police nor courts can pay back in money, they must pay back in protection and in justice. The accused of crime must be arrested, the innocent acquitted and exonerated, and the guilty sentenced to the penalties of the laws they have violated. But just here the careless mind slips into the mistake that the end is reached; that to punish crime, no matter how, is to deter crime; that when broken laws are *avenged* that is the end; that it is enough to have the culprit in limbo, if only he is made to suffer and not to cost. Hence the public resolve, expressed and enforced through legislators and executive officers, to spend no more money on the criminal than will promptly come back in cash—nay, worse, to make him pay in advance; and hence, too, a total disregard of all other results for good or bad that may be issuing from the prison walls. Thus it follows that that arm of the public service by whose workings a large part of all the immense labor and expenses of police and courts must become either profitable or unprofitable is handed over to the system which, whatever else of profound mischief its annual tables may betray or conceal, will show the smartest results on the cashbook. And thus we see, annually or biennially, the governors of some of our

States congratulating their legislatures upon the fact that, by farming out into private hands, whose single motive is money, the most delicate and difficult task in the whole public service, that task is changed from an outlay that might have been made nobly advantageous into a shameful and disastrous source of revenue.

XXVI

THE DEPENDENCE OF WOMEN[1]

CHARLOTTE PERKINS STETSON

Since we have learned to study the development of human life as we study the evolution of species throughout the animal kingdom, some peculiar phenomena which have puzzled the philosopher and moralist for so long begin to show themselves in a new light. We begin to see that, so far from being inscrutable problems requiring another life to explain, these sorrows and perplexities of our lives are but the natural results of natural causes, and that, as soon as we ascertain the causes, we can do much to remove them.

In spite of the power of the individual will to struggle against conditions, to resist them for a while, and sometimes to overcome them, it remains true that the human creature is affected by his environment, as is every other living thing. The power of the individual will to resist natural law is well proven by the life and death of the ascetic. In any one of those suicidal martyrs may be seen the will, misdirected by the ill-informed intelligence, forcing the body to defy every natural impulse—even to the door of death, and through it.

But, while these exceptions show what the human will can do, the general course of life shows the inexorable effect of conditions upon humanity. Of these conditions we share with other living things the environment of the material universe. We are affected by climate and locality, by physical, chemical, electrical forces, as are all animals and plants. With the animals, we further share the effect of our own activity, the reactionary force of exercise. What we do, as well as what is

1 [Charlotte Perkins Stetson, *Women and Economics* (Boston, 1900 ed.), pp. 1-18. Chapter title supplied by editor.]

done to us, makes us what we are. But, beyond these forces, we come under the effect of a third set of conditions peculiar to our human status, namely, social conditions. In the organic interchanges which constitute social life, we are affected by each other to a degree beyond what is found even among the most gregarious of animals. This third factor, the social environment, is of enormous force as a modifier of human life. Throughout all these environing conditions, those which affect us through our economic necessities are most marked in their influence.

Without touching yet upon the influence of the social factors, treating the human being merely as an individual animal, we see that he is modified most by his economic conditions, as is every other animal. Differ as they may in color and size, in strength and speed, in minor adaptation to minor conditions, all animals that live on grass have distinctive traits in common, and all animals that eat flesh have distinctive traits in common—so distinctive and so common that it is by teeth, by nutritive apparatus in general, that they are classified, rather than by means of defense or locomotion. The food supply of the animal is the largest passive factor in his development; the processes by which he obtains his food supply, the largest active factor in his development. It is these activities, the incessant repetition of the exertions by which he is fed, which most modify his structure and develop his functions. The sheep, the cow, the deer, differ in their adaptation to the weather, their locomotive ability, their means of defense; but they agree in main characteristics, because of their common method of nutrition.

The human animal is no exception to this rule. Climate affects him; weather affects him; enemies affect him; but most of all he is affected, like every other living creature, by what he does for his living. Under all the influence of his later and wider life, all the reactive effect of social institutions, the individual is still inexorably modified by his means of livelihood—"the hand of the dyer is subdued to what he works in." As one clear, world-known instance of the effect of economic conditions upon the human creature, note the marked race-modification of the Hebrew people under the enforced restrictions of the last two thousand years. Here is a people rising to national prominence, first as a pastoral, and then as an agricultural nation; only partially commercial through race affinity with the Phoenicians, the pioneer traders of the world. Under the social power of a united Christendom—united at least in this most unchristian deed—the Jew was forced to get his livelihood by commercial methods solely. Many effects can be traced in him to the fierce pressure of the social conditions to which he was subjected: the intense family devotion of a people who had no country, no king, no room for joy and pride except the family; the reduced size and tremendous vitality and endurance of the pitilessly selected survivors of the ghetto; the repeated bursts of erratic genius from the human spirit so inhumanly restrained. But more patent still is the effect of the economic conditions—the artificial development of a race of traders and dealers in money, from the lowest pawnbroker to the house of Rothschild; a special kind of people, bred of the economic environment in which they were compelled to live.

One rough but familiar instance of the same effect, from the same cause, we can all see in the marked distinction between the pastoral, the agricultural, and the manufacturing classes in any nation, though their other conditions be the same. On the clear line of argument that functions and organs are developed by use, that what we use most is developed most, and that the daily processes of supplying economic needs are the processes that we most use, it follows that, when we find special economic conditions affecting any special class of people, we may look for special results, and find them.

In view of these facts, attention is now called to a certain marked and peculiar economic condition affecting the human race, and unparalleled in the organic world. We are the only animal species in which the female depends on the male for food, the only animal species in which the sex relation is also an economic relation. With us, an entire sex lives in a relation of economic dependence upon the other sex, and the economic relation is combined with the sex relation. The economic status of the human female is relative to the sex relation.

It is commonly assumed that this condition also obtains among other animals, but such is not the case. There are many birds among which, during the nesting season, the male helps the female feed the young, and partially feeds her; and, with certain of the higher carnivora, the male helps the female feed the young, and partially feeds her. In no case does she depend on him absolutely, even during this season, save in that of the hornbill, where the female, sitting on her nest in a hollow tree, is walled in with clay by the male, so that only her beak projects; and then he feeds her while the eggs are developing. But even the female hornbill does not expect to be fed at any other time. The female bee and ant are economically dependent, but not on the male. The workers are females, too, specialized to economic functions solely. And with the carnivora, if the young are to lose one parent, it might far better be the father—the mother is quite competent to take care of them herself. With many species, as in the case of the common cat, she not only feeds herself and her young, but has to defend the young against the male as well. In no case is the female throughout her life supported by the male.

In the human species the condition is permanent and general, though there are exceptions, and though the present century is witnessing the beginnings of a great change in this respect. We have not been accustomed to face this fact beyond our loose generalization that it was "natural," and that other animals did so, too.

To many this view will not seem clear at first; and the case of working peasant women or females of savage tribes, and the general household industry of women, will be instanced against it. Some careful and honest discrimination is needed to make plain to ourselves the essential facts of the relation, even in these cases. The horse, in his free natural condition, is economically independent. He gets his living by his own exertions, irrespective of any other creature. The horse, in his present condition of slavery, is economically dependent. He gets his living at the hands of his master; and his exertions, though strenuous, bear no direct relation to his living. In fact, the horses who are the best fed and cared for and the horses who are the hardest worked are quite different animals. The horse works, it is true, but what he gets to eat depends on the power and will of his master. His living comes through another. He is economically dependent. So with the hard-worked savage or peasant women. Their labor is the property of another; they work under another will; and what they receive depends not on their labor, but on the power and will of another. They are economically dependent. This is true of the human female both individually and collectively.

In studying the economic position of the sexes collectively, the difference is most marked. As a social animal, the economic status of man rests on the combined and exchanged services of vast numbers of progressively specialized individuals. The economic progress of the race, its maintenance at any period, its continued advance, involve the collective activities of all the trades, crafts, arts, manufactures, inventions, discoveries, and all the civil and military institutions that go to maintain them. The economic status of any race at any time, with its involved effect on all the constituent individuals, depends on their world-wide labors and their free exchange. Economic progress, however, is almost exclusively masculine. Such economic processes as women have been allowed to exercise are of the earliest and most primitive kind. Were men to perform no economic services save such as are still performed by women, our racial status in economics would be reduced to most painful limitations.

To take from any community its male workers would paralyze it economically to a far greater degree than to remove its female workers. The labor now performed by the women could be performed by the men, requiring only the setting back of many advanced workers into earlier forms of industry; but the labor now performed by the men could not be performed by the women without generations of effort and adaptation. Men can cook, clean, and sew as well as women; but the making and managing of the great engines of modern industry, the threading of earth and sea in our vast systems of transportation, the handling of our elaborate machinery of trade, commerce, government—these things could not be done so well by women in their present degree of economic development.

This is not owing to lack of the essential human faculties necessary to such achievements, nor to any inherent disability of sex, but to the present condition of woman, forbidding the development of this degree of economic ability. The male human being is thousands of years in advance of the female in economic status. Speaking collectively, men produce and distribute wealth; and women receive it at their hands. As men hunt, fish, keep cattle, or raise corn, so do women eat game, fish, beef, or corn. As men go down to the sea in ships, and bring coffee and spices and silks and gems from far away, so do women partake of the coffee and spices and silks and gems the men bring.

The economic status of the human race in any nation, at any time, is governed mainly by the activities of the male; the female obtains her share in the racial advance only through him.

Studied individually, the facts are even more plainly visible, more open and familiar. From the day laborer to the millionaire, the wife's worn dress or flashing jewels, her low roof or her lordly one, her weary feet or her rich equipage—these speak of the economic ability of the husband. The comfort, the luxury, the necessities of life itself, which the woman receives, are obtained by the husband, and given her by him. And, when the woman, left alone with no man to "support" her, tries to meet her own economic necessities, the difficulties which confront her prove conclusively what the general economic status of the woman is. None can deny these patent facts—that the economic status of women generally depends upon that of men generally, and that the economic status of women individually depends upon that of men individually, those men to whom they are related. But we are instantly confronted by the commonly received opinion that, although it must be admitted that men make and distribute the wealth of the world, yet women earn their share of it as wives. This assumes either that the husband is in the position of employer and the wife as employee, or that marriage is a "partnership," and the wife an equal factor with the husband in producing wealth.

Economic independence is a relative condition at best. In the broadest sense, all living things are economically dependent upon others—the animals upon the vegetables, and man upon both. In a narrower sense, all social life is economically interdependent, man producing collectively what he could by no possibility produce separately. But, in the closest interpretation, individual economic independence among human beings means that the individual pays for what he gets, works for what he gets, gives to the other an equivalent for what the other gives him. I depend on the shoemaker for shoes, and the tailor for coats; but, if I give the shoemaker and the tailor enough of my own labor as a housebuilder to pay for the shoes and coats they give me, I retain my personal independence. I have not taken of their product, and given nothing of mine. As long as what I get is obtained by what I give, I am economically independent.

Women consume economic goods. What economic product do they give in exchange for what they consume? The claim that marriage is a partnership, in which the two persons married produce wealth which neither of them, separately, could produce, will not bear examination. A man happy and comfortable can produce more than one unhappy and uncomfortable, but this is as true of a father or son as of a husband. To take from a man any of the conditions which make him happy and strong is to cripple his industry, generally speaking. But those relatives who make him happy are not therefore his business partners, and entitled to share his income.

Grateful return for happiness conferred is not the method

of exchange in a partnership. The comfort a man takes with his wife is not in the nature of a business partnership, nor are her frugality and industry. A housekeeper, in her place, might be as frugal, as industrious, but would not therefore be a partner. Man and wife are partners truly in their mutual obligation to their children—their common love, duty, and service. But a manufacturer who marries, or a doctor, or a lawyer, does not take a partner in his business when he takes a partner in parenthood, unless his wife is also a manufacturer, a doctor, or a lawyer. In his business, she cannot even advise wisely without training and experience. To love her husband, the composer, does not enable her to compose; and the loss of a man's wife, though it may break his heart, does not cripple his business, unless his mind is affected by grief. She is in no sense a business partner, unless she contributes capital or experience or labor, as a man would in like relation. Most men would hesitate very seriously before entering a business partnership with any woman, wife or not.

If the wife is not, then, truly a business partner, in what way does she earn from her husband the food, clothing, and shelter she receives at his hands? By house service, it will be instantly replied. This is the general misty idea upon the subject—that women earn all they get, and more, by house service. Here we come to a very practical and definite economic ground. Although not producers of wealth, women serve in the final processes of preparation and distribution. Their labor in the household has a genuine economic value.

For a certain percentage of persons to serve other persons, in order that the ones so served may produce more, is a contribution not to be overlooked. The labor of women in the house, certainly, enables men to produce more wealth than they otherwise could; and in this way women are economic factors in society. But so are horses. The labor of horses enables men to produce more wealth than they otherwise could. The horse is an economic factor in society. But the horse is not economically independent, nor is the woman. If a man plus a valet can perform more useful service than he could minus a valet, then the valet is performing useful service. But, if the valet is the property of the man, is obliged to perform this service, and is not paid for it, he is not economically independent.

The labor which the wife performs in the household is given as part of her functional duty, not as employment. The wife of the poor man, who works hard in a small house, doing all the work for the family, or the wife of the rich man, who wisely and gracefully manages a large house and administers its functions—each is entitled to fair pay for services rendered.

To take this ground and hold it honestly, wives, as earners through domestic service, are entitled to the wages of cooks, housemaids, nursemaids, seamstresses, or housekeepers, and to no more. This would of course reduce the spending money of the wives of the rich, and put it out of the power of the poor man to "support" a wife at all, unless, indeed, the poor man faced the situation fully, paid his wife her wages as house servant, and then she and he combined their funds in the support of their children. He would be keeping a servant; she would be helping keep the family. But nowhere on earth would there be "a rich woman" by these means. Even the highest class of private housekeeper, useful as her services are, does not accumulate a fortune. She does not buy diamonds and sables and keep a carriage. Things like these are not earned by house service.

But the salient fact in this discussion is that, whatever the economic value of the domestic industry of women is, they do not get it. The women who do the most work get the least money, and the women who have the most money do the least work. Their labor is neither given nor taken as a factor in economic exchange. It is held to be their duty as women to do this work; and their economic status bears no relation to their domestic labors, unless an inverse one. Moreover, if they were thus fairly paid—given what they earned, and no more—all women working in this way would be reduced to the economic status of the house servant. Few women—or men either—care to face this condition. The ground that women earn their living by domestic labor is instantly forsaken, and we are told that they obtain their livelihood as mothers. This is a peculiar position. We speak of it commonly enough, and often with deep feeling, but without due analysis.

In treating of an economic exchange, asking what return in goods or labor women make for the goods and labor given them—either to the race collectively or to their husbands individually—what payment women make for their clothes and shoes and furniture and food and shelter, we are told that the duties and services of the mother entitle her to support.

If this is so, if motherhood is an exchangeable commodity given by women in payment for clothes and food, then we must of course find some relation between the quantity or quality of the motherhood and the quantity and quality of the pay. This being true, then the women who are not mothers have no economic status at all; and the economic status of those who are must be shown to be relative to their motherhood. This is obviously absurd. The childless wife has as much money as the mother of many—more; for the children of the latter consume what would otherwise be hers; and the inefficient mother is no less provided for than the efficient one. Visibly, and upon the face of it, women are not maintained in economic prosperity proportioned to their motherhood. Motherhood bears no relation to their economic status. Among primitive races, it is true—in the patriarchal period, for instance—there was some truth in this position. Women being of no value whatever save as bearers of children, their favor and indulgence did bear direct relation to maternity, and they had reason to exult on more grounds than one when they could boast a son. Today, however, the maintenance of the woman is not conditioned upon this. A man is not allowed to discard his wife because she is barren. The claim of motherhood as a factor in economic exchange is false today. But suppose it were true. Are we willing to hold this ground, even in theory? Are we willing to consider motherhood as a business, a form of commercial exchange?

Are the cares and duties of the mother, her travail and her love, commodities to be exchanged for bread?

It is revolting so to consider them; and, if we dare face our own thoughts, and force them to their logical conclusion, we shall see that nothing could be more repugnant to human feeling, or more socially and individually injurious, than to make motherhood a trade. Driven off these alleged grounds of women's economic independence; shown that women, as a class, neither produce nor distribute wealth; that women, as individuals, labor mainly as house servants, are not paid as such, and would not be satisfied with such an economic status if they were so paid; that wives are not business partners or coproducers of wealth with their husbands, unless they actually practice the same profession; that they are not salaried as mothers, and that it would be unspeakably degrading if they were—what remains to those who deny that women are supported by men? This (and a most amusing position it is)—that the function of maternity unfits a woman for economic production, and, therefore, it is right that she should be supported by her husband.

The ground is taken that the human female is not economically independent, that she is fed by the male of her species. In denial of this, it is first alleged that she is economically independent—that she does support herself by her own industry in the house. It being shown that there is no relation between the economic status of woman and the labor she performs in the home, it is then alleged that not as house servant, but as mother, does woman earn her living. It being shown that the economic status of woman bears no relation to her motherhood, either in quantity or quality, it is then alleged that motherhood renders a woman unfit for economic production, and that, therefore, it is right that she be supported by her husband. Before going farther, let us seize upon this admission—that she *is* supported by her husband.

Without going into either the ethics or the necessities of the case, we have reached so much common ground: the female of genus homo is supported by the male. Whereas, in other species of animals, male and female alike graze and browse, hunt and kill, climb, swim, dig, run, and fly for their livings, in our species the female does not seek her own living in the specific activities of our race, but is fed by the male.

XXVII

PROGRESS AND POVERTY

HENRY GEORGE

PRIVATE PROPERTY IN LAND INCONSISTENT WITH THE BEST USE OF LAND [1]

There is a delusion resulting from the tendency to confound the accidental with the essential—a delusion which the law writers have done their best to extend, and political economists generally have acquiesced in, rather than endeavored to expose—that private property in land is necessary to the proper use of land, and that again to make land common property would be to destroy civilization and revert to barbarism.

This delusion may be likened to the idea which, according to Charles Lamb, so long prevailed among the Chinese after the savor of roast pork had been accidentally discovered by the burning down of Ho-ti's hut—that to cook a pig it was necessary to set fire to a house. But, though in Lamb's charming dissertation it was required that a sage should arise to teach people that they might roast pigs without burning down houses, it does not take a sage to see that what is required for the improvement of land is not absolute ownership of the land, but security for the improvements. This will be obvious to whoever will look around him. While there is no more necessity for making a man the absolute and exclusive owner of land in order to induce him to improve it, than there is of burning down a house in order to cook a pig; while the making of land private property is as rude, wasteful, and uncer-

1 [Henry George, *Progress and Poverty. An Inquiry into the Cause of Industrial Depressions, and of Increase of Want with Increase of Wealth: The Remedy* (New York, 1892 ed.), pp. 357-61.]

tain a device for securing improvement, as the burning down of a house is a rude, wasteful, and uncertain device for roasting a pig, we have not the excuse for persisting in the one that Lamb's Chinamen had for persisting in the other. Until the sage arose who invented the rude gridiron (which according to Lamb preceded the spit and oven), no one had known or heard of a pig being roasted, except by a house being burned. But, among us, nothing is more common than for land to be improved by those who do not own it. The greater part of the land of Great Britain is cultivated by tenants; the greater part of the buildings of London are built upon leased ground; and even in the United States the same system prevails everywhere to a greater or less extent. Thus it is a common matter for use to be separated from ownership.

Would not all this land be cultivated and improved just as well if the rent went to the State or municipality, as now, when it goes to private individuals? If no private ownership in land were acknowledged, but all land were held in this way, the occupier or user paying rent to the State, would not land be used and improved as well and as securely as now? There can be but one answer: Of course it would. Then would the resumption of land as common property in nowise interfere with the proper use and improvement of land.

What is necessary for the use of land is not its private ownership, but the security of improvements. It is not necessary to say to a man, "this land is yours," in order to induce him to cultivate or improve it. It is only necessary to say to him, "whatever your labor or capital produces on this land shall be yours." Give a man security that he may reap, and he will sow; assure him of the possession of the house he wants to build, and he will build it. These are the natural rewards of labor. It is for the sake of the reaping that men sow; it is for the sake of possessing houses that men build. The ownership of land has nothing to do with it.

It was for the sake of obtaining this security that, in the beginning of the feudal period, so many of the smaller landholders surrendered the ownership of their lands to a military chieftain, receiving back the use of them in fief or trust, and kneeling bareheaded before the lord, with their hands between his hands, swore to serve him with life and limb, and worldly honor. Similar instances of the giving up of ownership in land for the sake of security in its enjoyment are to be seen in Turkey, where a peculiar exemption from taxation and extortion attaches to *vakouf,* or church lands, and where it is a common thing for a landowner to sell his land to a mosque for a nominal price, with the understanding that he may remain as tenant upon it at a fixed rent.

It is not the magic of property, as Arthur Young said, that has turned Flemish sands into fruitful fields. It is the magic of security to labor. This can be secured in other ways than making land private property, just as the heat necessary to roast a pig can be secured in other ways than by burning down houses. The mere pledge of an Irish landlord that for twenty years he would not claim in rent any share in their cultivation induced Irish peasants to turn a barren mountain into gardens; on the mere security of a fixed ground rent for a term of years the most costly buildings of such cities as London and New York are erected on leased ground. If we give improvers such security, we may safely abolish private property in land.

The complete recognition of common rights to land need in no way interfere with the complete recognition of individual right to improvements or produce. Two men may own a ship without sawing her in half. The ownership of a railway may be divided into a hundred thousand shares, and yet trains be run with as much system and precision as if there were but a single owner. In London, joint-stock companies have been formed to hold and manage real estate. Everything could go on as now, and yet the common right to land be fully recognized by appropriating rent to the common benefit. There is a lot in the center of San Francisco to which the common rights of the people of that city are yet legally recognized. This lot is not cut up into infinitesimal pieces nor yet is it an unused waste. It is covered with fine buildings, the property of private individuals, that stand there in perfect security. The only difference between this lot and those around it is that the rent of the one goes into Common School fund, the rent of the others into private pockets. What is to prevent the land of a whole country being held by the people of the country in this way?

It would be difficult to select any portion of the territory of the United States in which the conditions commonly taken to necessitate the reduction of land to private ownership exist in higher degree than on the little islets of St. Peter and St. Paul, in the Aleutian Archipelago, acquired by the Alaska purchase from Russia. These islands are the breeding places of the fur seal, an animal so timid and wary that the slightest fright causes it to abandon its accustomed resort, never to return. To prevent the utter destruction of this fishery, without which the islands are of no use to man, it is not only necessary to avoid killing the females and young cubs, but even such noises as the discharge of a pistol or the barking of a dog. The men who do the killing must be in no hurry, but quietly walk around among the seals who line the rocky beaches, until the timid animals, so clumsy on land but so graceful in water, show no more sign of fear than to lazily waddle out of the way. Then those who can be killed without diminution of future increase are carefully separated and gently driven inland, out of sight and hearing of the herds, where they are dispatched with clubs. To throw such a fishery as this open to whoever chose to go and kill—which would make it to the interest of each party to kill as many as they could at the time without reference to the future—would be to utterly destroy it in a few seasons, as similar fisheries in other oceans have been destroyed. But it is not necessary, therefore, to make these islands private property. Though for reasons greatly less cogent, the great public domain of the American people has been made over to private ownership as fast as anybody could be got to take it, these islands have been leased at a rent of $317,500 per year,[2] probably not very much less than they could have been sold for at the time of the Alaska purchase. They have already yielded two millions and a half to the national treasury, and they are still, in unimpaired value (for under the careful management of the Alaska Fur Company the seals increase rather than diminish), the common property of the people of the United States.

So far from the recognition of private property in land being necessary to the proper use of land, the contrary is the case. Treating land as private property stands in the way of its proper use. Were land treated as public property it would be used and improved as soon as there was need for its use or improvement, but being treated as private property, the individual owner is permitted to prevent others from using or improving what he cannot or will not use or improve himself. When the title is in dispute, the most valuable land lies unimproved for years; in many parts of England improvement is stopped because, the estates being entailed, no security to improvers can be given; and large tracts of ground which, were they treated as public property, would be covered with buildings and crops, are kept idle to gratify the caprice of the owner. In the thickly settled parts of the United States there is enough land to maintain three or four times our present population, lying unused, because its owners are holding it for higher prices, and immigrants are forced past this unused land to seek homes where their labor will be far less productive. In every city, valuable lots may be seen lying vacant for the same reason. If the best use of land be the test, then private property in land is condemned, as it is condemned by every other consideration. It is as wasteful and uncertain a mode of securing the proper use of land, as the burning down of houses is of roasting pigs.

[2] The fixed rent under the lease to the Alaska Fur Company is $55,000 a year, with a payment of $2.62½ on each skin, which on 100,000 skins, to which the take is limited, amounts to $262,500—a total rent of $317,500.

XXVIII

EQUALITY

EDWARD BELLAMY

WHY THE REVOLUTION DID NOT COME EARLIER[1]

Absorbed in our talk, we had not heard the steps of Dr. Leete as he approached.

"I have been watching you for ten minutes from the house," he said, "until, in fact, I could no longer resist the desire to know what you find so interesting."

"Your daughter," said I, "has been proving herself a mistress of the Socratic method. Under a plausible pretext of gross ignorance, she has been asking me a series of easy questions, with the result that I see as I never imagined it before the colossal sham of our pretended popular government in America. As one of the rich I knew, of course, that we had a great deal of power in the state, but I did not before realize how absolutely the people were without influence in their own government."

"Aha!" exclaimed the doctor in great glee, "so my daughter gets up early in the morning with the design of supplanting her father in his position of historical instructor?"

Edith had risen from the garden bench on which we had been seated and was arranging her flowers to take into the house. She shook her head rather gravely in reply to her father's challenge.

"You need not be at all apprehensive," she said; "Julian has quite cured me this morning of any wish I might have had to inquire further into the condition of our ancestors.

[1] [Edward Bellamy, *Equality* (New York, 1897), pp. 14-23.]

I have always been dreadfully sorry for the poor people of that day on account of the misery they endured from poverty and the oppression of the rich. Henceforth, however, I wash my hands of them and shall reserve my sympathy for more deserving objects."

"Dear me!" said the doctor, "what has so suddenly dried up the fountains of your pity? What has Julian been telling you?"

"Nothing, really, I suppose, that I had not read before and ought to have known, but the story always seemed so unreasonable and incredible that I never quite believed it until now. I thought there must be some modifying facts not set down in the histories."

"But what is this that he has been telling you?"

"It seems," said Edith, "that these very people, these very masses of the poor, had all the time the supreme control of the government and were able, if determined and united, to put an end at any moment to all the inequalities and oppressions of which they complained and to equalize things as we have done. Not only did they not do this, but they gave as a reason for enduring their bondage that their liberties would be endangered unless they had irresponsible masters to manage their interests, and that to take charge of their own affairs would imperil their freedom. I feel that I have been cheated out of all the tears I have shed over the sufferings of such people. Those who tamely endure wrongs which they have the power to end deserve not compassion but contempt. I have felt a little badly that Julian should have been one of the oppressor class, one of the rich. Now that I really understand the matter, I am glad. I fear that, had he been one of the poor, one of the mass of real masters, who with supreme power in their hands consented to be bondsmen, I should have despised him."

Having thus served formal notice on my contemporaries that they must expect no more sympathy from her, Edith went into the house, leaving me with a vivid impression that if the men of the twentieth century should prove incapable of preserving their liberties, the women might be trusted to do so.

"Really, doctor," I said, "you ought to be greatly obliged to your daughter. She has saved you lots of time and effort."

"How so, precisely?"

"By rendering it unnecessary for you to trouble yourself to explain to me any further how and why you came to set up your nationalized industrial system and your economic equality. It you have ever seen a desert or sea mirage, you remember that, while the picture in the sky is very clear and distinct in itself, its unreality is betrayed by a lack of detail, a sort of blur, where it blends with the foreground on which you are standing. Do you know that this new social order of which I have so strangely become a witness has hitherto had something of this mirage effect? In itself it is a scheme precise, orderly, and very reasonable, but I could see no way by which it could have naturally grown out of the utterly different conditions of the nineteenth century. I could only imagine that this world transformation must have been the result of new ideas and forces that had come into action since my day. I had a volume of questions all ready to ask you on the subject, but now we shall be able to use the time in talking of other things, for Edith has shown me in ten minutes' time that the only wonderful thing about your organization of the industrial system as public business is not that it has taken place, but that it waited so long before taking place; that a nation of rational beings consented to remain economic serfs of irresponsible masters for more than a century after coming into possession of absolute power to change at pleasure all social institutions which inconvenienced them."

"Really," said the doctor, "Edith has shown herself a very efficient teacher, if an involuntary one. She has succeeded at one stroke in giving you the modern point of view as to your period. As we look at it, the immortal preamble of the American Declaration of Independence, away back in 1776, logically contained the entire statement of the doctrine of universal economic equality guaranteed by the nation collectively to its members individually. You remember how the words run:

" 'We hold these truths to be self-evident: that all men are created equal, with certain inalienable rights; that among these are life, liberty, and the pursuit of happiness; that to secure these rights governments are instituted among men, deriving their just powers from the consent of the governed; that whenever any form of government becomes destructive of these rights it is right of the people to alter or to abolish it and institute a new government, laying its foundations on such principles and organizing its powers in such form as may seem most likely to effect their safety and happiness.'

"Is it possible, Julian, to imagine any governmental system less adequate than ours which could possibly realize this great idea of what a true people's government should be? The cornerstone of our state is economic equality, and is not that the obvious, necessary, and only adequate pledge of these three birthrights—life, liberty, and happiness? What is life without its material basis, and what is an equal right to life but a right to an equal material basis for it? What is liberty? How can men be free who must ask the right to labor and to live from their fellow men and seek their bread from the hands of others? How else can any government guarantee liberty to men save by providing them a means of labor and of life coupled with independence; and how could that be done unless the government conducted the economic system upon which employment and maintenance depend? Finally, what is implied in the equal right of all to the pursuit of happiness? What form of happiness, so far as it depends at all on material facts, is not bound up with economic conditions; and how shall an equal opportunity for the pursuit of happiness be guaranteed to all save by a guarantee of economic equality?"

"Yes," I said, "it is indeed all there, but why were we so long in seeing it?"

"Let us make ourselves comfortable on this bench," said the doctor, "and I will tell you what is the modern answer to the very interesting question you raise. At first glance, certainly, the delay of the world in general, and especially of the American people, to realize that democracy logically meant the substitution of popular government for the rule of the rich in regulating the production and distribution of wealth seems incomprehensible, not only because it was so plain an inference from the idea of popular government, but also because it was one which the masses of the people were so directly interested in carrying out. Edith's conclusion that people who were not capable of so simple a process of reasoning as that did not deserve much sympathy for the afflictions they might so easily have remedied, is a very natural first impression.

"On reflection, however, I think we shall conclude that the time taken by the world in general and the Americans in particular in finding out the full meaning of democracy as an economic as well as a political proposition was not greater than might have been expected, considering the vastness of the conclusions involved. It is the democratic idea that all human beings are peers in rights and dignity and that the sole just excuse and end of human governments is, therefore, the maintenance and furtherance of the common welfare on equal terms. This idea was the greatest social conception that the human mind had up to that time ever formed. It contained, when first conceived, the promise and potency of a complete transformation of all then existing social institutions, one and all of which had hitherto been based and formed on the principle of personal and class privilege and authority and the domination and selfish use of the many by the few. But it was simply inconsistent with the limitations of the human intellect that the implications of an idea so prodigious should at once have been taken in. The idea must absolutely have time to grow. The entire present order of economic democracy and equality was indeed logically bound up in the first full statement of the democratic idea, but only as the full-grown tree is in the seed; in the one case, as in the other, time was an essential element in the evolution of the result.

"We divide the history of the evolution of the democratic idea into two broadly contrasted phases. The first of these we call the phase of negative democracy. To understand it we must consider how the democratic idea originated. Ideas are born of previous ideas and are long in outgrowing the characteristics and limitations impressed on them by the circumstances under which they came into existence. The idea of popular government, in the case of America as in previous republican experiments in general, was a protest against royal government and its abuses. Nothing is more certain than that the signers of the immortal Declaration had no idea that democracy necessarily meant anything more than a device for getting along without kings. They conceived of it as a change in the forms of government only, and not at all in the principles and purposes of government.

"They were not, indeed, wholly without misgivings lest it might some time occur to the sovereign people that, being sovereign, it would be a good idea to use their sovereignty to improve their own condition. In fact, they seem to have given some serious thought to that possibility, but so little were they yet able to appreciate the logic and force of the democratic idea that they believed it possible by ingenious clauses in paper Constitutions to prevent the people from using their own power to help themselves even if they should wish to.

"This first phase of the evolution of democracy, during which it was conceived of solely as a substitute for royalty, includes all the so-called republican experiments up to the beginning of the twentieth century, of which, of course, the American Republic was the most important. During this period the democratic idea remained a mere protest against a previous form of government, absolutely without any new positive or vital principle of its own. Although the people had deposed the king as driver of the social chariot, and taken the reins into their own hands, they did not think as yet of anything but keeping the vehicle in the old ruts, and naturally the passengers scarcely noticed the change.

"The second phase in the evolution of the democratic idea began with the awakening of the people to the perception that the deposing of kings, instead of being the main end and mission of democracy, was merely preliminary to its real program, which was the use of the collective social machinery for the indefinite promotion of the welfare of the people at large.

"It is an interesting fact that the people began to think of applying their political power to the improvement of their material condition in Europe earlier than in America, although democratic forms had found much less acceptance there. This was, of course, on account of the perennial economic distress of the masses in the old countries, which prompted them to think first about the bearing any new idea might have on the question of livelihood. On the other hand, the general prosperity of the masses in America and the comparative ease of making a living up to the beginning of the last quarter of the nineteenth century account for the fact that it was not till then that the American people began to think seriously of improving their economic condition by collective action.

"During the negative phase of democracy it had been considered as differing from monarchy only as two machines might differ, the general use and purpose of which were the same. With the evolution of the democratic idea into the second or positive phase, it was recognized that the transfer of the supreme power from king and nobles to people meant not merely a change in the forms of government, but a fundamental revolution in the whole idea of government, its motives, purposes, and functions—a revolution equivalent to a reversal of polarity of the entire social system, carrying, so to speak, the entire compass card with it, and making north south, and east west. Then was seen what seems so plain to us that it is hard to understand why it was not always seen, that instead of its being proper for the sovereign people to confine themselves to the functions which the kings and classes had discharged when they were in power, the presumption was, on the contrary, since the interest of kings and classes had always been exactly opposed to those of the people, that whatever the previous governments had done, the people as rulers ought not to do, and whatever the previous governments had not done, it would be presumably for the interest of the people to do; and that the main use and function of popular government was properly one which no previous government had ever paid any attention to, namely, the use of the power of the social organization to raise the material and moral welfare of the whole body of the sovereign people to the highest possible point at which the same degree of welfare could be secured to all—that is to say, an equal level. The democracy of the second or positive phase triumphed in the great Revolution, and has since been the only form of government known in the world."

"Which amounts to saying," I observed, "that there never was a democratic government properly so called before the twentieth century."

"Just so," assented the doctor. "The so-called republics of the first phase we class as pseudo-republics or negative democracies. They were not, of course, in any sense, truly popular governments at all, but merely masks for plutocracy, under which the rich were the real though irresponsible rulers! You will readily see that they could have been nothing else. The masses from the beginning of the world had been the subjects and servants of the rich, but the kings had been above the rich, and constituted a check on their dominion. The overthrow of the kings left no check at all on the power of the rich, which became supreme. The people, indeed, nominally were sovereigns; but as these sovereigns were individually and as a class the economic serfs of the rich, and lived at their mercy, the so-called popular government became the mere stalking-horse of the capitalists.

"Regarded as necessary steps in the evolution of society

from pure monarchy to pure democracy, these republics of the negative phase mark a stage of progress; but if regarded as finalities, they were a type far less admirable on the whole than decent monarchies. In respect especially to their susceptibility to corruption and plutocratic subversion they were the worst kind of government possible. The nineteenth century, during which this crop of pseudo-democracies ripened for the sickle of the great Revolution, seems to the modern view nothing but a dreary interregnum of nondescript, *fainéant* government intervening between the decadence of virile monarchy in the eighteenth century and the rise of positive democracy in the twentieth. The period may be compared to that of the minority of a king, during which the royal power is abused by wicked stewards. The people had been proclaimed as sovereign, but they had not yet assumed the sceptre."

"And yet," said I, "during the latter part of the nineteenth century, when, as you say, the world had not yet seen a single specimen of popular government, our wise men were telling us that the democratic system had been fully tested and was ready to be judged on its results. Not a few of them, indeed, went so far as to say that the democratic experiment had proved a failure when, in point of fact, it seems that no experiment in democracy, properly understood, had as yet ever been so much as attempted."

The doctor shrugged his shoulders.

"It is a very sympathetic task," he said, "to explain the slowness of the masses in feeling their way to a comprehension of all that the democratic idea meant for them, but it is one equally difficult and thankless to account for the blank failure of the philosophers, historians, and statesmen of your day to arrive at an intelligent estimate of the logical content of democracy and to forecast its outcome. Surely, the very smallness of the practical results thus far achieved by the democratic movement as compared with the magnitude of its proposition and the forces behind it ought to have suggested to them that its evolution was yet but in the first stage. How could intelligent men delude themselves with the notion that the most portentous and revolutionary idea of all time had exhausted its influence and fulfilled its mission in changing the title of the executive of a nation from king to President, and the name of the national Legislature from Parliament to Congress? If your pedagogues, college professors, and presidents, and others who were responsible for your education had been worth their salt, you would have found nothing in the present order of economic equality that would in the least have surprised you. You would have said at once that it was just what you had been taught must necessarily be the next phase in the inevitable evolution of the democratic idea."

Edith beckoned from the door and we rose from our seat.

"The revolutionary party in the great Revolution," said the doctor, as we sauntered toward the house, "carried on the work of agitation and propaganda under various names more or less grotesque and ill-fitting, as political party names were apt to be, but the one word democracy, with its various equivalents and derivatives, more accurately and completely expressed, explained, and justified their method, reason, and purpose than a library of books could do. The American people fancied that they had set up a popular government when they separated from England, but they were deluded. In conquering the political power formerly exercised by the king, the people had but taken the outworks of the fortress of tyranny. The economic system which was the citadel and commanded every part of the social structure remained in possesssion of private and irresponsible rulers, and so long as it was so held, the possession of the outworks was of no use to the people, and only retained by the sufferance of the garrison of the citadel. The Revolution came when the people saw that they must either take the citadel or evacuate the outworks. They must either complete the work of establishing popular government which had been barely begun by their fathers, or abandon all that their fathers had accomplished."

XXIX

THE POLICY OF EXPANSION[1]

MOORFIELD STOREY

The citizen of Porto Rico today has no American citizenship, no constitutional rights, no representation in the legislature which imposes the important taxes that he pays, no voice in the selection of his executive or judicial officers, no effective voice in his own legislature. He is governed by a foreign nation under law which he had no part whatever in framing, and the Republican party offers the island no hope either of independence or of statehood. This is government without the the consent of the governed. This is what is meant by "imperialism." In the words of Abraham Lincoln, this is "despotism." To this policy under whatever name our people have always been opposed.

Is it really true that this treatment of a people who received us with open arms, and to whom our representative, General [Nelson A.] Miles promised "the immunities and blessings of the liberal institutions of our government," is generous? Does it really "accord with the most liberal thought of our own country"? When he says that it does, has the President[2] forgotten that only last December he said:

> It must be borne in mind that since the cession Porto Rico has been denied the principal markets she had long enjoyed, and our tariffs have continued against her products as when she was under Spanish sovereignty. . . . She has lost her free intercourse with Spain and Cuba without any compensa-

[1] [Moorfield Storey, *Our New Departure* (Boston, 1901), pp. 20-27. Chapter title supplied by editor.]

[2] [Reference is to William McKinley.]

> ting benefits in this market. . . . Our plain duty is to abolish all customs tariffs between the United States and Porto Rico, and give her products free access to our markets.

Does he not remember the revolt which followed his change of policy? Do we not know that the tariff which was enforced was laid in the interest of America, and not of Porto Rico? As Senator Henry Cabot Lodge so frankly admitted, we did "regard the welfare of the American people first." Can the supporters of the President pretend, with these facts fresh in their memory, that the treatment of Porto Rico "accords with the most liberal thought of our country?" Or can we be surprised that Mr. Semple, the agent of the treasury, on his return from a recent trip in Porto Rico, reported as follows:

> I traveled from San Juan to Ponce, through Arecibo and Aquadillo, and covered the entire island. I found the majority of the natives opposed to the United States, whereas I had been led to believe that they welcomed Americans with open arms.

This evidence tends to show that "the best aspirations of the people" need further encouragement; and no one who reads the law under which Porto Rico is governed can doubt its truth, or expect to find any friendship for the United States among its inhabitants, save perhaps that eye friendship, which is simulated from fear of loss or hope of gain.

When we pass to the Philippine Islands, we are met at once by a difficulty which should not exist. In the summer of 1899 the staff correspondents of the leading American newspapers stationed in Manila united in a statement to the public, in which they said:

> We believe that, owing to official dispatches from Manila made public in Washington, the people of the United States have not received a correct impression of the situation in the Philippines. . . . The censorship has compelled us to participate in this misrepresentation by excising or altering uncontroverted statements of facts, on the plea, as General Elwells Otis stated, that 'they would alarm the people at home' or 'have the people of the United States by the ears.'

This disclosure led to an outburst of public indignation, which was met on October 9, 1899, by a statement from the Adjutant General's office that the censorship was abolished. Somewhat later, on December 2, the censor himself declared that this statement was not true, and that the censorship had never been abolished. On July 30 of this year appeared a dispatch to the Associated Press from Manila, "edited by the censor"; and it is now in full force. Why General Henry C. Corbin authorized the false statement has never been explained. It was a supporter of the President's policy who spoke of this censorship as "utterly un-American and insolently tyrannous." The result is that the American people are called upon to decide the most important question of policy ever presented to them in ignorance of the facts. The administration has kept the truth not from the Filipinos, but from us. General Otis' anxiety was not to avoid informing the enemy, but to avoid alarming "the people at home." The President owes us the whole truth. Why should we not have it?

Is not this subject of vital interest to every American? Will the truth weaken or injure us? No one can pretend that. It can injure the administration by setting "the people of the United States by the ears." This explains the censorship, explains the false statement that it was abolished, explains its persistent maintenance after we are told that the insurrection is over. The Philippine correspondent of the Associated Press says, "The censor had repeatedly told us, in ruling out plain statements of undisputed facts, that he was instructed, 'to let nothing go that can hurt the administration.' " This confirmation, however, is not needed. No one can doubt the motive which induces the administration to keep the facts from the people. There is no court of law and no jury which does not draw the most unfavorable inferences against him who suppresses evidence; nor can the President complain if such inferences are drawn against him. We must deal with the question in the light of such knowledge as we have. Fortunately, the whole truth cannot be suppressed. There are facts enough by which to test the President's statements.

And, first, it is clear that from the time when the President originally asserted sovereignty over the Philippines until now, a period of nearly two years, the President alone has dealt with the inhabitants. He has undertaken to govern them as he has seen fit, without consulting Congress. So far as they are ruled by the United States at all, they are ruled by him, who thus by his unfettered will controls millions of men. This certainly is unknown in our history heretofore.

When the Spanish War ended, the future of the Philippine Islands became a pressing question. It was a question of the deepest interest to the people of the United States. To annex these islands or to control their government in any way meant an absolutely new departure from the policy of this country. Whether we admitted them as citizens or held them as subjects, the consequences must be far-reaching and momentous. To impose our sway upon them against their will, to conquer a nation of Asiatics by fire and sword, was the abandonment of every principle for which this country had stood. It was "criminal aggression." Surely, at such a crisis, it would have been natural under a republican government to consult the people. Before they were embarked in a "criminal aggression," their consent might have been asked. No one could pretend that the question had ever been decided by them. It was absolutely new. Yet Congress was not summoned; nor was even the advice of the Senate asked, as Mr. Lincoln and other presidents have asked it, before committing the country to an important step. The American people were not consulted upon this issue, involving, though it did, their whole future and the future of the free government throughout the world.

This question was of vital interest also to the people of the Philippine Islands. These millions of men, of whose language, whose history, whose capacities and possibilities we were absolutely ignorant, were surely entitled to be consulted as to their own future. The President knew that they desired and thought they had secured their independence. He knew that they had established a government which rested apparently on the consent of the people, and which was maintaining order outside of our lines. They regarded us as deliverers, and would have responded readily to kindly influences. The native leaders were certainly able to give us information as to their needs and desires. But the Filipino people were not consulted. Their ambassador was not received at Washington, and the doors of the Paris conference were closed against their envoys. Of the two peoples now unhappily engaged in a war which everyone deplores, neither was permitted to express its will before the Treaty of Paris was made.

Not even all the commissioners whom he appointed to make the treaty approved the document which they signed. This is known, though the President has declined to allow his correspondence with them to be published. It was one man, and that man the President, who insisted upon taking the Philippine Islands against the will of their people, and who, to do it, departed from all the traditions of our country. This proposition the President takes pains to establish by extracts from his instructions to the commissioners, which he has refused to publish in full—a singular use of public documents under a free government. From the opening sentence in the first quotation, "It is my wish," down to the statement, "Again on November 13 I instructed the commission," the responsibility is clear. It was the President who, to quote his own words, could "see but one plain path of duty, the acceptance of the archipelago." No emperor in the world could have exercised more absolute power than did the President in deciding to take the Philippines. It is true that the Senate had to ratify the treaty; but the President's influence was controlling, and was fully exerted to secure ratification.

But what did the treaty mean? Let me answer in the words of Senator Lodge spoken on January 24, 1899, while urging ratification: "The treaty cedes the Philippines to us. When that treaty is ratified, we have full power, and are absolutely free to do with those islands as we please. . . . Suppose we ratify the treaty. The islands pass from the possession of Spain into our possession without committing us to any policy." This was the position of the administration's friends. What the Senate meant by ratification was shown by the resolution of Mr. Augustus D. Bacon, from which I quote the following words: "That in demanding and in receiving the cession of the Philippine Islands it is not the purpose of the government of the United States to secure and maintain permanent dominion over the same as a part of the territory of the United States, or to permanently incorporate the inhabitants thereof as citizens of the United States, or to hold said inhabitants as vassals or subjects of this government; and the United States hereby disclaim any disposition or intention to exercise permanent sovereignty, jurisdiction, or control over said islands." The fact that upon this resolution the Senate stood equally divided must have informed the President that upon the question of how we should deal with the Philippines the country was not decided.

Who should determine the question of policy which the treaty left open? The President himself gave the only answer, when a few days after it was ratified, in his speech to the Home Market Club in Boston on February 16, he said: "The whole subject is now with Congress; and Congress is the voice, the conscience, and the judgment of the American people. Upon their judgment and conscience can we not rely? . . . Our priceless principles undergo no change under a tropical sun. They go with the flag." And Secretary John D. Long, who followed him, emphasized this answer when he said that the rejection of the treaty "would have taken out of the hands of the people and put into the hands of one man, the President, absolute authority over the Philippines, limited only to the indefinite scope of what is called the war power, wielded by a purely military arm holding a naked sword. Think of that for imperialism. It is a great credit to the President that, like Julius Caesar and George Washington, he has refused this offer of a 'kingly crown.' On the contrary, the good old democratic plan has been adopted of putting the disposition of these islands into the hands of the American people, who will duly express their will through their representatives in Congress assembled. I have no doubt the President is delighted to have the elephant off his hands, and on theirs."

When these words were uttered, the war in the Philippines was in its first and most acute stage. General Otis had a few days before refused [Emilio] Aguinaldo's request for a truce. Spoken under these circumstances, these speeches meant that the President would undertake no policy of his own, but would let Congress deal with the question. Least of all would he assume "absolute authority over the Philippines, limited only to the indefinite scope of what is called the war power, wielded by a purely military arm holding a naked sword" which Secretary Long described as real "imperialism." Yet from the day when those words were spoken till now we have had exactly this, and nothing else. It is Secretary Long who says, *"Think of that for imperialism."*

"The voice, the conscience, and the judgment of the American people" has never been consulted. Congress was not called in extra session to decide the question upon which the Senate was equally divided or to make such a declaration of our purpose as might have ended the war. The President alone assumed "that absolute authority over the Philippines" which Secretary Long praised him for refusing. Congress met in regular session on December 5, 1899. Did the President hasten to express his pleasure that "the elephant was off his hands, and on theirs?" This is what he said:

> It does not seem desirable that I should recommend at this time a specific and final form of government for these islands. When peace shall be restored, it will be the duty of Congress to construct a plan of government which shall establish and maintain freedom and order and peace in the Philippines. The insurrection is still existing; and, when it terminates, further information will be required as to the actual condition of affairs before inaugurating a permanent scheme of civil government. . . . As long as the insurrection continues, the military arm must necessarily be supreme.

This was a distinct invitation to Congress to leave "the elephant" on his hands, and the invitation was accepted. But it will be observed that the question of holding the islands—the question upon which the Senate divided equally, the question which the treaty left open—was treated by the President as settled. His words are: "The islands lie under the shelter of our flag. They are ours by every title of law and equity. They cannot be abandoned."

Who settled this question? Not a Congress which had never considered it. Not the Senate which was divided. It was the President who on December 21, 1898, weeks before the treaty was ratified, before it was even submitted to the Senate, and, therefore, before he had a shadow of authority beyond "the city, harbor, and bay of Manila," as he himself admitted at Pittsburgh, issued the proclamation which announced to the Filipinos that "the future control, disposition, and government of the Philippine Islands" had been "ceded to the United States," and proceeded, "In fulfilment of the right of sovereignty thus acquired and the reponsible obligations of government thus assumed, the actual occupation and administration of the entire group of the Philippine Islands become immediately necessary; and the military government heretofore maintained by the United States in the city, harbor, and bay of Manila, is to be extended with all possible dispatch to the whole of the ceded territory. . . . All persons who, either by active aid or by honest submission, co-operate with the government of the United States, . . . will receive the reward of its support and protection. All others will be brought within the lawful rule we have assumed with firmness, if need be, but without severity so far as may be possible."

When we remember that there was an organized government in Luzon recognized in the other principal islands, and that the army of this government, till then acting in alliance with us, lay just outside our lines; when we remember also that this army had been raised to win the independence of the islands, and that this government had proclaimed this independence—it is clear that the President's proclamation was a declaration of war. It ignored the established government, and proposed to occupy its territory by military force.

General Otis admits that he thought it unsafe to publish it, and that he modified it in essential respects; but General Miller published it unchanged. It was the President, in the exercise of the war power, who from that day till now has wielded all of the power of the United States in the Philippines. He has appointed two commissions; but Congress has never been asked to authorize either, to define their duties or to fix their salaries. They are the representatives of the President, responsible to him, and paid out of public funds such sums as he sees fit. He has instructed them "to devote their attention in the first instance to the establishment of municipal government, in which the natives of the islands . . . shall be afforded the opportunity to manage their own local affairs to the fullest extent of which they are capable"; that is, of which these commissioners think them capable.

BIOGRAPHICAL NOTES

CHARLES FRANCIS ADAMS, JR. (1835-1915) brought a rich training in the ideals of his father and other leading lights of New England to the problem of railroads as they developed in post-Civil War America. His *Chapters of Erie and Other Essays* (1871)—to which his brother Henry contributed – revealed dangers being posed by the railroads to social standards of honesty and responsibility. As chairman of the Massachusetts Board of Railroad Commissioners, he produced valuable reports on railroad conditions. His *Railroads: Their Origin and Problems* (1878) and *Notes on Railroad Accidents* (1879) reflect his studies and experiences. See also, *Charles Francis Adams 1835-1915: an Autobiography* (1916).

JANE ADDAMS (1860-1935) came from a well-to-do Illinois family. Frail of body and serious in outlook, she traveled and investigated possible careers in art and medicine. In 1887 her visit to the pioneer settlement, Toynbee Hall, in a London slum, crystallized her determination to enter into social work. In 1889 she opened Hull House in Chicago, and made it a center for the poor and afflicted as well as a training ground for others who were learning to write or minister to social problems. In later years she became an outstanding worker for international peace. Her many writings include her particularly notable *Twenty Years at Hull House* (1910).

JOHN PETER ALTGELD (1847-1902), the son of German immigrants, drifted west to become a lawyer and a financier in Chicago. As a Democrat, he advanced in his party's councils; as a judge and humanitarian, he was critical of the prison system. In 1893, he was elected governor of Illinois. His pardon of the imprisoned anarchist survivors of the Haymarket riot of 1886 subjected him to harsh criticism in the conservative press. In July, 1894, President Grover Cleveland sent troops to Chicago during the Pullman Strike, despite Altgeld's insistence that peace would be maintained by state troops, if necessary. Altgeld's protests against Cleveland's action made Altgeld the leading liberal in high position in the land. His financial position suffered, and he lost conventional political status, but he was a major force in turning the Democratic party to Populism in 1896. Following his death, Altgeld became a legend of liberalism and integrity. See Harry Barnard, *Eagle Forgotten: The Life of John Peter Altgeld* (1938).*

EDWARD BELLAMY (1850-1898), born and raised in Chicopee Falls, Massachusetts, was a thoughtful, studious young man. At the age of eighteen, he lived abroad, for the most part in Germany, where he first began to think about social problems. He returned home to become a journalist and writer of fiction. His early essay, unpublished in his lifetime, "The Religion of

* Reprinted in 1962 in the Bobbs-Merrill Charter Books series.

Solidarity," argued for an emphasis on what people had in common, rather than on their distinguishing qualities. *Looking Backward* (1888) portrayed a world in the twentieth century which was spiritually as well as economically at peace. It thrilled a generation disturbed by nineteenth-century social disorder. Bellamy Clubs multiplied throughout the country. In 1892, a delegation from these clubs at the Populist Convention wrote the nationalizing planks into its political platform. Bellamy now undertook a crusade in behalf of public ownership of railroads and other social necessities. He was careful to avoid the label of socialist, to which he believed Americans were cold. His health, never good, deteriorated, and he died shortly after completing his *Equality,* the lengthier and more detailed sequel to *Looking Backward.* In many ways superior to its predecessor, *Equality* sold far fewer copies. See Arthur E. Morgan, *Edward Bellamy* (1944).

William Jennings Bryan (1860-1925) was raised in Illinois, and became a lawyer. He moved to Lincoln, Nebraska, where his agreeable personality and eloquence gave him a place among its citizens, as well as in the courts. He turned to politics, and served in Congress. The Populist excitement of the early 1890's, and the extreme importance which was attached to the issue of "free silver," gave him his opportunity. He was but thirty-six years of age, and relatively unknown, when his speech at the Chicago Convention of the Democratic party won him its Presidential nomination. (Its famous passage, "You shall not crucify mankind upon a cross of gold," may have come from a passage in Bellamy's *Looking Backward:* "I have been in Golgotha, . . . I have seen Humanity hanging on a cross!") Bryan's failure to win the election seemed to his followers no more than a prelude to victory. His subsequent defeats, however, in 1900 and in 1908, underscored that he had been the spokesman for important, but not decisive elements of western thought. The most incisive biography — though a more definitive one is needed — is that of Paxton Hibben, *The Peerless Leader: William Jennings Bryan* (1929).

George Washington Cable (1844-1925) was born in New Orleans, and raised under straitened financial conditions which matured him early. A proud Southerner, he served as a Confederate soldier, and was afterward employed in business. Laboring to educate himself, he became steeped in the lore of New Orleans and of the Creole. His learning found expression in stories which were resoundingly successful, the most famous being *Old Creole Days* (1879) and *The Grandissimes* (1884). Cable now emerged, not only as a master of pungent prose, but as a reformer who urged prison improvements, more democratic government in the South, and equal treatment for the Negro. Local resentment called forth by the first of his books in the field, *The Silent South* (1885), was a factor in his moving north. This action largely concluded what had been a major attempt to establish a northern type of liberal theory in a southern locale. See Arlin Turner, *George W. Cable* (1956).

Helen Campbell (1839-1918) was a writer whose published works went back to 1864. She produced stories for children, books and articles on household arts, and a number of popular novels. Her earliest book on the needy was *The Problem of the Poor* (1882); others included *Prisoners of Poverty* (1887), *Darkness and Daylight: or, Lights and Shadows of New York Life* (1891), *Women Wage-Earners: Their Past, Their Present and Their Future* (1893).

JOHN DEWEY (1859-1952) was raised in Vermont, and graduated from the state university. Following two years of high school teaching in Pennsylvania, he attended the graduate school of Johns Hopkins University. He studied assiduously the German metaphysical philosopher Hegel, but later, as a professor of philosophy at the University of Michigan and the University of Minnesota, began to emphasize the principle of action, as interrelated with reason and intelligence. Dewey became director of the Experimental School of the University of Chicago, where his famous concept of learning to do by doing was developed as an educational principle. In subsequent years, Dewey became a symbol of pragmatism and of "progressive education," both of which were ultimately to attract a variety of criticisms. For an analysis of the circumstances from which Dewey and neo-Deweyans arose, see Louis Filler, "Main Currents in Progressivist American Education," *History of Education Journal,* Winter, 1957, pp. 33-57.

IGNATIUS DONNELLY (1831-1901), an orator and a writer, was a founder of Minnesota, and became its Republican lieutenant-governor after it achieved statehood in 1858. He served in Congress, 1863-1869, but a quarrel with Republican leaders ended his career among them. Thereafter, he wrote and spoke as the tribune of western farmers, whom he saw as oppressed by monopolists and cheated through evil currency and tariff policies. As a writer, he caused a sensation with *Atlantis: the Antediluvian World* (1882) and *Ragnarok: the Age of Fire and Ice* (1883), which advanced theories about the earth's development. *The Great Cryptogram* (1888) sought to prove Sir Francis Bacon the author of Shakespeare's works. *Caesar's Column: a Story of the Twentieth Century* (1891) rivaled Bellamy's *Looking Backward* in popularity, but it depicted catastrophe rather than peace. Donnelly was the author of the Preamble to the Populist Platform of 1892. There is no adequate account of his life in print.

HENRY GEORGE (1839-1897) was raised in a religious family in Philadelphia. His schooling was brief and irregular, its most significant aspect being the love of poetry which he developed and which later influenced his prose. In 1855 he became a sailor and left for Melbourne and Calcutta. Back home, the next year, he entered a printing office, which opened a new world of books and pamphlets to him. Impetuous in temper, he planned inadequately and hoped for quick returns. He found his way to San Francisco where he suffered want and disappointments, and compounded his troubles by marrying. During the hard years following, he managed to augment his experience as a printer, and, in addition, to concern himself with the problem of religion and social justice. This found ultimate expression in his *Progress and Poverty* (1879), a book which was read throughout the world. In the United States, George inspired such followers as Tom Johnson and Bolton Hall, who were active and influential in municipal affairs. In 1884, George made a strong campaign for mayor of New York. Throughout the last years of the century he was a famous lecturer and writer, and left numerous admirers to carry on in particular his campaign for the single tax. At his death, he received unprecedented obsequies. See Charles A. Barker, *Henry George* (1955).

EDWIN LAWRENCE GODKIN (1831-1902) was an English Protestant, born in Ireland. He was precocious, publishing a history of Hungary at the age of twenty-two, and brilliantly reporting the Crimean War for the London *Daily Mail* during the next two years. Godkin was a Manchester Liberal, and entirely without humanitarian sentiments; but within his limited set of principles he wrote with matchless clarity and effect. Emigrating to America, he won distinguished friends among the genteel classes, and became the first and greatest among the editors of the *Nation*. Later, he was also editor of the New York *Evening Post*. He was made pessimistic by an increased democracy which he thought made war and corruption increasingly certain. For an introduction to Godkin, see Louis Filler, "The Early Godkin: Toward a Revaluation of a Significant Victorian," *The Historian*, Autumn, 1954, pp. 43-66.

LAURENCE GRONLUND (1846-1899) came in 1867 from Denmark to the United States. He was a schoolteacher and lawyer, and a theoretic socialist. The argument that his *The Coöperative Commonwealth* (1884) influenced the form and content of Edward Bellamy's *Looking Backward* (1888) is analyzed in Arthur E. Morgan, *Plagiarism in Utopia* (1944).

GEORGE D. HERRON (1862-1925) fulfilled an intensely religious youth by becoming a minister. In 1891 his address, "The Message of Jesus to Men of Wealth," called him to public attention. Throughout the 1890's, he was one of the symbols of active Christianity. As professor of applied religion at what became Grinnell College, Iowa, he waxed more radical in approach, and in 1899 resigned his post. His subsequent adherence to the Socialist party was accompanied by an increased skepticism regarding the virtues of Christianity. As co-founder of the Rand School of Social Sciences in New York, and still later as President Woodrow Wilson's personal emissary to Germany, he made further changes in his outlook and philosophy. There is no adequate study of his life.

ROBERT G. INGERSOLL (1833-1899), the son of a clergyman, though descended from established New England stock, was raised in the West. Here he became a successful lawyer. Following the Civil War, in which he served, he became attorney-general of Illinois. Fully won over by the Darwinian hypothesis, he became the outstanding American agnostic, and an opponent of religion and revelation in any form. His orthodox Republicanism protected him from ostracism or financial difficulties. He was chief counsel for highly placed Republicans involved in the notorious "Star Route" mail frauds, and offered James G. Blaine, inculpated in railroad frauds, to the Republican Convention of 1884 as the "Plumed

Knight." Ingersoll was outspoken in his contempt for the Bible and its proponents, and loyal to the cause of free speech, as well as of freethinkers. His speeches on nonreligious subjects like Shakespeare and Burns, as well as his patriotic addresses, contributed to his reputation as one of the country's great orators. See Clarence H. Cramer, *Royal Bob: the Life of Robert G. Ingersoll* (1952).

HELEN HUNT JACKSON (1830-1885) was raised in Massachusetts and was a friend of Emily Dickinson. Her first husband was an Army officer, who was accidentally killed in 1863. She became a writer and poet. She settled in Colorado Springs, where she remarried. There, she became interested in the cause of the Indian, for whose welfare she labored and about whom she wrote her most significant works. In addition to *A Century of Dishonor* (1881), she wrote *Ramona* (1884), a fictionalized account of the injustice accorded Indians, which has a significant place in the literature of its time. See Ruth Odell, *Helen Hunt Jackson (H. H.)* (1939).

ERNEST LACY (1863-1916) was the product of a genteel, but demoralizing, upbringing. Though he shared his period's admiration for classical models of literature and distaste for a commercial civilization, his personal troubles and sympathy for the rebellious career of the English poet Thomas Chatterton taught him a sympathy and compassion which reflected itself in a natural verse form and in democratic attitudes. For biographical data and critical comment, see Louis Filler, ed., *Chatterton,* by Ernest Lacy (1952).

EMMA LAZARUS (1849-1887) was a poet and littérateur, whose precocious gifts attracted the attention of Ralph Waldo Emerson. Her verse was more notable for ardor and integrity than for originality. She was at first universal in her outlook rather than loyal to Judaism, but was turned into an active partisan of her people by the Russian persecutions of 1879-1883 and those following. A defense of the anti-Semitic atrocities in Russia, in *Century Magazine,* April, 1882, called forth in the following issue a reply by Emma Lazarus, "Russian Christianity *versus* Modern Judaism." Her 1882 volume of verse was proudly entitled *Songs of a Semite.* Her increasing fame was the product of the liberalism of the period, plus her adherence to the poetic conventions of the time. For an example of late nineteenth-century liberalism in this field, see, by a Baptist clergyman, Madison C. Peters, *Justice to the Jew . . .* (1899).

HENRY DEMAREST LLOYD (1847-1903) was a New Yorker of liberal, free-trade principles, who settled in Chicago as an editor on the *Tribune.* His marriage to a woman of wealth freed him for more complex examinations of social problems. As early as 1881, he published in the *Atlantic Monthly* his "Story of a Great Monopoly," an exposé of the methods by which the Standard Oil Company was fastening its grip on the oil industry. Not until 1894 was Lloyd ready to publish his classic *Wealth against Commonwealth,* a detailed and eloquent study of the Standard Oil Company, and a forerunner of later muckraking literature. Thereafter, Lloyd moved slowly but steadily toward acceptance of the idea of a co-operative form of society. His travels to Great

Britain, New Zealand, and Switzerland were directed at discovering social and political systems which could be adapted to American conditions. See Caro Lloyd, *Henry Demarest Lloyd* (1912).

EDWIN MARKHAM (1852-1940) spent a distraught youth in a broken family, a fact which was forgotten or ignored after he had achieved world fame. This fame came to him after January 15, 1899, when "The Man with the Hoe" was published in the San Francisco *Examiner*. The attention the poem received was unprecedented, and Markham was accorded status not only as a major poet, but as part of the humanitarian conscience of America. His subsequent career left him inconsequential, on the one hand, and the "Dean of American Poets," on the other. His *Children in Bondage* (1914) is a landmark in the crusade against child labor. For an approach to the problem of Markham, see Louis Filler, *Dictionary of American Biography, Supplement Two* (1958).

WILLIAM VAUGHN MOODY (1869-1910) attended Harvard University and became a professor of English literature at the University of Chicago. His verse and prose fell between his desire to emulate classical Greek dramatists, as in *The Fire-Bringer* (1904), and his effort to make contact with contemporary themes, as in *The Great Divide* (1906). His work was inordinately well received, not only among fanciers of verse, but even on the commercial stage. His poetic commentary on the implications of Darwinism, of imperialism, and other problems of the time secures his place in American literary history, as distinguished from American literature. See the introduction by Robert Morss Lovett to *Selected Poems of William Vaughn Moody* (1931).

TERENCE V. POWDERLY (1849-1924) was the son of Irish immigrants, who worked in the coal mines of Pennsylvania. He became a machinist, and rose in labor's ranks. In 1876, he was initiated into the Knights of Labor, and by 1879 had been chosen Grand Master Workman of that dynamic labor organization. He was elected mayor of Scranton, Pennsylvania, in 1878, and served in that capacity for six years. A man of moderate principles, he believed in labor education, favored an industrial form of organization which welcomed workers, rather than excluded them, on trade union principles, and sought arbitration with employers to prevent class war. He later served on governmental boards and commissions. See his posthumous autobiography, *The Path I Trod* (1940).

JACOB AUGUST RIIS (1849-1914) was born the son of a schoolteacher in Denmark, and became a carpenter. In 1870 he left his country for the United States, where, after following various vicissitudes, he became a journalist, serving on the New York *Tribune* and the New York *Evening Sun* as a police reporter. He waged a constant war against the slums, his reports inspiring not only the sympathy of the newly developing class of social workers, but also the co-operation of such energetic men of affairs as Theodore Roosevelt. His autobiography, *The Making of an American* (1901), is a classic among autobiographical works.

CHARLOTTE PERKINS GILMAN STETSON (1860-1935) was raised in poverty and a broken home. An unhappy marriage resulted in divorce. Bellamy's *Looking Backward* first brought her into social movements. Her *Women and Economics* (1898) made her a leading feminist. Though she wrote many other books, it remained her most effective work. See her *The Living of Charlotte Perkins Gilman: an Autobiography* (1935).

MOORFIELD STOREY (1845-1929), of New England heritage, was secretary to Charles Sumner, and himself became a distinguished lawyer. Engaged in various social and political reforms, he consistently fought in the interests of honest politics and reasonable legal procedure. He approved the death penalty for Sacco and Vanzetti, in 1927. His most notable cause was anti-imperialism.

WILLIAM GRAHAM SUMNER (1840-1910) left a ministerial career in 1872 to fill the new chair of political and social science at Yale University. He was an indefatigable worker, and fearless in his expression of opinion. As a leading social Darwinian in America, he opposed imperialism, advocated laissez-faire principles of industry, and decried socialism, as evidenced in his well-known essay "What the Social Classes Owe to Each Other." His numerous works also include studies of banking, and biographies of Andrew Jackson, Alexander Hamilton, and Robert Morris. His *Folkways* (1907) is a milestone in the scientific study of society. See Harris E. Starr, *William Graham Sumner* (1925).

THORSTEIN VEBLEN (1857-1929) grew up in Minnesota among Norwegians who retained much of their old-world background. He attended Carleton College, in Minnesota, learned American ways slowly and painfully, and studied literature, philosophy, and economics. Uncertain of a career, unhappy and in debt, he attended Johns Hopkins University for a year, then transferred to Yale University where he studied social theory with William Graham Sumner. Though manifestly talented and having a Ph.D. degree, he had no place in the academic world. He endured seven jobless years, during which he married. In 1891, he entered Cornell University, hoping that further graduate work would show him a way. A sympathetic professor and a sudden crystallization of ideas landed him in the University of Chicago in 1892, though it was not until 1900 when he was forty-two years of age, after the success of his *The Theory of the Leisure Class* (1899), that he was advanced to assistant professor. His writing, a product of frustration and of a nonconforming point of view natural to one who had been rejected by society, was a long, complex criticism of a social order based on pecuniary values. His early work was liberal in premises. In his eccentric career in the twentieth century, Veblen moved toward bolder, more revolutionary perspectives in a unique system of social analysis; see, for example, *The Vested Interests and the State of the Industrial Arts* (1919). The indispensable reference work is that of Joseph Dorfman, *Thorstein Veblen and His America* (1934).

BOOKER T. WASHINGTON (1856-1915) was born a slave. Following emancipation, he struggled for an education and attended Hampton Institute, from which he graduated in 1875, becoming a teacher. In 1881, he was chosen by Southern philanthropists to head a Negro normal school at Tuskegee, Alabama; and in following years, he developed his gifts as orator and spokesman for the Negro people. His desire to teach Negroes the dignity of labor, and to find grounds for mutual respect between Negroes and white people, offered one program to Negroes. It was denounced as servile and inadequate by some later critics. Washington wrote numerous works, the most famous being his autobiographical *Up from Slavery* (1901).

JAMES BAIRD WEAVER (1833-1912) was raised on the Iowa frontier, and became a lawyer and a Republican. He served with distinction in the Civil War, from which he emerged a brigadier general. Opposing monopolists and machine politicians, and possessing a magnetic presence and oratorical power, Weaver became a leader of western revolt. He was the Presidential candidate of the Greenback party in 1880, and also served in Congress. In 1892, the Populists nominated him again for the Presidency. He polled over a million votes, and received twenty-two votes in the electoral college. He helped create the fusion of Democratic and Populist forces which ran William Jennings Bryan for President in 1896. See Frederick E. Haynes, *James Baird Weaver* (1919).

INDEX

THE AMERICAN HERITAGE SERIES

THE COLONIAL PERIOD

Adams, John *The Political Writings of John Adams: Representative Selections* AHS 8 George A. Peek, Jr.
The English Libertarian Heritage: From the Writings of John Trenchard and Thomas Gordon in The Independent Whig *and* Cato's Letters AHS 32 David L. Jacobson
The Great Awakening AHS 34 Alan Heimert, Perry Miller
Puritan Political Thought AHS 33 Edmund S. Morgan

THE REVOLUTIONARY ERA

The American Revolution as a Democratic Movement AHS 36 Alfred Young
The Antifederalists AHS 38 Cecelia Kenyon
Early American Libertarian Thought: Freedom of the Press from Zenger to Jefferson AHS 41 Leonard W. Levy
Franklin, Benjamin *The Political Thought of Benjamin Franklin* AHS 64 Ralph Ketcham
Paine, Thomas *Common Sense and Other Political Writings* AHS 5 Nelson F. Adkins

THE YOUNG NATION

Calhoun, John C. *Disquisition on Government and Selections from the* Discourse AHS 10 C. Gordon Post
Channing, William Ellery *Unitarian Christianity and Other Essays* AHS 21 Irving H. Bartlett
Democracy, Liberty, and Property: The State Constitutional Conventions of the 1820's AHS 43 Merrill D. Peterson

The Federal Convention and the Formation of the Union of American States AHS 19 Winton U. Solberg

From the Declaration of Independence to the Constitution: The Roots of American Constitutionalism AHS 6 Carl J. Friedrich, Robert G. McCloskey

Gallatin, Albert *Selected Writings* AHS 40 E. James Ferguson

Hamilton, Alexander *Papers on Public Credit, Commerce, and Finance* AHS 18 Samuel McKee, Jr., J. Harvie Williams

Hamilton, Madison, and Jay on the Constitution: Selections from the Federalist Papers AHS 7 Ralph H. Gabriel

Jefferson, Thomas *The Political Writings of Thomas Jefferson: Representative Selections* AHS 9 Edward Dumbauld

Social Theories of Jacksonian Democracy: Representative Writings of the Period 1825–1850 AHS 1 Joseph L. Blau

The Writings of Justice Joseph Story AHS 45 Henry Steele Commager

THE MIDDLE PERIOD

The Antislavery Argument AHS 44 Jane and William Pease

Lincoln, Abraham *The Political Thought of Abraham Lincoln* AHS 46 Richard Current

The Radical Republicans and Reconstruction AHS 47 Harold Hyman

THE LATE NINETEENTH CENTURY

Bryan, William Jennings *The Mind and Thought of William Jennings Bryan* AHS 52 Ray Ginger

The Forging of American Socialism: Origins of the Modern Movement AHS 24 Howard H. Quint

Late Nineteenth-Century American Liberalism AHS 26 Louis Filler

The Populist Mind AHS 50 Norman Pollack

THE TWENTIETH CENTURY

Addams, Jane *The Social Thought of Jane Addams* AHS 69 Christopher Lasch

The American Writer and the Great Depression AHS 63 Harvey Swados

Negro Protest Thought in the Twentieth Century AHS 56 Francis Broderick, August Meier

New Deal Thought AHS 70 Howard Zinn

The Progressives AHS 54 Carl Resek

Roosevelt, Theodore *The Writings of Theodore Roosevelt* AHS 53 William H. Harbaugh

The Supreme Court: Law Versus Discretion AHS 72 Wallace Mendelson

Wilson, Woodrow, *The Political Thought of Woodrow Wilson* AHS 68 E. David Cronon

TOPICAL VOLUMES

The American Economic System: Representative Selections AHS 27 Massimo Salvadori

American Military Thought AHS 75 Walter Millis

The Churches and the City AHS 61 Robert Cross

Freedom of the Press: 1800–1965 AHS 74 Harold L. Nelson

Nonviolence in America: A Documentary History AHS 60 Staughton Lynd

The Library of Liberal Arts

AESCHYLUS, Prometheus Bound
D'ALEMBERT, J., Preliminary Discourse to the Encyclopedia of Diderot
AQUINAS, ST. T., The Principles of Nature, On Being and Essence, On Free Choice, *and* On the Virtues in General
ARISTOTLE, Nicomachean Ethics
On Poetry and Music
On Poetry and Style
ARNAULD, A., The Art of Thinking (Port-Royal Logic)
AUGUSTINE, ST., On Christian Doctrine
On Free Choice of the Will
BACON, F., The New Organon
BARON and BLAU, eds., Judaism
BAUDELAIRE, C., The Prophetic Muse: Critical Essays of Baudelaire
BAYLE, P., Historical and Critical Dictionary (Selections)
BECCARIA, C., On Crimes and Punishments
BERGSON, H., Duration and Simultaneity
Introduction to Metaphysics
BERKELEY, G., Principles, Dialogues, *and* Philosophical Correspondence
Principles of Human Knowledge
Three Dialogues Between Hylas and Philonous
Works on Vision
BOCCACCIO, G., On Poetry
BOETHIUS, The Consolation of Philosophy
BOILEAU, N., Selected Criticism
BOLINGBROKE, H., The Idea of a Patriot King
BONAVENTURA, ST., The Mind's Road to God
BOSANQUET, B., Three Lectures on Aesthetic
BOWMAN, A., The Absurdity of Christianity
BRADLEY, F., Ethical Studies
BURKE, E., An Appeal from the New to the Old Whigs
Reflections on the Revolution in France
Selected Writings and Speeches on America
BURKE, K., Permanence and Change
BUTLER, J., Five Sermons
CALVIN, J., On the Christian Faith
On God and Political Duty
CATULLUS, Odi et Amo: Complete Poetry
CICERO, On the Commonwealth
Cid, The Epic of the

CROCE, B., Guide to Aesthetics

DESCARTES, R., Discourse on Method
- Discourse on Method *and* Meditations
- Discourse on Method, Optics, Geometry, *and* Meteorology
- Meditations
- Philosophical Essays
- Rules for the Direction of the Mind

DEWEY, J., On Experience, Nature, and Freedom

DIDEROT, D., Encyclopedia (Selections)
- Rameau's Nephew and Other Works

DOSTOEVSKI, F., The Grand Inquisitor

DRYDEN, J., An Essay of Dramatic Poesy and Other Essays

DUNS SCOTUS, J., Philosophical Writings

EPICTETUS, The Enchiridion

EPICURUS, Letters, Principal Doctrines, *and* Vatican Sayings

ERASMUS, D., Ten Colloquies

EURIPIDES, Electra

FEUERBACH, L., Principles of the Philosophy of the Future

FICHTE, J., The Vocation of Man

GOETHE, J., Faust I and II (verse)
- Faust I (prose)
- Faust II (prose)

GRANT, F., ed., Ancient Roman Religion
- Hellenistic Religions

GRIMMELSHAUSEN, J., Simplicius Simplicissimus

GROTIUS, H., Prolegomena to The Law of War and Peace

HAMILTON, C., ed., Buddhism

HANSLICK, E., The Beautiful in Music

HENDEL, C., Jean-Jacques Rousseau: Moralist
- Studies in the Philosophy of David Hume

HERDER, J., God, Some Conversations

HESIOD, Theogony

HOBBES, T., Leviathan I and II

HORACE, The Odes of Horace *and* The Centennial Hymn

HUME, D., Dialogues Concerning Natural Religion
- Inquiry Concerning Human Understanding
- Inquiry Concerning the Principles of Morals
- Of the Standard of Taste, and Other Essays
- Philosophical Historian
- Political Essays

JEFFERY, A., ed., Islam

KANT, I., Analytic of the Beautiful
- Critique of Practical Reason
- First Introduction to the Critique of Judgment
- Foundations of the Metaphysics of Morals
- The Metaphysical Elements of Justice, Part I of *Metaphysik der Sitten*
- The Metaphysical Principles of Virtue, Part II of *Metaphysik der Sitten*
- On History
- Perpetual Peace
- Prolegomena to Any Future Metaphysics

KLEIST, H., The Prince of Homburg

LAO TZU, The Way of Lao Tzu

Lazarillo de Tormes, The Life of

LEIBNIZ, G., Monadology and Other Philosophical Essays
LESSING, G., Laocoön
LOCKE, J., A Letter Concerning Toleration
Second Treatise of Government
LONGINUS, On Great Writing (On the Sublime)
LUCIAN, Selected Works
LUCRETIUS, On Nature
MACHIAVELLI, N., The Art of War
Mandragola
MARCUS AURELIUS, Meditations
MEAD, G., Selected Writings
MILL, J., An Essay on Government
MILL, J. S., Autobiography
Considerations on Representative Government
Nature *and* Utility of Religion
On Liberty
On the Logic of the Moral Sciences
Theism
Utilitarianism
MOLIÈRE, Tartuffe
MONTESQUIEU, C., The Persian Letters
NIETZSCHE, F., The Use and Abuse of History
NOVALIS, Hymns to the Night and Other Writings
OCKHAM, W., Philosophical Writings
PAINE, T., The Age of Reason
PALEY, W., Natural Theology
PARKINSON, T., ed., Masterworks of Prose
PICO DELLA MIRANDOLA, On the Dignity of Man, On Being and the One, *and* Heptaplus

PLATO, Epistles
Euthydemus
Euthyphro, Apology, Crito
Gorgias
Meno
Phaedo
Phaedrus
Protagoras
Statesman
Symposium
Theaetetus
Timaeus
Commentaries:
BLUCK, R., Plato's Phaedo
CORNFORD, F., Plato and Parmenides
Plato's Cosmology
Plato's Theory of Knowledge
HACKFORTH, R., Plato's Examination of Pleasure
Plato's Phaedo
Plato's Phaedrus
PLAUTUS, The Haunted House
The Menaechmi
The Rope
POPE, A., An Essay on Man
POST, C., ed., Significant Cases in British Constitutional Law
QUINTILIAN, On the Early Education of the Citizen-Orator
REYNOLDS, J., Discourses on Art
Roman Drama, Copley and Hadas, trans.
ROSENMEYER, OSTWALD, and HALPORN, The Meters of Greek and Latin Poetry
RUSSELL, B., Philosophy of Science
Sappho, The Poems of

SCHILLER, J., Wilhelm Tell

SCHLEGEL, J., On Imitation and Other Essays

SCHNEIDER, H., Sources of Contemporary Philosophical Realism in America

SCHOPENHAUER, A., On the Basis of Morality
 Freedom of the Will

SELBY-BIGGE, L., British Moralists

SENECA, Medea
 Oedipus
 Thyestes

SHAFTESBURY, A., Characteristics

SHELLEY, P., A Defence of Poetry

SMITH, A., The Wealth of Nations (Selections)

Song of Roland, Terry, trans.

SOPHOCLES, Electra

SPIEGELBERG, H., The Socratic Enigma

SPINOZA, B., Earlier Philosophical Writings
 On the Improvement of the Understanding

TERENCE, The Brothers
 The Eunuch
 The Mother-in-Law
 Phormio
 The Self-Tormentor
 The Woman of Andros

Three Greek Romances, Hadas, trans.

TOLSTOY, L., What is Art?

VERGIL, Aeneid

VICO, G. B., On the Study Methods Our Time

VOLTAIRE, Philosophical Letters

WHITEHEAD, A., Interpretation of Science

WOLFF, C., Preliminary Discourse on Philosophy in General

XENOPHON, Recollections of Socrates *and* Socrates' Defense Before the Jury

The Library of Literature

CRANE, STEPHEN, *The Red Badge of Courage,* ed. Frederick C. Crews, 6

DICKENS, CHARLES, *Great Expectations,* ed. Louis Crompton, 2

HAWTHORNE, NATHANIEL, *The Scarlet Letter,* ed. Larzer Ziff, 1

MELVILLE, HERMAN, *Moby Dick,* ed. Charles Feidelson, 5

One Hundred Middle English Lyrics, ed. Robert D. Stevick, 7

SWIFT, JONATHAN, *Gulliver's Travels,* ed. Martin Price, 3

TWAIN, MARK, *The Adventures of Huckleberry Finn,* ed. Leo Marx, 4